MODERN CHINA:

A Topical History

By
Su Kaiming

NEW WORLD PRESS
BEIJING, CHINA

First edition   1985
Second printing   1986

Cover design by Sun Chengwu

ISBN 0-8351-1397-3

Published by
New World Press
24 Baiwanzhuang Road, Beijing, China

Printed by
Foreign Languages Printing House
19 West Chegongzhuang Road, Beijing, China

Distributed by
China International Book Trading Corporation (Guoji Shudian)
P.O. Box 399, Beijing, China

Printed in the People's Republic of China

To

**The Millions of Unknown Heroes
Who Gave Their Lives
in the Long and Bitter Struggle for
a New China**

CONTENTS

PART II: THE FAILURE OF THE REPUBLIC

PART III: PEOPLE'S CHINA

AFTERWORD

APPENDICES:

INDEX

TO THE READER

To understand a person, one has to know not only his present condition and conduct but also his family and social background and stages of growth. So it is with a nation. To really understand present-day China, one must go beyond appearances and delve into roots and developments. This book aims to provide some historical facts to help the reader gain a deeper understanding of the events and people of China today.

Instead of giving an outline of modern Chinese history covering all aspects of life, this book presents to the general reader a series of topics which will hopefully be of interest. If one wants to acquire a basic knowledge of this momentous period of Chinese history, it is preferable to read the book from beginning to end. But the reader is welcome, of course, to choose only those topics which particularly interest him.

The editors of the New World Press showed active interest in this book and gave me help and encouragement. In the course of writing, I consulted a wide range of materials, Chinese and foreign. As I wanted to avoid the use of cumbersome footnotes, I did not give the credit due to many scholars and writers. Also, many friends offered valuable criticisms and suggestions to improve the manuscript. To them all I wish to express my deepest appreciation. Whatever mistakes in facts or judgments should be found, the responsibility is solely mine.

Su Kaiming

Beijing
1984

INTRODUCTION

Chinese history from 1840 to the present is a record of one of the greatest transformations the world has ever known. Only recently a semi-feudal and semi-colonial country, China is today being built into a modern socialist nation through the struggles and efforts of its people. The process is far from complete, which accounts for the continuing presence of the old in the new. Only with a basic knowledge of the historical background can one begin to understand the events and the people of China today.

The hundred and fifty years or so which have elapsed since this transformation began can be roughly divided into three major periods: (1) the collapse of the empire (1840-1911), (2) the failure of the nominal republic (1912-1949), and (3) the struggle for socialist revolution and reconstruction (from the founding of the People's Republic in 1949 to the present). The first two periods were both filled with dramatic ups and downs, heroic deeds and unexpected betrayals. Even in the period of socialist revolution and reconstruction with the nation united under the leadership of the Communist Party, the road has by no means been smooth. Here, too, there have been sudden twists and turns, remarkable achievements and serious mistakes. However, after thirty years of trial and error, the Party and the people seem to have found the correct approach to building a new nation along socialist principles that takes China's own special conditions into account.

To understand the sharp contrast between the old and the

11

new China, a brief review of the historical events of the last 150 years is necessary.

In 1840, when the British government decided to dispatch gunboats to open the door of China by force, the Qing dynasty rulers still considered themselves to be masters of a great empire that bestowed civilization upon all the "barbarian" states clustered around its periphery. The disastrous defeats in the First and Second Opium Wars brought not only national humiliation but also unequal treaties which reduced China to a *de facto* semi-colony. Westerners began to enjoy a growing range of privileges that infringed upon her sovereignty. Further military defeats coupled with economic penetration placed ever greater burdens on the laboring people and their plight became increasingly miserable. Uprisings broke out in many parts of the country. The greatest of these, the mid-century Taiping peasant revolution, was stamped out only with the help of foreign troops.

To bolster its power, the Qing government built Western-style arsenals and navy yards to produce modern weapons and warships. The attempts were so inept, however, that China was defeated in 1895 by its smaller neighbor Japan. Its impotence fully exposed, China fell an easy prey in the scramble for territory and concessions by imperialist powers. Some well-meaning scholars still sought to shore up the tottering regime by introducing comparatively drastic reforms, but these attempts were crushed by the Empress Dowager Cixi and her reactionary coterie. Having alienated the last of their popular support, the Qing rulers were toppled by revolution in 1911, and China became a nominal republic.

But the establishment of the Republic would bring no new dawn for the Chinese people, for it was quickly and forcefully betrayed by President Yuan Shikai, who made himself emperor. Taking advantage of World War I when the Western powers were locked in their own gigantic struggle, Japan presented the weak Chinese government with a series of demands which, if granted, would have all but reduced China to a Japanese colony. Many intellectuals were already searching for a way out of this deplorable situation when the October Revolution in Russia in 1917 suddenly gave the world a glimpse of the possibilities for radical change.

In 1919 a great patriotic upsurge known as the "May Fourth Movement" spread the ideas of a far-reaching cultural reform effort across the land. Democratic ideals and socialist theories poured into China like a flood-tide. A few intellectuals, attracted to Marxism, founded the Chinese Communist Party in 1921. At about the same time, Dr. Sun Yat-sen decided to reorganize his own party, the Kuomintang,* and adopt three major policies: (1) cooperation with the Chinese Communists, (2) alliance with the Soviet Union, and (3) promotion of the interests of peasants and workers. On this basis a Kuomintang-Communist united front against foreign imperialism and domestic reaction (namely, the northern warlords) was formed, and a new revolutionary storm erupted in south China which was soon scoring important victories. But after Dr. Sun died in 1925, the Kuomintang's military strong man Chiang Kai-shek suddenly turned against the Communists and began to slaughter militant workers and peasants. Once again China fell into the morass of terror and chaos.

Chiang Kai-shek had nearly succeeded in bringing the entire country under his control by 1928, and it seemed that he would be able to build China into a modern nation with the help of technicians and administrators trained in the United States and Europe. His repeated "encirclement campaigns" against rural strongholds held by the Communist Party, however, invited an ambitious imperial Japan to invade, first the Northeast and then the rest of China. Under tremendous pressure from all sides, Chiang promised to stop the civil war and once again unite with the Communists and all other patriotic forces to resist Japanese aggression. Throughout the War Against Japan from 1937 to 1945, however, he still refused to share power in democratic coalition with any other parties. Instead, he continued a sometimes covert, sometimes open campaign against

---

* Sometimes also referred to as the Nationalist Party.

them in the hope of perpetuating a personal dictatorship after the war, while waiting idly for the United States and Russia to defeat Japan for him.

When Japan's surrender in August 1945 brought an end to the war, Chiang Kai-shek dreamed of wiping out the popular Communist forces within a few months, counting on unlimited U.S. support. But his basic instincts were his undoing. While he and his kin amassed huge fortunes, rampant inflation and skyrocketing prices drove many businessmen to bankruptcy and brought untold misery to the common people. Having alienated even his former supporters, the big capitalists and landowners as well as Western-trained intellectuals, his regime collapsed under the powerful blows of the Communists' armed forces, the People's Liberation Army. "Generalissimo" Chiang, miffed and rejected, was forced to seek refuge on the island of Taiwan under U.S. protection. The so-called Republic of China was brought to an end after a short life of 38 years.

The founding of the People's Republic of China took place on October 1, 1949. On that occasion, Chairman Mao Ze-dong, standing atop Tian An Men, the "Gate of Heavenly Peace" in front of the age-old Forbidden City, spoke from the heart of China when he declared, "Our nation will never again be insulted, for we have stood up." Indeed, this marked the beginning of a new era for the Chinese people.

After clearing away the war debris of many years and the dross left over from the old society, the people's government began to lay the foundations for a new social order. Economic planning was inaugurated with Soviet help, and China began to develop its own heavy industry. Land reform and the building of irrigation and other rural construction projects promoted farm production to feed its huge population. Agriculture, private industry, commerce and handicrafts were soon transformed from private to socialist (state or collective) ownership.

Unfortunately, with so many successes to their credit, some of China's leaders became swell-headed and over-confident. They first invited people to offer criticisms in order to improve their work. But when a few individuals attacked the Party, many who out of good intentions criticized its style of work, were punished for being "rightists" opposed to Party leadership. They thought that by merely arousing the enthusiasm of the masses, China could catch up with and overtake the advanced industrial countries within two or three decades. In the Great Leap Forward of 1958, excessively high targets were set for industrial production, and communes were hastily established in the countryside. Fundamental differences arose between the Chinese and Soviet leaders, and all Soviet technicians were abruptly withdrawn from China. Then followed three difficult years (1959-1961) in which the government tried to correct its mistakes by readjusting the economy. Once again China started moving forward through its own efforts, becoming self-sufficient in oil and petroleum products, exploding its first atom bomb, and repaying all debts to the Soviet Union by 1964.

But in 1966 Chairman Mao Zedong suddenly launched a rash new campaign, the "cultural revolution," which brought turmoil to the land for a full ten years. In the name of destroying the "Four Olds" (outdated culture, ideas, customs and habits), young and naive "Red Guards" wrought havoc, going as far as to smash national treasures carefully handed down for hundreds or even thousands of years. Numerous veteran revolutionaries were wrongly accused of being "capitalist-roaders"; intellectuals, writers, artists, university professors and school teachers were accused of being "reactionary bourgeois authorities"; and returned overseas Chinese were suspected of being "foreign agents". The flight and sudden death of Lin Biao (in 1971) and the toppling of the Gang of Four (in 1976) finally brought this tragedy to an end. Yet not until December 1978 did the Party decide to make the "four modernizations" (of agriculture, industry, science and technology, and national defense) the main priority of the Chinese government for the rest of the 20th century.

Despite serious errors and setbacks, new China has made tremendous strides in industrial and agricultural production, education and scientific research, medicine and public health.

The living conditions of the people have vastly improved. To give just one illustration, the average life span had risen from an estimated 36 years prior to Liberation to 68 years in 1982. And today the aged enjoy respect and security in China.

The profound transformation from the old to a new China affected the life of every Chinese person. My own experience is a case in point. I was born in Henan Province north of the Yellow River in 1903, during the last years of the moribund Qing dynasty. From early childhood I was taught to be an absolutely loyal subject of the emperor, who was regarded as the "Son of Heaven". My mother was a devout Buddhist, and I remember how she used to take me to a Buddhist temple and have me burn incense and kowtow before *Guanyin*, the "Goddess of Mercy". One day my father suddenly announced his conversion to Christianity, an act which was to bring the family friction and ultimately tragedy. At seven, I was sent to a mission school where one of my tasks was to memorize passage after passage from the New Testament. I too became a Christian. I thought that since the missionaries were dauntless enough to cross oceans in order to save our heathen souls, I should not hesitate when I grew up to go to remote places like Tibet to spread the gospel.

The news of the Revolution of 1911 and the establishment of the Republic came as a gust of fresh air to our school. Our Chinese teachers told us that henceforth the country no longer belonged to the emperor but to the whole people, who had become citizens of the new Republic. In our school all pupils were asked to cut off their pigtails. I was too young to have a queue yet, but I remember there was another boy from the countryside who refused to do so. When he was fast asleep at night, his queue was clipped off by some older schoolmates. The following morning when he discovered his pigtail had disappeared, he cried his heart out, thinking his life would be in danger when the emperor returned to the throne. In fact, to most people of our town, monarchy was the normal order of things and the Republic seemed destined to be shortlived.

While the Republic did not change our lives very much, it

did open our minds to new ideas. I began to read about George Washington and Abraham Lincoln, heroes of the American people. I remember when World War I broke out in Europe in 1914 how I wondered why the soldiers of Britain and France on one side and Germany and Austria-Hungary on the other, all supposedly Christian nations, killed one another with such equanimity. Japan's Twenty-One Demands in 1915, aimed at securing political, economic and military control of China, shocked my national pride and sense of fair play. Together with my schoolmates I joined students from other schools in patriotic demonstrations and a boycott of Japanese goods, though our missionary authorities forbade us to get "involved". As the Christian missionaries loved their own countries, I thought we Chinese students had the right to love ours, too.

Like a great wave the ensuing May Fourth Movement of 1919 swept over our land and reached our school. Some teachers showed me copies of progressive magazines such as *New Youth* and *New Tide,* published in Shanghai and Beijing. I myself subscribed to *Social Reconstruction,* in which I came for the first time across the motto: "From each according to his ability, to each according to his needs." I remember that when I showed this to a missionary teacher, she merely cast me a blank stare. But I also read newspaper accounts of speeches by people like John Dewey, Bertrand Russell and George Sherwood Eddy (representative of the Young Men's Christian Association) given in China's major cities at that time. My mind was awakening to all kinds of new ideas.

In the summer of 1922 I passed the entrance examination for Qinghua (Tsinghua) College in Beijing, then a school for preparing students to study in American universities on government scholarships (the funds came from the U.S. portion of the Boxer indemnity, set aside by U.S. government decision from China's own maritime customs revenue). Here I met young men from all parts of China. Through the introduction of a fellow-student from south China, I became a member of Sun Yat-sen's party, the Kuomintang. I came to believe that Dr. Sun's Three People's Principles — nationalism, democracy and people's livelihood — would lead China out of its backwardness. That was the period of the first Kuomintang-Communist united front, and a few of my schoolmates had become Communists. I regarded them as revolutionary comrades, although I thought at the time communism was too high an ideal for China. I felt that if China could develop into a strong capitalist country like the United States, I would be satisfied.

In the spring of 1927 I was stunned by Chiang Kai-shek's sudden coup against the Communists in Shanghai. But still living under the rule of the warlords in Beijing, I could not uncover the real reason. Upon graduation from Qinghua that summer, I was to embark from Shanghai for the United States. Before leaving for a strange country so far away, I traveled to Nanjing to see how the new Kuomintang regime recently set up by Chiang Kai-shek was faring. To my disappointment I found that the same discredited officials we students had denounced in Beijing were flocking there and obtaining high positions. Meanwhile, thousands of poor inhabitants had been left homeless as the new government had torn down their dilapidated shacks to make way for the projected Sun Yat-sen mausoleum and their new, modern capital. To my mind the Kuomintang no longer carried a revolutionary aura and I departed from China a disillusioned and sad young man.

Our steamship stopped in Japan and Hawaii before arriving in San Francisco in September 1927. Wherever I went, I was impressed by the peaceful life and prosperity of the people. The United States, in particular, fascinated me with its high buildings, broad highways, beautiful parks and glittering city lights. The people appeared well-dressed, well-fed, and each busy in his or her own pursuits. As I saw it then, everyone was enjoying material well-being and a happy life in this "Land of Opportunity". What a sharp contrast with the Chinese people who were struggling for mere existence in the midst of foreign encroachments, civil wars and constant famines!

I went to the University of Wisconsin to study, and decided to immerse myself in study in order to learn the truth. I took up world history as my major, and read widely in my spare hours. The American and French revolutions, and particularly the Russian October Revolution, interested me. Some Chinese students started a group to study the ongoing Chinese struggle, Dr. Sun Yat-sen's principles and Marxism-Leninism, and I was invited to join them. Through our heated discussions I began to see the applicability of Marxism-Leninism to Chinese conditions. It wasn't long before I had become an ardent supporter of the Chinese Communist Party.

After graduating from the University of Wisconsin in the summer of 1929, I entered Harvard University in the fall. Then the Great Depression hit hard. The shutdown of many factories, the closure of banks, the crash of the stock market and sudden bankruptcy of many middle-class families, including the parents of some of my American friends, and the long lines outside soup kitchens all convinced me of the truth of Marxism. When from time to time I was asked to speak on China, I praised the Communists and condemned Chiang Kai-shek and the Nanjing government. After the War Against Japan broke out in 1937, as a representative of the China Aid Council, I collected funds for the support of the Communist-led Eighth Route Army and guerrilla fighters behind Japanese lines and had them forwarded through Soong Ching Ling (Madame Sun Yat-sen), then Chairperson of the China Defense League in Hongkong.

In the anti-Communist atmosphere that followed World War II, life in the United States became less than pleasant. During the McCarthy era, knowing full well that I had become suspected of being a "subversive element", I decided to return to my native land where a new day was dawning. My European-born American wife, Sonia, and my young daughter were willing to come with me, though they knew that life in China would not be easy. Our family reached Beijing in the winter of 1953.

Thirty years have passed since we arrived in new China. At first, everybody we met felt enthusiastic at being liberated from the oppression of the "three great mountains" — imperialism, feudalism and bureaucrat-capitalism. We saw the socialist revolution in which private ownership of the means of production was transformed into state or collective ownership. We took part in the Great Leap Forward and shared the hardships with other Chinese people in the three difficult years. During the "cultural revolution", like many other returned students from abroad, I was confined for almost five years for investigation as a suspected American spy, but was finally declared innocent. I was restored to my old position and continued my work where I had left off.

Looking back over the years, I am amazed at the long road I have traveled: from Buddhist idol worshipper to Christian, to nationalist, and finally to a participant in the building of socialism. But I am not alone. I am but one of China's millions, who have been or are being transformed, in different ways, into builders of a new socialist society — a noble task unprecedented in Chinese history.

China today is no paradise. It has difficult problems to tackle like any other country. We have to find ways to improve the material and cultural life of its huge population of over 1,000 million. We have to train our young people adequately and find work for them. We have to overcome bureaucracy, corruption, nepotism and other bad habits inherited from our old society. But I believe I am voicing the opinion of the overwhelming majority of the Chinese people when I say that hard work will make for a more promising future.

Napoleon once compared China to a sleeping giant. "Let him sleep," he said. "For when he wakes, he will shake the world. . . ." We all hope that new China's impact on the rest of the world will be a beneficial one. In a world beset by incessant wars, hunger and oppression, and threatened by an atomic holocaust that endangers the very survival of mankind, I trust China will be a promoter of world peace, freedom and progress.

Su Kaiming

Beijing

June 1984

PART I
THE COLLAPSE OF THE EMPIRE

1. 1840 — THE STARTING POINT OF MODERN CHINESE HISTORY

The year 1840 saw the outbreak of the First Opium War with Great Britain. This event marked a great turning point for China, which has a continuous history of 4,000 years.

Earlier incursions — the Portuguese occupation of Macao in 1533, the Dutch seizure of Taiwan during the first part of the 17th century, and the Russian invasion of the Heilong River region in the same century — had not fundamentally disturbed the political and social fabric of old China. The Opium War was different. As a result of its defeat in this war, China began to sink from the level of a great empire to that of a semi-colony. Thereafter, her feudal foundations were rapidly eroded by the penetration of capitalism. For a time she was near partition — with her very existence as an independent state in danger.

In the First Opium War China for the first time met an adversary more advanced in military technique as well as superior in economic and political organization. It was a clash between two empires — one representing Oriental decadent feudalism and the other, expanding Western capitalism. She had to either transform herself to survive, or stick to her old ways and perish. Only after more than 100 years of struggle did the Chinese people regain their independence, with the prospect before them of building a socialist society. For these reasons historians are of the opinion that the First Opium War marked the beginning of a new period and that the year 1840 was the demarcation line between ancient and modern Chinese history.

2.   CHINA BEFORE 1840

China is one of the oldest civilizations in the world, having a written history of 4,000 years and a prehistory which stretches back much further.

The remains of a 7,000 year-old Neolithic matriarchal commune society can be seen today at Banpo Village near Xi'an in Shaanxi Province. Slave society in China lasted almost 2,000 years, covering the Xia, Shang and Zhou dynasties (c. 21st century-221 B.C.). For a time China was divided into many local kingdoms, organized for wars of plunder and aggrandizement. It was Qin Shi Huang, the first emperor of the Qin dynasty (221-207 B.C.), who first unified China, established a centralized feudal empire and ordered the building of the Great Wall.

For over 2,000 years, in spite of dynastic wars and invasions by the nomads along its extensive frontiers, China developed a unique culture. Inventions included silk, paper, gunpowder, porcelain, printing, the seismoscope and the maritime compass. China sent silk and other valuable products down the Silk Road, opened in the second century B.C., to Central and Western Asia, whence they were shipped to Europe and Egypt. A fleet of seagoing vessels in the early 15th century carried gold, silk and porcelain to Southeast Asia and as far as the east coast of Africa. China's dauntless sailors braved the dangerous elements to accomplish these deeds at least half a century before

Columbus discovered America and the Portuguese navigator Vasco da Gama rounded the Cape of Good Hope.

Although China produced many great statesmen, philosophers, poets, artists and military strategists, its social and political structure never broke out of the shell of feudalism. Long isolated from the rest of the world and ignorant of other countries and peoples, the emperor regarded himself as the supreme ruler of "all under heaven" and his Celestial Empire as the center of the universe, surrounded by "barbarians". As the "Son of Heaven", he wielded absolute power over all his subjects. He ruled through trusted members of his imperial family as well as officials selected by a civil service-type examination based on the Confucian classics. Steeped in Confucian philosophy, these officials looked back to an imaginary "golden age" of sage kings. Lacking scientific and technical knowledge, they were not interested in social progress and the better utilization of the natural resources of the country. While professing loyalty to the emperor and benevolence to the people, they were chiefly concerned with the consolidation of the power and privileges they and their families had acquired.

No independent powerful merchant class existed as in the West, because trade in major commodities like iron and salt became a state monopoly and the once powerful merchants of the Warring States period (475-221 B.C.) were degraded in the social scale in the Western Han dynasty (206 B.C.-A.D. 24). Indeed, a landlord in old China was usually a four-in-one combination of landowner, usurer, merchant and bureaucratic official. The peasants at the bottom end of the social ladder had no rights but only duties. They were literally beasts of burden, illiterate and tied to the soil, producing the essentials of life and supporting a hierarchy of parasitic rulers and masters.

Lacking any democratic process to redress their grievances, the peasants frequently rebelled against their intolerable position by organizing large-scale peasant uprisings. However, without any change in the economic structure and the emergence of a new progressive class, a peasant leader who succeeded in overthrowing a decadent despot often became an emperor himself, repeating the cycle of the rise and fall of another dynasty. By 1840, when the Qing dynasty had begun its decline and was no longer capable of resisting Western capitalist aggression, a new chapter opened in China's history.

3. ORIGINS OF THE FIRST OPIUM WAR

Toward the end of the 18th century, the British merchants found the sale of opium the easiest way to make great profit from their trade with China.

At that time, China still had a self-sufficient pre-capitalist economy. The peasants worked in the fields, their wives wove cloth at home, and artisans and craftsmen produced luxury articles for the upper classes and even for export. In 1793, in his reply to a proposal for wider trade relations by King George III of England, Emperor Qian Long (r. 1736-1795) declared: "The Celestial Empire possesses all things in prolific abundance and lacks no product within its borders. There is therefore no need to import the manufactures of outside barbarians in exchange for our own products."

Under these circumstances, the British merchants were able to sell very little to China, and for most of what they bought, such as tea, silks and porcelain, they had to pay in silver. For them this meant a serious drain on their silver reserves, and the British East India Company, which held the British trade monopoly in China, was looking for another way to pay for Chinese goods. It found the sale of opium to be the answer. The British had just become masters of India, and they paid the people in the northern and central parts of that country to grow poppies for that purpose. In 1781, the Company made its first big shipment of opium to China. After that the trade grew by leaps and bounds, and increasing amounts of silver flowed out of China instead of into it.

In 1800 Emperor Jia Qing (r. 1796-1820), disturbed by the dire effects of the opium trade, proclaimed a ban on it. But the ban was ignored by the British and their Chinese accomplices. Many Chinese officials and merchants were eager to grow rich through the opium trade even though it meant defying imperial orders, undermining the health of the Chinese people and bankrupting their families. Smuggling and bribery became widespread.

The import of opium increased from 4,000 chests (each containing 100 to 120 catties, or 60 to 72 kilograms) in 1800, to over 40,000 chests in 1838. Opium then constituted 57 per cent of Chinese imports. Out of the huge profits derived from the sale of this debilitating narcotic grew a number of the "merchant princes" of Britain, and of the United States as well.

The Chinese government, now under the rule of Emperor Dao Guang (r. 1821-1850), became alarmed by the enormous drain of silver from its territory. Toward the end of 1838, Commissioner Lin Zexu (1785-1850) was appointed to deal with the problem. Upon his arrival in Guangzhou Lin forced the British and a number of American merchants to surrender their stocks of opium. Some 20,000 chests (out of which over 1,000 belonged to American merchants) were handed in and publicly destroyed on the beaches.

The pretext under which the British government declared war on China was freedom of trade. The Industrial Revolution and victory over its maritime rivals in the Napoleonic Wars had made Britain the leading capitalist power seeking overseas markets and sources of raw materials. Free trade and gunboat diplomacy had become the order of the day.

In 1834 the British House of Commons had revoked the British East India Company's trade monopoly in the Far East, clearing the way for "free trade". It was under this banner that the British government declared war on China to promote British interests. In 1840 troop carriers and men-of-war were dispatched eastward to force open China's "closed door".

4. THE CAUSES OF CHINA'S DEFEAT IN THE FIRST OPIUM WAR

The First Opium War lasted more than two years, from June 1840 to August 1842. The Chinese people fought heroically, but they were defeated because of (1) the wavering of the emperor and betrayal by capitulationist officials; and (2) the superior fire power of the British aggressors and China's lack of modern weapons.

The patriotic Lin Zexu, after destroying the seized opium in Guangzhou, prepared for defense. Wooden stakes were driven into the bed of the sea and linked together by iron chains at the approaches to the Zhujiang (Pearl) River, and people were organized into local militia units. Unable to capture such a well-fortified city, the British fleet veered northward along the coast, took Dinghai in Zhejiang Province and proceeded to Tianjin, maritime gateway to the capital. When news of this reached Beijing, capitulationist officials in the court denounced Lin Zexu, blaming him for having stirred up the trouble. The emperor wavered, dismissed Lin Zexu and ordered Qi Shan (Kishen in Western historical works), a Manchu aristocrat, to negotiate with the British invaders.

After this, the situation went from bad to worse. The British commander agreed to return to Guangzhou for talks. Upon Qi Shan's arrival in Guangzhou, he ordered all the defenses dismantled and the people's militia disbanded, in an attempt to placate the enemy. He readily yielded to the British demands: the cession of Hongkong and the payment of an indemnity of 6,000,000 silver dollars.

Feeling this too bitter a pill to swallow, the emperor decided to fight again and ordered Yi Shan, another Manchu aristocrat, to defend Guangzhou. The latter hoisted the white flag when the British fleet was approaching the city. Finally, when the reinforced British fleet under Sir Henry Pottinger had occupied Zhenjiang and was approaching Nanjing, Qi Ying (Kiying), a third official, was sent by the emperor to beg for peace at any price. On August 29, 1842, Qi Ying boarded a British warship to sign the humiliating Treaty of Nanjing.

5. POPULAR REACTIONS TO BRITISH AGGRESSION

The large-scale smuggling of opium brought tragedy to many families in south and central China. To obtain this drug, many addicts sold their land and houses, and even their wives and children. Thus, outside of the small number of merchants and officials who profited from this illicit trade, the overwhelming majority of the Chinese people were filled with indignation and wholeheartedly supported the war against the British invaders.

The British troops also went on raids in the villages along the seacoast. They plundered, killed, and molested the womenfolk. In self-defense the peasants organized themselves into militia units, and neighboring villages pledged to help one another in case of emergency. The struggles of the people to defend themselves were the only heartening aspect of an otherwise gloomy story of official appeasement and capitulation.

On May 30, 1841, a bloody clash took place at Sanyuanli, a village near Guangzhou, between the peasants and the British marauders. When the gongs were sounded, thousands of peasants from 103 nearby villages flocked to the scene. They raised banners bearing the characters "Ping Ying Tuan" (Subdue-the-British Corps), and women and children also joined in. They lured the enemy to a hilly area and surrounded them from all sides.

A rainstorm broke out. The soaked ammunition rendered the British firearms useless. The peasants fought the pillagers with spears, swords, hoes, pitchforks and other farm tools. The British soldiers, in panic, ran about in the muddy fields, and many were killed or wounded. Finally, it was the Chinese city prefect who came and dispersed the crowd by cajolery and threat, and the British were able to escape.

The fight at Sanyuanli was not an isolated case. Wherever the British invaders went, they met with determined resistance from the masses of the people. A popular saying went, "The officials fear the foreigners, and the foreigners fear the people."

6. OUTCOME OF THE FIRST OPIUM WAR

The First Opium War was brought to an end by the signing of the Treaty of Nanjing in 1842. It was the first of the humiliating "unequal treaties" forced on China by the foreign powers. Its 13 articles included the following main points:

• The cession of Hongkong, which later became a British military, political and economic base for further aggression in China;

• The opening of five ports — Guangzhou, Xiamen, Fuzhou, Ningbo and Shanghai — to British trade;

• The payment of an indemnity of 21,000,000 silver dollars; and

• The fixing of tariff rates on British goods by mutual agreement, thus depriving China of her sovereign right to determine import duties.

In the following year, the Chinese government was forced to sign with the British a supplementary protocol, which, among other things, laid down the following conditions:

• The fixing of a limit of five per cent on import tariffs for British goods, thereby hindering China's development of its own home industry;

• The handing over to the British consulates of British nationals involved in disputes with Chinese merchants, thus giving extraterritorial rights to the British in China;

• Permission for British settlements in certain districts of the treaty ports, embryos of foreign concessions in the large cities of China; and

• Most-favored-nation status, extending to Britain all privileges which might be granted to any other power in the future.

Together the provisions of the treaty and the protocol began to transform China from an independent nation into a semi-colony.

7. U.S. AND OTHER POWERS' POLICY TOWARD CHINA AFTER THE FIRST OPIUM WAR

American merchants were early collaborators with the British traders. During the Opium War the United States government sent a squadron to China as a gesture of support to the British aggressors. In 1843 it sent the blustering Caleb Cushing as an envoy to conclude a treaty with China. Upon his arrival in Macao, he demanded passage to Beijing to negotiate directly with the emperor. If this request were refused, he warned, U.S. warships would soon sail to Tianjin and knock at the door of the capital.

The emperor hastily sent his trusted official Qi Ying to deal with Cushing. In July 1844, the Treaty of Wangxia was signed between the two countries. It gave the United States most-favored-nation status, under which American merchants could enjoy all the privileges granted to the British in the Treaty of Nanjing and supplementary agreements. It provided that any change in the import tariffs had to have the consent of the United States consular authorities, thus limiting China's import duties on foreign goods to five per cent (*ad valorem*) until 1928. Furthermore, the treaty greatly expanded the principle of extraterritoriality — from that time on, foreigners in other parts of China besides the treaty ports were protected; civil as well as criminal cases were included; and the nationals of even those Western countries having no treaty relations with China were covered. The result was to greatly undermine China's independence in the administration of justice. American war vessels as well as merchant ships were allowed to visit the trading ports, where American missionaries could build churches and hospitals.

The French government followed closely, and in the same year forced the Qing government to sign the Treaty of Huangpu. It granted to France as many privileges as had been ceded to Britain and the United States. In addition, it secured for Roman Catholics the right to freely propagate their faith in the trading ports of China. Under the most-favored-nation clause the British too acquired these additional benefits.

Following the examples of the United States and France, other Western countries, such as Belgium, Sweden and Norway, demanded the same privileges for their nationals. Under the principle of granting "equal treatment for all", the Qing rulers agreed to these demands.

8. SOCIAL IMPACT OF THE FIRST OPIUM WAR

The defeat in the First Opium War was a hard blow to the Chinese empire, and the old social and economic structure began to break down. The importation of opium, though still illegal, grew faster than ever — from 40,000 chests in 1838 to 52,000 in 1850 and 80,000 in 1853. On top of this, the Qing government had to pay a huge indemnity to the British victors in the war. The outflow of silver had become a torrent. This pushed up its value in relation to the cash (copper coins) in general circulation and increased the peasants' burden. In a "memorial to the throne" in 1852, Zeng Guofan, a high official who later became one of the chief suppressors of the Taiping Revolution, stated:

> The distress among the people cannot appeal to the emperor . . . the silver price is too high so it is difficult to pay taxes. . . . In former days a tael (Chinese ounce) of silver was worth 1,000 cash; then a picul of rice could be sold for three taels of silver. Nowadays one tael of silver is worth 2,000 cash and one picul of rice only brings one tael and a half of silver. In former days, through the sale of three pecks of rice, the peasants could pay the land tax of one *mu*** and there was still something left over. Nowadays to sell six pecks of rice to pay the land tax for one *mu* is still not enough. The court naturally collects the regular amount but the small people actually have to pay double. Those who have no power to pay are innumerable. . . .

Forced to borrow from the landlords, the peasants were charged an exorbitant rate of interest. For grain borrowed in the spring, they had to pay double the amount in the autumn of the same year. Countless families deserted the land and drifted around as beggars. The strong joined bandit gangs or secret revolutionary societies.

While peasants were becoming destitute and losing their land, craftsmen in the cities fared no better. The limit of a five per cent import tariff on foreign goods opened the door wide to an influx of cheap British and American textiles and other merchandise. This ruined China's traditional cottage industries, and millions of weavers and other handicraftsmen. In addition, the enforced opening of new ports besides Guangzhou to foreign trade destroyed the old inland transport system. Thousands of boatmen and porters in south China could no longer find work.

While people were hard pressed for mere survival, the Qing court increased its levies time and again to maintain its luxuri-

---

* One *mu* = 1/15 hectare or 1/6 acre.

ous life and pay the indemnity to the British government as well.

Under these circumstances, the people were driven to revolt. Between 1841 and 1849 more than 100 uprisings took place in different parts of the country. The Taiping Revolution, with its capable leadership and equalitarian program, attracted people like a magnet, uniting them into a movement that shook the foundation of China's feudal society and nearly toppled the Qing rulers.

9.   THE SECOND OPIUM WAR

The Second Opium War broke out in 1856 because Great Britain and the other Western powers were not satisfied with what they had acquired in the First Opium War. They had not achieved their aims in China, either in Guangzhou or the country as a whole.

• The British could not enter the walled city of Guangzhou because of popular opposition;

• Foreign trade with China had not grown as much as the West had expected. Western traders and their governments wanted to have more ports opened in north China and along the Changjiang (Yangtze) River to increase foreign business;

• The lucrative opium trade was still formally illegal; and

• Instead of dealing with local authorities, Western governments wanted to negotiate directly with the Qing court in Beijing.

All these points were included in a paper presented to the Chinese authorities in 1854 by the ministers of Britain, France and the United States, demanding that the old treaties be revised.

The Qing court, however, convinced it had already yielded too much to the Western powers, refused to change the treaties in any way.

In this stalemate, another armed clash between China and the West was inevitable. Two minor incidents served as pretexts for the outbreak of the Second Opium War.

On October 8, 1856, the *Arrow*, a Chinese vessel registered in Hongkong, was laying off the city of Guangzhou. Chinese maritime police boarded it in search of a notorious pirate. In the process they hauled down its British flag and arrested the Chinese crew together with the pirate. Despite the fact that the boat's Hongkong license had expired some 10 days earlier, the British consul H. S. Parkes chose to regard the incident as an insult to the British flag and a violation of British rights. In a letter to the Chinese High Commissioner Ye Mingchen (1807-1859), he demanded a written apology and the return of the Chinese crew. Commissioner Ye rejected these demands. Thinking that this "tempest in a teapot" would blow over by itself, Commissioner Ye took no active steps for defense.

By coincidence a French missionary, one Father Chapedelaine, was arrested and executed about the same time in a county town of neighboring Guangxi Province. Fresh from his victories with his British ally in the Crimean War against Russia, and eager to imitate the exploits of his uncle Napoleon I, Napoleon III quickly dispatched a fleet under Baron Gros to join in a war against China. In December 1857, the Anglo-French forces bombarded the city of Guangzhou, took the inept Commissioner Ye prisoner and shipped him to Calcutta where he died in captivity two years later.

After the capture of Guangzhou, the Anglo-French forces under Lord Elgin and Baron Gros sailed northward toward Tianjin, the sea gateway only 80 miles from Beijing. This action was supported by the ministers of the United States and tsarist Russia, who pretended to be mediators in the conflict.

In May 1858, the Anglo-French forces took the Dagu forts protecting Tianjin's seaward flank and threatened to attack Tianjin and march on to the capital unless imperial representatives were sent immediately to negotiate revision of the original treaties.

Greatly alarmed, the Qing rulers yielded once again. In June unequal treaties were signed one after another with Britain and France as well as Russia and the United States. By these "Treaties of Tianjin", the Western powers extracted the following additional privileges:

• Foreign representatives would be allowed to reside in Beijing, so that they might deal with the central government directly;

• Several new ports were to be opened to foreign trade and new foreign settlements were to be established along China's seacoast and the Changjiang River;

• Foreign missionaries were to be allowed to travel and preach freely anywhere in China;

• Foreign gunboats would be allowed to visit the treaty ports and sail on the Changjiang River; and

• Huge indemnities to cover the cost of the war operations were to be paid to Britain and France.

Further injury and insult were added the following November when, through negotiations in Shanghai, the Qing government agreed to legalize the opium trade and legitimize foreign control of China's customs and the fixed low tariff rate.

10. DESTRUCTION OF THE OLD SUMMER PALACE

Yuan Ming Yuan, the old summer palace, was destroyed in October 1860 by British and French troops as the Second Opium War was coming to a close.

The Treaties of Tianjin stipulated that the ratified documents should be exchanged in Beijing within a year. When the Qing court delayed ratification, Britain and France again used force to achieve their aims.

In the spring of 1860, 18,000 British troops under Lord Elgin and 7,000 French troops under Baron Gros were assembled in Chinese waters. Toward the end of July, they arrived off the Dagu forts guarding the approaches to Tianjin. The Russian Minister, Ignatieff, who had arrived earlier, had found that Beitang to the north had been left defenseless. Under his guidance, the British-French allied forces took it without meeting any resistance. Then they attacked the Dagu forts from both land and sea. On August 21, they captured the forts and three days later entered the city of Tianjin.

The Qing court hurriedly sent special representatives to beg for peace. But in the meantime Chinese troops had captured a group of British and French emissaries and, determined to teach the Qing rulers a lesson with the mailed fist, the British-French allied forces marched toward Beijing. The emperor fled in panic to Chengde (Jehol) beyond the Great Wall. On October 6, the allied troops occupied the old summer palace, a few miles to the northwest of the capital. Finding the halls and pavilions filled with priceless articles — "nothing in our Europe can give any idea of such luxury," in the words of the French commander Montauban — the officers and men looted for days on end. Using the death of 21 of the emissaries as an excuse, Lord Elgin on October 18 gave the order to set fire to the palace, so as to "hurt the personal pride of the emperor".

Victor Hugo wrote acidly of this act of brigandage and vandalism:

> Two bandits, France and England, entered a cathedral in Asia. One plundered and the other set fire. . . . One of the two victors filled his pockets, the other filled his boxes, and they came back to Europe, arm-in-arm, laughing.

Later he added, "Governments are sometimes robbers, the people never."

11. CONCLUSION OF THE SECOND OPIUM WAR

Meanwhile, the British-French allied troops had entered the city of Beijing itself on October 13, 1860. Completely humiliated, the Qing rulers yielded to every demand put forward by the victors. In addition to recognizing the validity of the Treaties of Tianjin, they concluded the "Treaties of Beijing" with Britain and France, giving them the following advantages:

• The opening of Tianjin as a trading port, thus bringing the gateway to the capital under foreign domination;

• The freedom to transport Chinese laborers to work abroad, thus starting the "coolie trade" whereby Chinese peasants and the urban poor were indentured to work in the mines and plantations of Malaya, Australia, Latin America or the Caribbean Islands. In the United States, many worked under the system of contract labor, receiving extremely low wages in the construction of the transcontinental railway. Others came as immigrants under the credit-ticket arrangement by which Chinese merchants in America advanced passage money to workers and kept collecting money from them for years;

• The right of French Catholic missionaries to purchase land and build churches inside China, thus giving the Chinese people the impression that gunboats and the Bible went hand-in-hand and that the Western powers were intent on subduing China spiritually as well as militarily;

• The cession to Britain of Kowloon, the area on the mainland adjacent to Hongkong; and

• An increase in the war indemnities to 8,000,000 silver taels each to Britain and France.

To quote the British historian H. B. Morse, as a result of the Opium Wars, "The Chinese learned ... that, whereas formerly it was China which dictated the conditions under which international relations were to be maintained, now it was the Western nations which imposed their will on China." China was now well on its way to becoming a semi-colony of the Western powers.

12. RUSSIA'S ROLE IN THE SECOND OPIUM WAR

In the 19th century Russia was pushing outward in several directions. Having been blocked in the Middle East by defeat in the Crimean War, its leaders were eager to take advantage of China's weakness in their drive to the Pacific.

Early in the 17th century when the Qing dynasty was still young and vigorous, Russia had met strong resistance to its expansion in Siberia. In 1689 the two countries signed the Treaty of Nerchinsk, by which Russia recognized that its domain extended only to the Lake Baikal region and that the territory to the east belonged to China. For many years a limited overland trade was carried on at Kyakhta, a Mongolian frontier town to the south of the lake.

By the middle of the 19th century, however, despite repeated protests from a weakened Qing government, Russian forces had obtained a foothold on the Pacific coast, building forts and establishing settlements north of the Heilong River. The outbreak of the Second Opium War was regarded by Russia as an opportunity to consolidate its gains and extract more concessions from China.

To realize its ambitions, Russia on the one hand worked together with the British-French allied troops in subduing the Qing court by military force. On the other, Russia posed as a "friend" of China, claiming to be a "mediator", but actually demanding an exorbitant price for "services rendered".

While the Chinese forces were engaged in resisting the British-French allied troops elsewhere in China, Russian forces occupied Haishenwai on the Pacific coast in Siberia and renamed it, significantly, Vladivostok (Ruler of the East). Russia also imposed on China three unequal treaties:

1. The Treaty of Aihui, May 28, 1858, allowed Russia to

claim exclusively the area north of the Heilong River and obtain the right to rule jointly with China the area east of the Wusuli River.

2. The Treaty of Tianjin, June 13, 1858, gave Russia the same rights granted the other powers to carry on trade in China's coastal cities in addition to the original overland trade with China. Russian missionaries were allowed to travel and reside in any part of China, and Russian nationals could enjoy the same extraterritorial rights extended to other foreigners in China.

3. The Treaty of Beijing, November 11, 1860, was signed under pressure applied by the Russian Minister Ignatieff as a reward for his role as "honest broker" in the Second Opium War. The treaty contained the following main points:

• Formal recognition of the vast area north of the Heilong River (600,000 square kilometers) and east of the Wusuli River (400,000 square kilometers) as Russian territory;

• The opening of Kashgar in Xinjiang as a trading center and permission to set up a Russian consulate there;

• Permission for Russian merchants to carry on trade in Kulun and Zhangjiakou, from where they could travel freely to Beijing; and

• A projected survey and re-demarcation of China's western boundary with Russia.

Through these treaties Russia obtained all the privileges enjoyed by other Western powers in China, confirmed the annexation of 1,000,000 square kilometers of territory (more than the combined areas of France and Germany) in Siberia, and prepared the ground for further land annexations in Central Asia by incorporating large chunks of territory on China's northwest frontiers.

13.   THE TAIPING REVOLUTION AND ITS LEADERS

The Taiping Revolution (1851-1864) was China's biggest

peasant revolt and the world's greatest civil war in the 19th century. A democratic movement springing from the grass-roots, it took place almost simultaneously with the 1848 Revolution in Europe and the American Civil War. Starting out from Guangxi near the Viet Nam border in the south, it swept like a prairie fire across the middle and lower Changjiang River region, approaching Shanghai in the east and, for a time, threatening the Qing court in Beijing in the north. Its supporters included not only impoverished peasants and craftsmen but also people from national minorities who suffered from unbearable oppression. Setting up its capital at Nanjing which it renamed Tianjing (Heavenly Capital) in 1853 and calling its revolutionary state the "Taiping Heavenly Kingdom", it ruled over millions of people for more than 11 years. When it was suppressed in 1864, more people had perished than the total number from the Napoleonic, Crimean, American Civil and Franco-Prussian wars.

The standard-bearer and moving spirit of the revolution was Hong Xiuquan (1814-1864), a village school teacher from a peasant family. Having repeatedly failed at the Confucian examinations, he was attracted to the teachings of Protestant Christian missionaries in Guangzhou. In 1843 he set up the God Worshipping Society in his native town and smashed the tablet of Confucius in a village private school. The sufferings of the people drove him to become a revolutionary pamphleteer. During a serious illness he had a "vision" that he was the second son of the true God, the younger brother of Jesus Christ, whose mission was to overthrow the evil rule of the false "Son of Heaven", the Qing emperor, and bring paradise down to earth by setting up the Taiping Heavenly Kingdom in China. An indomitable personality, Hong Xiuquan ruled the Taiping state until his death in June 1864.

Other leaders of the movement included Yang Xiuqing (c. 1820-1856), a landless charcoal burner, who later became the Taiping state's King of the East and an outstanding commander of its armed forces. Xiao Chaogui, a poor peasant and wood-cutter, also became a king in the Taiping regime, as did Feng

Yunshan, a village school teacher and Hong Xiuquan's intimate friend. Later, Hong Rengan, a cousin of Hong Xiuquan who had come into contact with missionaries in Hongkong, returned to become premier, and Li Xiucheng (1823-1864), another poor peasant, became the commander of the armed forces. Among the Taiping leaders were also representatives of the landowners and well-to-do scholar gentry, such as Wei Changhui and Shi Dakai.

14. DOMESTIC PROGRAM OF THE TAIPING HEAVENLY KINGDOM

The Taiping peasant revolutionaries were the first to attempt to modernize China by learning from the West. Their avowed aim was to build a "heavenly kingdom" on earth; in their social and political programs they tried to couple Christian morals (everyone was taught to observe the Ten Commandments) with the age-old equalitarian dream of the Chinese peasants.

The basic law of the Heavenly Kingdom was the Land Law of 1853. It declared: "All lands under heaven shall be farmed jointly by the people under heaven.... If there is a famine in one area, the surplus will be moved from another area where there is abundance to this area in order to feed the starving.... Land shall be farmed by all; rice, eaten by all; clothes, worn by all; money, spent by all. There shall be no inequality, and no person shall be without food or fuel.... Thus the people under heaven shall all enjoy the great happiness given by the Heavenly Father, Supreme Lord and August God."

The distribution of land was to be made according to the size of the family. Everyone over 16 years of age, man or woman, would receive a share, and those under 16, half a share. The land was to be divided into nine grades according to fertility of soil, and each family was to receive an allotment of both fertile as well as less fertile land so as to avoid inequalities.

Although it is difficult to know how far this law was actually carried out under the prevailing war conditions, many peasants did receive title deeds to the land they tilled from the new government or worked their plots without paying rent to the landlords. This brought great improvement in the life of the peasants, which was reflected in their support for the Taipings.

No less noteworthy was the raising of the status of women. Not only were they entitled to a share of land, but they were also given social and political equality with men. Prostitution, concubinage, adultery, foot-binding, infanticide and the sale of slaves (mainly the traffic in girls) were prohibited. Women, like men, could become officials through taking civil service examinations or could be appointed commanders in the fighting forces. One eyewitness account related that in the areas ruled by the Taipings women freely walked or rode on horseback in the streets, a thing unheard of in feudal China.

The basic administrative unit remained the family. Every 25 families formed a communal unit with a common storehouse, a church, and a head in charge of temporal and spiritual affairs. After the harvest this chief was responsible for keeping back sufficient grain for his group and for sending the surplus to national storehouses which would then supply the grain-deficient areas. The monthly tax was considerably lighter than that levied by the Qing government.

To ensure that everyone should be justly treated, the Taipings adopted their own judicial system. Two large drums were always kept hanging outside the gate of the yamen, the headquarters and residence of government officials. Anyone who had a complaint to make or wished to speak on behalf of one unjustly treated was free to strike the drums and demand justice from the magistrate. No lawyer was needed at a trial; plaintiffs, defendants and prisoners pleaded their own cases. Neither torture nor cruel physical punishment was allowed.

The Taipings also trained a disciplined army. Prohibiting looting and corruption, it dealt summarily with Qing officials, big landlords and moneylenders, seizing their wealth and distributing it among the poor. Unpaid and serving voluntarily, the Taiping forces grew from an original 20,000 or so to over a million. The imperial troops, degenerate and corrupt, were no match for them.

These reforms gained the active support of the overwhelming majority of the people in the areas under the control of the Taipings. They also won the praise of many foreign visitors. In 1854, the Reverend E. C. Bridgman accompanied the U.S. Commissioner R. M. McLane on a diplomatic mission to Nanjing. He wrote: "All the people we saw were well-clad, well-fed, and well-provided for in every way. They all seemed content, and in high spirits, as if sure of success."

15. TAIPING FOREIGN POLICY AND THE WESTERN POWERS

From the very beginning, the Taiping leader Hong Xiuquan believed in the equality and friendship between nations. Even before the outbreak of the revolution in 1851, he had told his cousin Hong Rengan: "Every nation should keep its own wealth and should not encroach upon others. They should maintain friendly relations, exchange truth and knowledge, and treat one another with civility." Based on these ideas, the Taiping Heavenly Kingdom adopted a policy of national independence combined with equality and friendship with other countries.

The Western powers, however, were apprehensive of revolution in the Celestial Empire. They felt that the upsetting of the Qing dynasty "apple cart" could only bring them harm.

In the spring of 1853, while the Taiping troops swept toward the Changjiang River region, Sir George Bonham, British Governor of Hongkong and Minister to China at the time, secretly planned to help smother the revolution and then demand "rewards" from the Qing court. He dispatched British warships to Shanghai, hoping to occupy Zhenjiang immediately, thus sealing off the mighty river and the Grand Canal to block the revolutionaries. The rapidity of the Taiping advance, however, thwarted his scheme. Before the British warships reached Shanghai, the Taipings had already captured Nanjing and Zhenjiang, two strategic cities on the lower Changjiang. Forced to change his plans, Bonham adopted a wait-and-see attitude and declared a policy of "neutrality" in China's civil war.

In April 1853 Bonham visited Tianjing (presently Nanjing) to sound out the attitude of the Taiping leaders toward the treaty and agreements concluded between the British and the Qing court. In a "yellow silk letter", the Taiping leaders stated: "The Heavenly Father, the Supreme Lord, the Great God, in the beginning created Heaven and Earth, land and sea, men and things in six days; from that time to this day, the whole world has been one family. . . . We therefore issue this special decree, permitting you, the English chief, to lead your brethren in or out, backward or forward, in full accordance with your own will or wish, whether to aid us in exterminating our devilish foes, or to carry on your commercial operations." However, traffic in opium was to be stopped once and for all.

Later the French Minister A. de Bourboulon and the U.S. Commissioner R. M. McLane also visited Tianjing. They asked the Taiping Kingdom to guarantee the validity of the treaties they both had signed with the Qing government. The Taiping leaders ignored their demands.

In June 1854, a representative of the new British Minister J. Bowring visited Tianjing. The Eastern King Yang Xiuqing, on behalf of the Taiping government, restated in a letter the fundamental principles of Taiping foreign policy: (1) all countries, including Britain, would have freedom of trade once peace was restored in China; (2) the opening of trading ports would be negotiated later on; and (3) all noxious goods were to be banned. In other words, the Taiping revolutionary government would not recognize the "unequal treaties" signed between the Western powers and the Qing rulers.

Disappointed at their failure to get the Taipings to respect the special privileges they had obtained, the Western powers began to link their future interests with the continued rule of the Qing dynasty. They provoked the Second Opium War in 1856 only in order to get more concessions. Ironically it was the assistance of these professed Christian gentlemen that enabled the decadent Qing rulers and the reactionary Chinese landlords to destroy this peasant revolutionary state whose program included many elements of Christianity.

16. CAUSES OF THE DEFEAT OF THE TAIPING REVOLUTION

In June 1864, the Heavenly King Hong Xiuquan died in his palace just before Nanjing, the long-besieged capital of the Heavenly Kingdom, fell to the Hunan provincial armies. The great peasant war, which had swept 17 provinces and lasted 14 years, was drowned in blood.

Three factors contributed to the defeat of this peasant movement: internal degeneration and strife, the growth of domestic reaction and foreign intervention.

1. **Internal degeneration and strife.** After setting up their capital at Nanjing in 1853, the Taiping leaders began to lead a luxurious life and indulge in personal pleasures. While the peasants were still supporting them wholeheartedly, they themselves lost their revolutionary spirit and forgot about their equalitarian ideals. Still full of feudal ideas, Hong proclaimed himself Heavenly King and tried to build a hierarchy of military leaders, whom he also made "kings".

In the summer of 1856 the Taipings were winning on all fronts and the future looked promising for the revolution. Just then, however, Yang Xiuqing, the capable strategist and administrator and Eastern King of the Heavenly Kingdom, attempted to seize the supreme power. The Northern King Wei marched his troops into the capital and out of personal jealousy murdered Yang's whole family and massacred tens of thousands of his supporters.   To "restore the balance", the Heavenly King had Wei and many of his followers killed. The following year the Assistant King Shi Dakai, disgruntled at the distrust shown toward him by the Heavenly King, withdrew his allegiance and led his army of 200,000 westward to fight the imperial troops on his own.   This internal dissension greatly weakened the Taipings.   During the Second Opium War, although the Taipings regained unity under the capable leadership of the Heavenly King's cousin Hong Rengan and the Loyal King Li Xiucheng, stubbornly fighting the forces allied with the emperor, they were unable to recover their former revolutionary fervor and win sufficiently wide support among the people.   Feudal mentality and habits were too deep-rooted to allow the carrying out of Hong Rengan's program for reform and modernization.

2.   **Domestic reaction.** The imperial troops were no match for the well-disciplined Taiping armies. To check the revolutionary tide, Emperor Xian Feng (r. 1851-1861) called on the landlord-gentry to organize local militia units with which to defend their own interests.

One prominent landlord-official who played a major role in defeating the Taipings was Zeng Guofan (1811-1872).   In 1853 he was asked to organize a self-defense corps in behalf of the landed gentry in his native Hunan Province.   In time these provincial militia units replaced the imperial troops as the mainstay of the Qing rulers in suppressing the Taiping Revolution.

By February 1854, Zeng's Hunan troops numbered 17,000 men.   In a declaration at the time, he defended the feudal land-owning system, the Qing imperial government and the teachings of Confucius.   At first he met with many defeats in his encounters with the Taiping armies.   However, with the aid of foreign rifles and advisers, his forces grew in numbers and combat power.   By 1862 they were laying siege to Nanjing.   Step by step they seized all the strategic cities around the Celestial Capital. Entirely cut off from the outside and with all their provisions exhausted, the army and people in the city fought to the last. They preferred death to living again under the old order of feudal oppression.

The organization of the provincial troops was entirely on feudal principles. Each officer recruited his own men, who were loyal to himself personally. All the officers swore allegiance to the commander-in-chief. Zeng Guofan's troops were the prototype of China's warlord armies of later years.

3. **Foreign intervention.** The foreign merchants and governments never had any love for the Taiping leaders who were determined to ban the lucrative opium trade and refused to recognize the special privileges the foreigners had obtained from the Qing rulers. But while the revolutionary forces were expanding territorially, they feigned neutrality and adopted a wait-and-see policy.

Following the Second Opium War, the foreign powers became more open in their opposition to the revolution. They linked their long-term interests to the continued rule of the Qing monarchs and propped up the tottering imperial regime with military aid and intervention.

Supplying modern weapons and steam-propelled gunboats to improve the fighting capabilities of the imperial Chinese troops, they also sent officers to train them in fighting techniques and transported Qing combat units to the battlefront at crucial moments in the anti-Taiping struggle.

The Western powers also engaged in direct military intervention to a limited extent. In June 1860, while the Loyal King Li Xiucheng was attacking Shanghai, the American adventurer Frederick Townsend Ward (1831-1862), at the request of local officials, organized a mercenary army of adventurers from many countries. Later called the "Ever-Victorious Army", it grew to 5,000 men (including some Chinese mercenaries) and fought the Taipings on many occasions. When Ward was killed in battle, the leadership was taken over by the British Major (later General) Charles George Gordon (1833-1885) with the official approval of his government.

This was the same Gordon who in 1885 was killed by Sudanese revolutionaries in the siege of Khartoum. British and French troops also took part in the fighting. With their aid, the Hunan and Anhui provincial armies recaptured many strategic cities in the lower Changjiang region and finally occupied Nanjing, capital of the Heavenly Kingdom, in July 1864.

The foreign powers resorted to every means to suppress the Taipings. British and French troops indiscriminately killed non-combatants. Captain Fishbourne, commander of the British vessel *Hermes*, then in Chinese waters, reported that the Western powers had hired Chinese pirates and promised them six dollars for each head they would bring in. These executioners dispersed in every direction in search of heads. As a result, countless men and women, including mothers and infants, lost their lives in this bloodbath.

Estimates put the overall loss of life in the Taiping peasant revolution at between 20 and 30 million people, the most destructive civil war in world history. The suppression of the Taiping Revolution brought devastation to the lower Changjiang region and other parts of south China. The population had dwindled to such an extent that large areas of farmland lay waste for years.

17. FOREIGN SYMPATHIZERS OF THE TAIPING REVOLUTION

The Taiping Revolution, because it fought for social justice and progress, had friends and sympathizers in many lands. In its early stages, its reforms were praised by many foreign visitors. Favorable reports and comments by eyewitnesses appeared in the foreign press.

The British government's intervention on the side of the reactionary and corrupt Qing rulers aroused wide public opposition at home. Workers and democratic elements demonstrated in London's Trafalgar Square in protest against their government's policy. In Parliament leading politicians like Richard Cobden and John Bright voiced strong criticism which was met with stormy applause.

A number of foreigners joined the Taiping army and fought with the revolutionaries. Among them were Englishmen, former officers of the French army, at least one Italian, one Greek and a number of Indians. Major Moreno, an Italian from Sardinia, served for a time as an undercover Taiping agent in Shanghai. Unlike those who served the Qing rulers, they were volunteers and refused any pay.

An outstanding fighter for the Taiping cause was the Englishman Augustus Frederick Lindley. Arriving in China in 1859 at the age of 19, he was shocked by the opium trade as well as the ineptitude and corruption of the Qing government. Finding that the Taiping cause was just and had the support of the Chinese people, in the autumn of 1860 he decided to join the Taipings and became an honorary officer on the staff of the Loyal King Li Xiucheng.

Lindley won many battle honors under Li Xiucheng's command. He taught gunnery to the Taiping soldiers and drilled them in both Chinese and Western formations. On his trips to Shanghai to buy munitions and grain, he spread among other foreigners the truth about the Taipings, urged Western merchants to trade with them, and arranged for influential foreigners to visit the Taiping capital at Nanjing.

In December 1863, after Suzhou had fallen to the enemy, Li Xiucheng ordered Lindley to go to Shanghai and Ningbo to procure warships for the Taipings. Early in 1864 he traveled to Shanghai, but, before long, his presence and activities were discovered by a Qing spy. Lindley's own health was undermined by years of hard campaigning, so he returned to England for medical treatment.

Not long afterwards the Taiping Revolution met with defeat. To fulfill his promise to the Taiping fighters to make the truth about them known, Lindley wrote in 1866 his two-volume *Ti-*

Ping Tien-Kwoh — the History of the Ti-Ping Revolution. He predicted correctly that the Chinese people would never cease to struggle against oppression until they achieved victory.

18. FOREIGN CONTROL OVER CHINA'S MARITIME CUSTOMS ADMINISTRATION

In 1853 a revolt later to become known as the Small Sword Uprising broke out in Shanghai, causing the prefect to flee the city. The British, French and American consuls got together and agreed that they would assume the task of collecting the customs dues themselves. When the prefect returned, the consuls persuaded him to entrust the collection of tariffs in Shanghai to a permanent body of foreign inspectors. In exchange they guaranteed that the arrears, collected over the previous two years, would be paid. The inspectors would be nominated by the consuls and formally appointed by the prefect, to whom they would hand over the taxes they collected. Originally a local expedient for Shanghai, this plan later spread to all other trading ports of China. By the Treaty of Tianjin of 1858, a nationwide Maritime Customs Administration was set up under the Zongli Yamen in Beijing, a new organ performing some of the functions of a foreign ministry, and this important part of the Chinese state's financial machinery came under foreign control.

From the beginning the Maritime Customs Service was headed by an Englishman. In 1863, Robert Hart (1835-1911), a former interpreter with the British consulate in Guangzhou, became the inspector general of imperial customs. As he was directly responsible to the Zongli Yamen, the customs headquarters were moved from Shanghai to Beijing. In every important port Hart employed foreigners as customs commissioners, men who often found themselves in an ambiguous position. On the one hand, they protected the interests of foreign merchants, with the backing of the governments concerned. Foreign goods were levied a fixed low tariff of five percent and, unlike Chinese native products, were exempt from the internal transit taxes (*li jin*) once a moderate surtax of 2.5 percent had been paid. Thus cheap foreign goods flooded the Chinese market and throttled domestic industry.

On the other hand, these foreign customs commissioners were part of a well-organized and efficiently run customs service which soon became an important source of revenue for the Qing government. Customs revenues totaled eight million taels in 1864 and grew to 15 million by 1886, when they constituted a quarter of the government's total revenues. This sizeable and dependable income was used to pay China's huge indemnities to foreign governments, secure loans from foreign banks and help bolster the decrepit Qing government.

As officials of the Qing government, the customs commissioners had easy access to Chinese officials at all levels and could thus exert influence on political affairs. Robert Hart served as the inspector general until 1908. In the 45 years that he held this position, his authority grew until he actually became a chief counselor to the Qing rulers. His memorandum of 1866 to the Qing government, for example, was a regular "manual of good conduct" for both domestic and foreign policy. He played an important role in the negotiation of treaties and agreements between China and foreign countries. Acting upon his suggestion, the Qing government appointed Anson Burlingame (1820-1870), an American diplomat, as head of the first Chinese diplomatic mission to visit the United States of America and European countries. Hart even had a say in the appointment of high Chinese officials who had nothing to do with foreign affairs. In 1867, for instance, both the candidates he proposed for the posts of governor-general of the southwestern provinces of Sichuan and Yunnan-Guizhou were appointed.

Not until 1933 did the foreigners hand back the customs administration to Chinese control under the pressure of the popular Nationalist movement. For nearly 80 years the low tariffs enjoyed by foreign merchants enabled them to sell all sorts of goods to China, including the kerosene for the lamps in town and country and even such small household items as sewing needles, nails and matches. Unable to develop her own productive and mercantile forces, China remained an economically backward semi-colony. After the overthrow of the Qing government in 1911, the revenues from the Maritime Customs mainly went to support first the warlord governments and then Chiang Kai-shek's Kuomintang regime.

19. THE QING GOVERNMENT'S ATTEMPTS AT MODERNIZATION

The suppression of the Taiping Revolution once again demonstrated the importance of modern weapons. To enable the Qing government to put down widespread peasant revolts (such as the uprisings of the Nian in north China, the Miao nationality in Guizhou Province in the southwest and the Muslim Hui nationality in the northwestern provinces of Shaanxi and Ningxia, etc.) and to save the regime from further foreign encroachment, some officials inaugurated a program of modernization over the opposition of diehards at the imperial court.

This program of modernization, known as the *yangwu* (foreign matters) movement, lasted about 30 years from 1865 to 1894. It can be divided into three phases:

1. 1865-1872, the establishment of modern arsenals and other directly military-related industries;

2. 1872-1885, the founding of modern enterprises less directly associated with the military industries; and

3. 1885-1894, the building up of a modern navy and establishment of Western-style iron and steel works.

In the first phase the slogan was *ziqiang* (self-strengthening), the aim being to build up the state's military power through the purchase and manufacture of modern weapons. Arsenals were set up in Shanghai, Nanjing, Fuzhou and Tianjin under the patronage of such officials as Zeng Guofan, Zuo Zongtang (1812-1885) and Li Hongzhang (1823-1901). The building and operating costs were covered by the customs revenues and provincial taxation. Machinery and equipment, sometimes outdated and of low quality, were imported from abroad, and foreign engineers and technicians were invited as advisers or directors.

As the sole purpose of the movement was to build up the military power of the Qing government without regard to the economic development of the country, procurement of all the necessary parts and even of raw materials was by way of foreign imports. Because of the incompetence and corruption of Qing officials, some of the foreign "engineers" were no better than semi-skilled mechanics. The outcome was the manufacture of low-quality weapons at outrageously high cost. While the rifles and ammunition turned out in these arsenals might be good enough to suppress peasant revolts at home, they were all but useless in fighting off foreign aggressors.

Some of the cannons built at the Nanjing arsenal under the direction of the English engineer Macartney to equip the Dagu forts guarding the sea approaches to Tianjin exploded during trials, killing several soldiers. The steam gunboats built at the Shanghai arsenal under the supervision of foreign engineers were so badly built that they could not be steered around at sea, amounting to no more than useless toys in any sea battle. When the French-equipped shipyard at Fuzhou did manage to build a few good ships, it became a target in the Sino-French War of 1884. A French flotilla bombarded the port of Fuzhou without warning, destroying not only the modern fleet which China had been creating there with the help of French technicians, but also the shipyard's installations.

The slogan for the second phase was *fuqiang* (wealth and power), and the aim was to build modern enterprises with the participation of private capital. Accordingly the China Merchant Steam Navigation Company was formed in Shanghai and the Kaiping Mining Company was set up in north China in 1877 on the basis of "government supervision and merchant operation". For a time these enterprises prospered. The ships of the Steam Navigation Company, using coal from the Kaiping Mines, carried goods and passengers on the Changjiang River as far as Yichang near the gorges which guard the access to Sichuan Province in the west, and all along the coast from Macao to Tianjin. However, as these enterprises were under the supervision of appointed officials, the merchant shareholders received only a fixed interest of 10 percent while the greedy bureaucrats in control pocketed huge profits for themselves. The supremacy of officialdom protected the traditional feudal order and prevented the development of capitalism. This benefited the foreigners as well as the bureaucrats, because it ensured that Chinese industry would never grow sufficiently strong to challenge foreign economic penetration.

The third phase was marked by the building up of a navy and the establishment of modern iron and steel works. By 1894 the number of warships had grown to 67 (from 24 in 1884) and the total tonnage had reached 72,800. The fleet was divided into four squadrons, the largest being the Beiyang (Northern Seas) Squadron controlled by Li Hongzhang. Its 29 vessels, including two cruisers armed with Krupp 30-cm. guns, made an impressive show. But with poor and uncoordinated leadership and heavy dependence on antiquated foreign equipment, the Chinese navy had little combat ability.

The iron and steel works founded by the Qing official Zhang Zhidong (1837-1909) at Guangzhou and later moved to Hanyang on the middle Changjiang was equipped with British machinery and directed by a Belgian engineer. The high salaries of the foreigners were a burden on its budget. Furthermore, the construction cost was so high that Zhang had to borrow four million taels from the Deutsche-Asiatische Bank to complete the project. The blast furnaces began working in June 1894, with an annual output of only 22,000 tons.

On the whole, the modernization movement did not bring real wealth or power to China. It merely strengthened the Qing rulers in their ability to oppress the Chinese people and enriched a few senior provincial officials and their hangers-on. By bolstering China's feudal bureaucracy, it prevented the development of China's modern capitalist industry. China's stinging defeat in the Sino-Japanese War of 1894 fully exposed the impotence of the Qing government and spelt an end to the movement.

20. WHY CHINA DIDN'T BECOME A STRONG POWER AS DID JAPAN

In the mid-19th century the Western powers broke open the closed door of Japan, imposing unequal treaties just as they did in China. Although China sank to the status of a semi-colony under the domination of the Western powers, Japan in a few decades rose to become a strong imperialist power. Why did the two countries develop in such contrasting ways?

To answer this question, which is still being widely debated by Chinese scholars, it is necessary to analyze the internal social and political structure and the foreign relations of the two countries.

Internally, Japan had a large body of military aristocrats and their retainers (samurai) who were eager to learn Western technology and military arts to buttress their regional power (especially in the fiefs of the southwestern part of the country). Aware of the subjugation of India and many parts of Africa and the brutality of the British and French troops in China, they became conscious of their own precarious future. Infuriated by the concessions granted to foreigners by the weak central authority known as the Tokugawa Shogunate (1603-1868), they rallied around the emperor under the slogan "revere the emperor, expel the barbarians!" In 1868 they overthrew the Shogunate and proclaimed the return of political power to the ancient monarchy. This Meiji Restoration paved the way for many economic, technological and political reforms, one of the most important of which being the creation of a strong, centralized regime.

In 1871 a mission headed by Iwakura Tomomi (1825-1883) was sent abroad to find out what could be learned from the West. Although the British economy won the admiration of the mission's members, politically the Prussian state impressed them the most. Some years later Ito Hirobumi (1841-1909) scoured Europe in search of ideas for a new constitution. Again it was to Prussia and its spokesmen that he turned for ideas and material assistance. Japan's state structure was thus patterned after that of Prussia, and a similarly militaristic policy was pursued.

The state was run by a new bureaucracy largely composed of ex-samurai. In the central government these ex-samurai constituted 78.3 percent of all office holders listed in the years immediately after 1868. In local governments their numbers exceeded 70 percent. What's more, the police and army were heavily staffed by members of this same class, who mercilessly suppressed any popular revolt.

Lacking almost all the raw materials for heavy industry, Japan seemed destined to develop mainly light industry based on agricultural raw materials, such as raw silk. However, in imitation of Prussia, the Japanese ruling class felt it must also develop heavy industry to provide for its military needs. From the beginning this sector was under government control and all the factories were equipped with modern machinery imported from abroad. Specially favored, this sector developed rapidly and a big military force was soon built up.

Another factor contributing to Japan's rapid industrialization was the existence of a relatively strong commercial and entrepreneurial class which had grown up along the post routes linking the local fiefs to Edo (now Tokyo), capital of the Shogunate. This stratum, uninhibited by either ideological concerns or government interference, was quick to adopt elements of Western technology.

Unlike Japan, China did not have a military aristocratic group corresponding to the samurai and her commercial class was comparatively weak. For many centuries China had been mainly ruled by scholar-bureaucrats who believed — in theory at least — in managing the nation according to Confucian moral principles instead of through military might or technical knowledge. The military arts were looked down upon. On the social ladder, scholars stood at the top and soldiers at the bottom. A common saying went, "Good iron is not used for nails, and good men do not become soldiers."

As China had long been more highly civilized relative to her northern nomadic neighbors and had been admired by peoples such as the Mongols and Manchus, the Chinese scholar-gentry considered itself a civilization dispenser rather than borrower. Even the few high officials who advocated modernization in the mid-19th century thought that Chinese learning should remain "the essence" and Western learning be adopted for "pragmatic" purposes only.

China's ruling scholar-bureaucrats derived from the landlord-gentry class. They were primarily concerned with maintaining the old feudal order against any kind of peasant unrest. Bound by tradition, they linked their fate with the continued rule of a conservative monarchy. They were apprehensive that any new ideas or new technology from the West might undermine their own privileged positions.

The foreign relations of China took a different course from that of Japan. With its vast territory, rich resources and huge population, China was in Western eyes a potentially unlimited market for manufactured goods and a rich source of raw materials. The exploitation of China was thus at the top of the list of priorities for the Western powers in the Far East. Japan, with a small territory and limited resources, was not regarded as such a worthy prize.

Thus, a combination of specific internal and external conditions enabled Japan to be modernized on a feudal foundation. China, on the other hand, sank deeper into the quagmire of semi-colonial misery under the rule of the reactionaries headed by the haughty and ignorant Empress Dowager Ci Xi.

21. THE EMPRESS DOWAGER, POWER BEHIND THE THRONE

Empress Dowager Ci Xi (Tzu Hsi, 1835-1908) was born into the aristocratic Yehenala family. At the age of 17 she was selected to enter the imperial palace as the concubine of the Xian Feng Emperor, who reigned from 1851-1861. In 1856 she gave birth to a son who was to be the emperor's successor, so she was raised in status to be the emperor's second consort, with the right of residence in the western inner court. Prudent and obedient in appearance though cruel and crafty at heart, she was able to win the emperor's trust.

In 1861 Xian Feng suddenly died in Chengde, the Manchu court's summer resort beyond the Great Wall. Her son, the new emperor, was only five years old. According to the Manchu court rules, the regency should have gone to the experienced elderly princes rather than the child emperor's mother. Determined to grasp power for herself, Ci Xi arranged to have the powerful Minister Sushun (1816-1861) killed during the emperor's funeral. With the imperial seal in hand, she was then able to issue edicts in the name of the emperor, thus becoming the real power behind the throne.

In her long rule of 48 years, China experienced one of the darkest and most reactionary periods in its history. In 1864 she was instrumental in suppressing the Taiping peasant revolution and other large-scale revolts with the support of other leading members of the ruling classes and foreign interests. In the First Sino-Japanese War of 1894-1895, she ordered her trusted representative Li Hongzhang to sign away the island of Taiwan and other vital rights to Japan. In 1898 she broke the Hundred Days' Reform and imprisoned the Guang Xu Emperor who had initiated the reforms. At the turn of the century, she first encouraged the Boxers in their efforts to kill foreigners in China; when this provoked the powers to dispatch an international army to suppress these patriotic but superstitious peasants, she turned around and ordered the ruthless suppression of the Boxers. In her attempt to strengthen her personal power and perpetuate dynastic rule, she shut the doors to all necessary reforms, thus weakening the regime against the rising popular discontent and foreign aggression.

In private life the Empress Dowager was arbitrary, pleasure-seeking and extravagant. To build the Summer Palace for her own enjoyment, she diverted 36,000,000 taels of silver from the fund for naval construction plus countless millions in "gifts" extracted from officials and the people. For her 60th birthday celebrations in 1894 she ordered all the provinces to set up separate decorations along the road from the Forbidden City to the Summer Palace in the northwestern suburbs of the capital. In 1873, when she was 39, Ci Xi mobilized millions of workers and artisans to begin building her tomb, an underground palace which was still not completed by the time of her death 35 years later. Buried with her were numerous priceless treasures which were later looted by warlord soldiers. Such extravagance depleted the national treasury and impoverished the people.

How could Ci Xi remain in power for so long? The secret lay in her ability to manipulate people in the factional strife among the Manchu princes, aristocrats and officials in the bureaucracy. With the help of her trusted eunuchs who catered to her every whim, she played one party against another for her own interests. Thus she was able to seize power after the death of the Xian Feng Emperor. Using the same method she maneuvered to have her nephew succeed her son the Tong Zhi Emperor instead of some one else from the younger generation in the imperial clan, according to law, so that she could retain power as regent. She repeatedly violated court laws and customs in order to enhance her own power, but she demanded strict observance of old rules from other members of the imperial clan and other subordinates.

During her long rule, China experienced serious famines, peasant uprisings and foreign encroachment. The times demanded a strong central government with popular support. The Empress Dowager's refusal to adopt any reforms that would reduce the power of the imperial house drove many reformers into the ranks of the revolutionaries, and thus brought about the downfall of the Qing dynasty.

22. THE FIRST SINO-JAPANESE WAR
(1894-1895)

In 1894 Japan, with a modern army and navy, was prepared for military adventures. Short of resources, its leaders cast their hungry eyes particularly on Korea and the adjoining parts of China, including both the northeast and the Shandong peninsula across the sea.

In June of that year the Qing government was called upon by the king of Korea to send troops to help quell an insurrection in his country. Citing the Sino-Japanese Treaty of Tianjin signed in 1885, by which both countries had pledged not to intervene directly in Korea without informing the other, Japan dispatched troops, too. China sent 3,000 men, Japan 18,000. In July Japan set up a puppet government and demanded the withdrawal of Chinese troops from Korea. Without warning, Japanese troops began to attack Chinese forces, and war was formally declared on August 1, 1894.

This war lasted only about six months. While the various groups in the Japanese government were united in the effort to win the war, the Qing government was rent by factional strife and intrigue. In the field, the Japanese army first drove the disorganized Chinese troops out of Korea; then its naval forces routed the poorly-led Chinese navy in the Yellow Sea. By February 1895, the Japanese forces had crossed the Yalu River into Chinese territory, conducted landings at the naval bases of Dalian ("Dairen" or "Dalny" in Japanese and Russian respectively) and Lüshun ("Port Arthur" in British parlance) on the Liaodong peninsula, smashed the "powerful" Beiyang naval squadron outside Weihaiwei on the Shandong peninsula, and threatened Beijing itself.

Despite this national crisis, the Empress Dowager Ci Xi went on busily preparing for her elaborate 60th birthday celebrations. Determined not to allow any "unpleasantness" to mar this happy occasion, she decided to sue for peace at any price. She sent the trusted official Li Hongzhang (with a former U.S. Secretary of State, John W. Foster, as adviser) to Japan to negotiate a peace treaty. Japan dictated extremely harsh conditions. Just at that time Li Hongzhang was seriously wounded by a Japanese assassin's bullet. Fearing the intervention by other big powers, the Japanese government softened its terms, which remained bitter for China. On April 17, 1895, the Treaty of Shimonoseki was signed. By the terms of the treaty, China was forced to renounce its suzerainty over Korea (which meant *de facto* recognition of Japanese control of that country), to cede the Liaodong peninsula in the northeast and Taiwan and the Penghu Islands off the southeast China coast, and to pay a huge indemnity of 200 million taels of silver (the Qing government's annual revenues totaled only 80 million taels at the time) to cover Japan's military expenditures in the war. In addition, China had to open Chongqing and Shashi on the upper Changjiang River as well as Suzhou and Hangzhou on the Grand Canal as trading ports which could be visited by Japanese ships, and to permit the establishment of Japanese-run factories in all the open ports.

But Japan's claims brought foreign repercussions. Japanese occupation of the Liaodong peninsula directly threatened Russia's ambitions in northeast China. Russia persuaded Germany and France to join in concerted action, and the three governments demanded that Japan hand Liaodong back to China. Japan disgorged the territory only after the Qing government agreed to pay an additional indemnity of 30 million taels of silver.

Japan's annexation of Taiwan met determined resistance from the local population. Yosaburo Takekoshi, a Japanese chronicler, writes: "Whenever our troops were defeated, the inhabitants of the surrounding villages instantly became our enemies, every one, even the young women, arming and joining the ranks with shouts of defiance. Our opponents were very stubborn and not at all afraid of death." Only by fighting a cruel war for almost eight years against guerrillas and wide popular opposition did Japan impose control over Taiwan.

23. CHINA'S INTERNATIONAL POSITION AFTER ITS DEFEAT

China's defeat in the Sino-Japanese War of 1894-1895 was an unprecedented humiliation. Defeat at the hands of the Western powers was hard enough, but now China had been beaten by a neighbor which it had always regarded as an inferior.

The exposure of the Chinese government's complete bankruptcy whetted the appetite of the Western powers. Lord Rosebery, British Foreign Minister under Gladstone, voiced the sentiment of many when he stated bluntly: "There we have a sick man worth many Turkeys, of more value to us as a people than all the Armenians that ever walked the earth; as a commercial inheritance, priceless, beyond all the ivory and peacocks that ever came out of Africa." (Quoted by William Langer, *Diplomacy of Imperialism*, p. 385.)

The powers started a scramble for concessions, for the granting of government loans, and for the right to build railways in various parts of China. In July 1895 a syndicate of Russian and French banks extended a loan of 100 million taels of silver to China to enable her to pay the first installment of her war indemnity to Japan. In return, France obtained the right to extend her railway from Viet Nam to Nanning and Kunming in southwest China, while Russia demanded the right to build a railway from Chita (in southeastern Siberia) straight through China's northeast to Vladivostok. Temporarily forestalled due to British protest, this demand was also granted by the Chinese government the following year. To counter the growth of the French and Russian influence, British and German banks in 1896 extended China a loan of the same amount (but with less favorable terms) to enable her to pay the second installment of the indemnity to Japan. For this Britain obtained a promise from the Chinese government not to change the British administration of the Maritime Customs, whose revenues served as security for the loan.

The building of the Beijing-Hankou Railway through the heart of China was a bone of contention among the powers. To avoid domination by any of the giants, in 1897 the Chinese government gave the contract to Belgium. However, the group of bankers financing the project was actually Franco-Belgian. Since France was an ally of Russia at that time, this vitally important railway fell under Franco-Russian influence. Britain reacted with a demand that an Englishman be appointed chief engineer of the projected Shanhaiguan-Shenyang Railway in order to check Russia's growing power in the northeast. The Qing government readily agreed to this demand as it was attempting to "use one barbarian to control another".

The appetite of the foreign powers continued to grow. Ever since the end of the Second Opium War in 1860, the Western powers had been swallowing up China's peaceful neighbors (Burma, Viet Nam, Nepal, Thailand, etc.) and nibbling at China's borderlands (Xinjiang in the northwest, Tibet in the southwest). Now, seeing China in a helpless situation, they began to seize territories within her very boundaries. In November 1897, using the killing of two German Roman Catholic missionaries as a pretext, Germany occupied the north China harbor of Qingdao on the Shandong peninsula. In a treaty the following March, Germany extorted a "leasehold" on this strategic naval base for 99 years (until 1997) as well as the right to build railways and open mines in Shandong Province. Russia, through a secret agreement between the Tsar and the German Kaiser, quickly obtained a lease of 25 years on the naval base of Lüshun and the commercial port of Dalian which she had helped force Japan to give up after the Sino-Japanese War in 1895. She also acquired the right to build a branch railway line to "south Manchuria", thus bringing all northeast China under Russian domination.

Five days after the Russian acquisitions were confirmed, Britain occupied the naval base of Weihaiwei on the north side of the Shandong peninsula, declaring that she would hold it as long as Russia held Lüshun. In April 1898, France seized Kuangzhouwan on the south China coast, where China's big trading port of Zhanjiang is situated today. In addition to a 99-year lease on the harbor, she forced the Chinese government to promise that it would not cede any territory in Yunnan, Guangdong or Guangxi to any other power, thus recognizing in effect that these three southern provinces were within its "sphere of influence". Under the pretext of counter-balancing French influence in the area, Britain enlarged its possessions in Hongkong, obtaining a 99-year lease on the adjacent territories north of Jiulong peninsula and neighboring islands, thus adding 974 square kilometers to the 75 square kilometers of the original Hongkong colony. Then, with the help of Britain, Japan obtained a promise from the Chinese government to respect the "territorial integrity" of Fujian Province facing Taiwan.

At this point, China's international position had sunk so low that it seemed she might be carved up like a melon among the powers and cease to be an independent nation.

24.   THE UNITED STATES' "OPEN DOOR" DOCTRINE

While the European powers were scrambling for concessions in China, the United States was busy with its war against Spain. By the time the United States had occupied the Pacific island of Guam and the Philippines, China's nearest neighbor in the

South China Sea, China had already been carved up into "spheres of influence" by the powers: the Changjiang valley and Tibet had been claimed by Britain, northeast China and Mongolia had been allotted to tsarist Russia, southwest China had fallen to both Britain and France, Shandong Province had become Germany's preserve, and Fujian Province had been brought under the influence of the rising Oriental power, Japan.

To protect the commercial interests of the United States under such circumstances, Secretary of State John Hay in the fall of 1899 addressed identical notes to Britain, France, Germany, Russia, Italy and Japan, asking that each of them:

1.   Refrain from any interference with the commercial activities of other powers within the sphere of interest or leased territory that each country might have in China;

2.   Recognize the right of the Chinese government alone to collect duties according to the Chinese treaty tariff; and

3.   Allow no preferential harbor dues or railway charges to benefit its own subjects.

Clearly, the notes were a reassertion of the most-favored-nation treatment provided in the unequal treaties concluded between China and the powers. While recognizing the existence of the "spheres of influence", the U.S. government was asking that U.S. interests not be discriminated against in any way. Whatever privileges other foreigners enjoyed in China should be accorded to Americans. Owen Lattimore, an American specialist in Chinese affairs, has called this the "me too" policy.

The other powers gave prompt attention to the Hay notes. Britain readily agreed to the policy outlined as it was then the leading capitalist power and feared competition from none. In fact, the very idea of the "open door" had originated in the British Colonial Office, which considered it the best means of maintaining Britain's predominant commercial position in the Chinese market. Russia made a reservation on the question of Chinese collection of customs duties, but renounced the intention of claiming any privileges for its own subjects to the exclusion of other foreigners. Germany, France and Italy declared their agreement one after another. While anxious to protect its own privileged positions in China, each power was also afraid that it might be pushed out by another. Japan had to give its consent, although the "open door" eventually became one of the major causes of the war with the United States.

In this whole process, China was never consulted as to whether it wanted its doors closed or open. Nominally an independent nation, China had in effect become a semi-colony to be exploited by all the powers.

25. THE "HUNDRED DAYS' REFORM" OF 1898

From June to September 1898, Emperor Guang Xu (r. 1875-1908), following the advice of the reformer Kang Youwei (1858-1927), issued a flood of edicts on the reform of administration, economy, education and military affairs. This attempt at reform from the top lasted about 100 days and is known as the "Hundred Days' Reform".

The moving spirit was Kang Youwei and his followers. A scholar from a landed-gentry family in the southern province of Guangdong, Kang recognized in his youth the danger of foreign imperialist aggression and the necessity of reform in order to maintain China's independence. He wrote his first memorial to the emperor as early as 1888, but it never reached the throne. Kang arrived in Beijing to take the metropolitan examinations in 1895, just as Japan was imposing the Treaty of Shimonoseki on China after the first Sino-Japanese War. In a second memorial, signed by 1,300 scholars who had come from the provinces for the examinations, Kang recommended that the treaty not be ratified, that the army be reorganized, and that reforms be carried out in the political, economic and cultural fields. Although this memorial also failed to reach the throne due to its interception by the Board of Censors, it was widely circulated among the scholars. "Study societies" sprang up in various parts of China, their aim being to promote reform. Newspapers began to be published to spread Western bourgeois democratic ideas and schools were set up to imbue the young with a new spirit. Demands for reform quickly became widespread among educated youth.

When Germany occupied Qingdao in Shandong Province in November 1897, Kang rushed from Guangdong to Beijing and wrote three more memorials to Emperor Guang Xu. To avoid the threatened partition of China by the powers, he proposed that the emperor immediately issue a reform declaration giving people the freedom to present suggestions and establishing the Administrative Systems Bureau as the leading reform organ. Soon thereafter, Societies for the Preservation of the Nation were formed in the capital and many provinces. Their newspapers had a tremendous impact on the educated classes throughout the country.

Meanwhile a struggle for power was going on in Beijing between Emperor Guang Xu and Empress Dowager Ci Xi. Emperor Guang Xu decided to assert his authority and institute reforms. On June 11, 1898, he issued an edict announcing the initiation of "discussions on national affairs"; this edict marked the beginning of the "Hundred Days". In subsequent decrees he ordered the elimination of large numbers of useless offices, posts and sinecures; abolition of the subsidies paid to all Manchus; disbandment of the corrupt and inefficient Army of the Green Standard and the formation of modern military units.

In the field of education and culture, old academies and temples which had fallen into disuse were to be converted into schools where science and politics would be included in the curriculum. Peking University was founded. The traditional examination system was reorganized and essays based solely on the Confucian classics were eliminated. Liang Qichao (1873-1929), a follower of Kang Youwei, was placed in charge of a new translation bureau responsible for introducing foreign books. Tan Sitong (1865-1898) and three other Kang supporters were appointed to high posts in order to implement the reform decrees.

Despite their broad appeal, the projected reforms met with determined opposition from conservative officials in the provinces. Only Chen Baochen (1831-1900), governor of Hunan Province in central China, wholeheartedly supported the reforms; the governors of the other provinces simply ignored the relevant decrees.

From the first, the Empress Dowager Ci Xi was hostile to the reforms, and she soon decided on a coup d'état to oust the emperor. She had her loyal follower Ronglu (1836-1903) appointed governor-general of Zhili (now Hebei) Province, where the capital was situated, and made him commander-in-chief of the armed forces. She took control of the garrison troops in Beijing and at the Summer Palace in the outskirts. Toward the beginning of September, rumors circulated that the Empress Dowager would soon take the emperor with her to review troops in Tianjin, where Ronglu would stage a coup and force the emperor to abdicate.

At this critical moment, the reformers put their trust in Yuan Shikai (1859-1916), an erstwhile member of the Society for the Preservation of the Nation, and now a subordinate of Ronglu in charge of the modern army units. In the small hours of the morning of September 18, Tan Sitong went to the home of Yuan Shikai, hoping to persuade him to murder Ronglu and protect the emperor. Yuan promised to do so, but he in fact immediately betrayed the plan to Ronglu, who rushed to inform the Empress Dowager in the Summer Palace.

The Empress Dowager struck on the morning of September 21. She returned to the Forbidden City, put the emperor under house arrest, and ordered the arrest and execution of the reformers. Kang Youwei fled to Hongkong, and Liang Qichao to Japan. Warned by his colleagues to flee, Tan Sitong refused. "In other countries," he said, "no reform has been accomplished without bloodshed. No one has yet shed any blood for it in China. ... I shall be the first." He and five other leading reformers were executed. All the reform decrees, except that founding Peking University, were revoked. The whole reform movement collapsed.

The "Hundred Days" was a progressive movement initiated by upper-class intellectuals of the day. They attempted to go beyond the mere copying of Western military science and technology as advocated by the *yangwu* movement, to transform China's centuries-old political system and to learn from Western bourgeois-democratic thought and culture. They played a great part in arousing the national consciousness of the Chinese people. However, because their program did not touch on the feudal landowning system, they failed to win support from the peasant masses. They relied on the emperor alone to carry out the reforms even while the Empress Dowager held the real power. Despite its failure, however, the reform movement served as a valuable lesson. Seeing that reform within the old framework led up a blind alley, many patriots turned to revolution as the only way out for China.

26. THE BOXER (YI HE TUAN) MOVEMENT

The "Boxer" Movement was a great popular uprising triggered by resentment against foreign aggression. As a demonstration of the strength and patriotic fervor of the ordinary Chinese people, it probably played a part in saving the country from partition at the beginning of the 20th century.

The movement started in Shandong Province on the north China coast. Here public indignation ran high against Germany's seizure in 1898 of Qingdao and Jiaozhou Bay as well as against the misdeeds of some Christian missionaries and their Chinese converts. The missionaries in many places became notorious for various activities, including land-grabbing, money-lending at exorbitant rates of interest, interference in lawsuits in favor of their followers against non-Christians, and even for maintaining armed thugs and protecting outright criminals. An exploited and oppressed population was easily stirred to regard the missionaries in their midst as the main source of all their sufferings.

The Boxers, originally known as *Yi He Quan* (Righteous and Harmonious Fists), practiced a type of martial arts and believed that amulets and incantations would protect them from bullets and shells. Their members were mostly young peasants, but included also some boatmen, porters, ruined craftsmen, small shopkeepers, peddlers, monks and soldiers. Protected by Provincial Governor Yuxian (Yuhsien) of Shandong, an imperial clansman and a protegé of Empress Dowager Ci Xi, the Boxers adopted the slogan, "Support the Qing dynasty and exterminate the foreigners." Their numbers grew rapidly and this grassroots uprising soon spread to other parts of north China and southern Manchuria.

By the beginning of June 1900, large numbers of Boxers had converged on Beijing. Joined by many local residents, they attacked Catholic and Protestant churches in the city and set up altars in the streets and lanes, practicing boxing and forging weapons night and day. In face of this militant mass movement, the Empress Dowager adopted a two-faced policy. While ordering the reorganization of the Boxers into the *Yi He Tuan* (Righteous and Harmonious Militia) and declaring war on the foreign powers, she secretly told the foreign diplomats that she was forced to do so and would suppress the Boxers at the earliest opportunity.

The foreign powers had no faith in the honeyed words of the Empress Dowager. Eight of them — Britain, Russia, the U.S.A., Germany, France, Japan, Italy and Austria-Hungary — formed an international army, which after arriving in north China, destroyed the forts at Dagu, occupied Tianjin, and on August 14 stormed into the capital itself. In this national emergency, the Empress Dowager, disguised as a peasant woman, fled to Xi'an, taking the emperor and a cortege of court officials and attendants with her.

Wherever the allied forces went, they burned, looted, massacred both old and young, and raped the womenfolk. Kaiser Wilhelm II, who regarded the Chinese people as a "yellow peril", had instructed his troops to give no quarter and take no prisoners. He told them to wield their weapons well "so that for a thousand years no Chinese will dare look askance at a German". Tsar Nicholas II of Russia sent 150,000 troops into China's northeast, where they razed cities to the ground and slaughtered the inhabitants. At the time Lenin wrote:

> If we are to call things by their right names, we must say that the European governments (the Russian government among the very first) have already started to partition China. They began to rob China as ghouls rob corpses, and when the seeming corpse attempted to resist, they flung themselves upon it like savage beasts, burning whole villages and drowning in the Amur River unarmed inhabitants, their wives and their children.

In the capital, B. L. Putnam Weale, a British eyewitness, described vividly how every house was robbed. He portrayed the foreign troops as "an endless procession of looting men". "On top of the blood and ruin, they began to sell and barter their spoils so that all our armies are becoming armies of traders." The American writer Mark Twain, in a letter to a friend, said, "My sympathies are with the Chinese. . . . I hope they will drive all foreigners out and keep them out for good."

In face of the depredations, the Empress Dowager sent Li Hongzhang as plenipotentiary to Beijing to beg for peace. In January 1901 he accepted a list of foreign demands, which were ratified as the "Boxer Protocol" in September of that year. The terms included:

• Payment of an indemnity of 450 million taels in gold in 39 annual installments (to 1940); (When interest and silver substitution rates are taken into account, the total amounted to well over 980 million taels, more than 12 times the total annual national revenue at that time!)

• Punishment of the chief offenders by death or exile, suspension of the examinations for five years in 45 districts where the Boxers had been active, banning of all anti-foreign societies, and the change of the Zongli Yamen (Office in Charge of Foreign Affairs) to Waiwubu (Ministry of Foreign Affairs) to take precedence over all other ministries; and

• Razing of all forts between Beijing and the sea, including those at Dagu, and the garrisoning of 12 points on the route by foreign troops. The Legation Quarter in the heart of the capital was also to be guarded by foreign troops and enlarged, and Chinese were forbidden to live there.

The settlement was disastrous for China. The huge indemnity became an enormous drain on the country's finances, making any real economic development impossible. The foreign diplomatic corps in Beijing, protected by foreign guards, became in reality the overlords of the Qing government, supervising its finances and dictating its domestic and foreign policies to suit their own interests.

Although the Boxers were ultimately slaughtered and suppressed, their fierce struggle against overwhelming odds made the foreign powers think twice before carving China up among themselves. Recognizing the potential of an enraged Chinese populace, Count Alfred von Waldersee (1832-1904), the German commander-in-chief of the allied army, wrote: "Neither any European nor American nation nor Japan has the intellectual or military strength to rule over such a country with a quarter of the world's population. . . . The partition of China is therefore the least feasible policy."

27. DR. SUN YAT-SEN, FATHER OF THE CHINESE REVOLUTION

Dr. Sun Yat-sen (1866-1925) was the first to advocate the overthrow of the Qing dynasty and the establishment of a Chinese democratic republic. Because he devoted his entire life to the achievement of these lofty goals, he is revered by the Chinese people to this day.

Dr. Sun was born to a peasant family on November 12, 1866, in a village of Xiangshan (now Zhongshan) County, in the southern part of Guangdong Province. His parents were so poor that the family subsisted on sweet potatoes (rice being too expensive), and he never had shoes to wear. As his village was near the birthplace of Hong Xiuquan, the leader of the Taiping Revolution, he was inspired in his childhood by this revolutionary tradition. At the age of 13 he went to Honolulu; his brother enrolled him in a missionary school where he came under the influence of Western ideas of Christianity and democracy. Later, he studied medicine in Hongkong. After graduation in 1892, he began to practice medicine in Guangzhou and Macao. But his mind was soon preoccupied with the problem of curing the ills of the old feudal China and making it a modern, strong nation.

At that time Dr. Sun was not yet a revolutionary and still had illusions about the Qing dynasty. In 1894 he wrote a letter to Li Hongzhang, the most powerful figure in the imperial court, recommending reforms in agriculture, industry, commerce and education. Certain of the correctness of his views, he traveled to Tianjin with the hope of convincing Li Hongzhang personally. But Li was not interested in the ideas of this unknown young man and refused to see him. Disappointed, Sun Yat-sen went on to Beijing, the capital. There he discovered that the Qing court was rotten to the core. Ignorance and intrigue were rife among the court officials. With the first Sino-Japanese War raging, the Empress Dowager Ci Xi and her courtiers were more concerned with preparing a grand celebration for her 60th birthday in the Summer Palace.

China's defeat by Japan intensified Sun Yat-sen's patriotic indignation. On his way back south he visited Wuhan and Shanghai, where he saw further evidence of the decay of the empire. Convinced that saving the moribund regime through reform was a hopeless task, he decided that the Qing dynasty must be overthrown and the monarchy replaced by a free and enlightened China. He had become a revolutionary.

In subsequent years, Dr. Sun's revolutionary activities took him far and wide — to Honolulu, the United States, Europe and Japan.

In 1894, together with some 20 Chinese shopkeepers and farm-owners in Honolulu, he formed the *Xing Zhong Hui* (Society for the Revival of China), China's first bourgeois revolutionary organization.* Convinced that the nation was in crisis, the organization adopted the slogan, "Regenerate China and maintain national independence." The following spring Sun Yat-sen returned to Hongkong with some followers and staged their first armed uprising against the Qing dynasty at Guangzhou. Although it failed, Sun Yat-sen began to be known at home and abroad as the leader of a revolutionary group.

Now under threat of arrest, Sun fled to Japan and then traveled to the United States and Europe. Wherever he went, he worked to spread revolutionary ideas among the Chinese residents and students. In October 1896, he was kidnapped in London by Chinese Legation officials, who intended to return him to China for execution. Thanks to the aid of Dr. James Cantlie (1851-1926), former dean of the medical college in Hongkong where he had studied, Sun was rescued, thus escaping certain death. This incident only strengthened Sun's determination to devote his life to revolution.

To work out guiding principles for the Chinese revolution, Dr. Sun began to study works on the American and European revolutions and to observe how Western political and social institutions operated. In June 1897, he went to Japan to plan more revolutionary uprisings in China.

During the Boxer Movement in 1900, Sun Yat-sen thought the time for the revolution had come. In October, he directed some *Xing Zhong Hui* leaders to stage with the support of 600 members of the *San He Hui* (a secret society) an uprising in Huizhou in his native province. The revolutionaries fought bravely against the government troops, but due to the inter-

---

* This term refers to the nature of the movement's social backing, which consisted of overseas Chinese businessmen and students who had been influenced by the ideas of the French and American revolutions.

ference of the Japanese government, Sun could not get the promised arms from Taiwan to the insurgents. Thus, this attempt also collapsed.

Still more failures awaited Dr. Sun in his revolutionary activities, but they could not shake his determination to destroy once and for all the monarchical system in China. His untiring efforts to achieve this aim eventually won the deep respect of the Chinese people, earning him the right to be considered the father of the Chinese revolution.

28. DR. SUN YAT-SEN'S REVOLUTIONARY THOUGHT

Dr. Sun Yat-sen was a staunch republican. His political ideas were the product of a childhood in a peasant village where he was influenced by the heritage of the Taiping Revolution, his education in an American school in Honolulu and a British medical college in Hongkong, and 10 years of exile in Japan, Europe and the United States.

His main political ideas are embodied in his "Three People's Principles" (*San Min Zhu Yi*).

Nationalism, the first principle, was directed chiefly against the Qing monarchy. In his book *Solution to China's Problems*, written in 1904, he argued: "The Manchu rule is like a building about to collapse. Its structure is completely rotten. No outside force can save it from falling." He called on the Chinese people to rise up and overthrow the monarchy and to establish an independent national state. He directed his attack only against the Qing rulers who were the real oppressors, and not against the ordinary Manchu people. He regarded people of all nationalities in China as equal citizens working together for a regenerated nation.

Democracy, the second principle, involved the establishment of a republic with a constitution guaranteeing democratic rule.

A popularly elected parliament was to be set up to discuss and decide on national affairs. Instead of being agents for a despotic emperor, officials would be "public servants" working for the welfare of the people, the real masters of the country. And the people were to rise up and condemn anyone who attempted to restore the monarchical structure.

People's livelihood, the third principle, involved the improvement of the common people's lot through land reform, a major change in a predominantly agricultural country. This was to be accomplished through non-violent means. As China was an economically underdeveloped country, the value of land was low. The state was to fix land values at this low level. The future development of industry and communications would inevitably raise land prices tremendously. This increase or increment should go to the state rather than to private landowners. With this increment and the land tax, the state would get enough revenues from the land alone to defray all governmental expenditures. Other taxes would be abolished; commodity prices would therefore remain low, and the people would become more prosperous. By preventing the polarization of society between the very rich and the very poor, bloody class struggle could be avoided in the future.

Dr. Sun Yat-sen's Three People's Principles were influenced by his knowledge of Western political history. Dr. Sun sometimes compared his principles to those of the French Revolution embodied in the slogan "liberty, equality and fraternity". Like Abraham Lincoln, he sought a "government of the people, by the people and for the people". However, having learned much through practice in his revolutionary activities, Dr. Sun re-interpreted his Three People's Principles a year before his death in 1925.

In the earlier period, Dr. Sun also put forward several other notable political ideas for China.

1. The constitutional powers should be divided into five branches — administrative, legislative, judicial, supervisory and impeachment, and the selection of civil servants would be through examinations.

2.   Real democracy had to be based on local self-government.

3.   The electorate should exercise direct supervision over their representatives, and anyone could be recalled if he no longer represented the interests of the people.

4.   The revolution should progress through three successive stages — military rule (three years or less), the achievement of local self-government (about six years), and constitutional government in which the President of the Republic and members of parliament would be elected by popular vote.

There were no doubt weaknesses in Dr. Sun's early political thought.   His proposed method to transform China's feudal land-ownership was rather utopian.   He imagined that the foreign imperialist powers were sympathetic enough to the Chinese revolution to aid and support the revolutionary cause. Afraid of mass actions, he thought they should be restricted and the revolution conducted "in an orderly way".   Nevertheless, Dr. Sun Yat-sen is revered by the Chinese people, because he was a devoted revolutionary who, in spite of repeated failures, strove unwaveringly to realize his noble dream of a modernized republican China.

29.   REVOLUTION VS. REFORM

After Japan's victory over China in the first Sino-Japanese War in 1895, thousands of Chinese students went to Japan to try to learn the "secret" of its success.   There many discussion groups were formed, with the patriotic students gradually polarizing into two opposite camps.   One, under the leadership of Dr. Sun Yat-sen, advocated the revolutionary overthrow of the Qing dynasty, while the other, headed by Kang Youwei and his capable disciple Liang Qichao, sought the preservation of the Manchu monarchy through constitutional reforms.

Although China's "Hundred Days' Reform" of 1898 collapsed, the two leaders, Kang and Liang, put the blame for their defeat on the Empress Dowager Ci Xi and her conservative followers. Regarding the young Emperor Guang Xu as a "progressive", they organized a *Bao Huang Hui* (Protect the Emperor Society) and published a journal *Xinmin Congbao* (*New People's Miscellany*). Kang extolled the old order and proposed to make Confucianism an official religion, based on a new interpretation of Confucian tenets. Liang, however, went beyond his mentor's teachings. Interested in Western history and philosophy, he became an admirer of Darwin, Martin Luther, Bacon, Descartes, Cavour and Mazzini. In a lucid and flowing style, his writings awakened the national consciousness of his readers and stirred them to demand the establishment of a constitutional monarchy in China. His biting criticism of the diehards in the Qing government also had a great influence on many upper-class gentry-scholars, so that they too began to call for constitutional reforms.

As the impotence of the Qing government in resisting foreign encroachment became more and more clearly exposed, increasing numbers of young students became disillusioned with the monarchy and turned toward revolution as the only way out for China. Among them were Zhang Taiyan (1869-1936) from Zhejiang Province, who in 1900 cut off his queue — an act of defiance against the Manchu rulers — to show his complete break with the reformers; Zou Rong (1885-1905) from Sichuan Province, who wrote the pamphlet *Revolutionary Army* in 1903 which called on all patriots to join the army of revolution; and Chen Tianhua (1875-1905) from Hunan Province, whose *Alarm Bell*, issued in 1903, urged the Chinese people to take up arms and fight foreign aggressors in order to achieve complete national independence.

In July 1905, Dr. Sun Yat-sen arrived in Japan from Europe. He called the revolutionary groups together and explained the importance of unity. As a result, *Tong Meng Hui* (China Revolutionary League) was established on August 20, and Dr. Sun was elected its General Director.

In its program, the Revolutionary League accepted Dr. Sun's Three People's Principles — nationalism, democracy and the people's livelihood. Its organ, *Min Bao* (*The People*), immediately launched into a battle of words with the *New People's Miscellany* of the Kang-Liang reformist camp. The ensuing heated polemic centered around three major questions:

1.   **Should there be a revolution in China?**   The reformers claimed that revolution would create internal chaos leading to the partition of China by the foreign powers. The revolutionaries countered with the argument that the Qing government was selling out the nation to the foreign powers, and every patriot was duty-bound to try to overthrow a monarchy which was betraying the interests of the people.

2.   **Should China become a republic?**   In the eyes of the reformers, the Chinese people were too ignorant to manage a democratic republic; the best form of government was a constitutional monarchy like that of Japan. The revolutionaries argued that, with the Qing dynasty gone, the way would be clear to adopt a more advanced form of government, the republican form.

3.   **Should China's feudal landowning system be changed?** The reformers wanted to perpetuate the old landowning system. They maintained that any change of the land system would lead to disturbances and breakdown of the social order. The revolutionaries argued that a new China must be built on a new social foundation in which equality and fraternity would be the guiding principle.

The revolutionaries won many young intellectuals to their side. The ranks of the Revolutionary League grew in Japan, and its ideas spread among the secret societies and the junior officers of the New Army, a military force being formed by the Qing court along modern lines. But it was too loose an organization of heterogeneous elements. While all agreed that the Qing government had to be destroyed by revolutionary means, few were firm republicans and still fewer supported Dr. Sun's ideal of "land to the tillers". This lack of a united purpose and the low level of organizational discipline reflected the weakness of China's newly rising bourgeoisie and foreshadowed the inevitable failure of China's first bourgeois democratic revolution.

30. QIU JIN — A WOMAN REVOLUTIONARY

Qiu Jin stood out like a brilliant star among the revolutionaries of her time.

Qiu Jin (1875-1907) was born to a wealthy family in Shaoxing County to the southeast of the beautiful lake city of Hangzhou, Zhejiang Province. During her childhood her father held minor official positions in the provinces of Fujian and Hunan. At 22 she was married to a wealthy scholar who later became an official in Beijing. During the Boxer Movement, she saw how the capital was plundered by the international army of the eight allied powers. Indignantly, she said, "I should try to save our nation from its present danger. How can I be tied down as a housewife, concerned with rice and salt and other chores?"

Qiu Jin decided to leave her husband, with whom she had few interests in common. In 1904, with money obtained from selling her jewelry and other valuables, she went to study in Japan.

There she met other patriotic Chinese students and took part in secret revolutionary activities. She was an eloquent orator; when she mounted the platform at student meetings, her fiery words against the Qing dynasty moved the listeners to tears.

In 1905, on a trip to Shanghai, she joined the *Guang Fu Hui* (Restoration Society) under the leadership of Cai Yuanpei (1868-1940, who later became Chancellor of Peking University during the May 4th Movement in 1919) and Xu Xilin (1873-1907). By the time of her return to Japan, the Japanese government, at the instigation of the Manchu rulers, was suppressing the Chinese students' revolutionary activities. She called on the students to return to their native land and develop the revolutionary movement at home. She organized a "Dare-to-Die Brigade", of which she herself became the commander.

Back in Shanghai again, she became a teacher in a private academy. Besides attending to her teaching duties, she set up China's first women's organization, the *Gong Ai Hui* (Mutual Love Association), and published *Chinese Women*, one of the earliest women's periodicals in China. She also wrote poems and articles calling on the people to overthrow the Qing government in order to save the nation and urging women to learn some skill so as to become economically independent, thus emancipating themselves from the domination of men. Qiu Jin was not only a patriot but a forerunner of women's liberation in China.

The revolutionary tide was rising. When Dr. Sun Yat-sen's China Revolutionary League staged an uprising in northern Hunan Province, Qiu Jin returned to her native county to take charge of the Datong School, with the aim of training revolutionary leaders. She started military drilling for the students and secretly organized a "Restoration Army" of which Xu Xilin was the commander-in-chief and she his assistant.

In May 1907, Xu Xilin was planning an uprising to take place in Anqing, the capital of the neighboring province of Anhui. Unfortunately, the secret leaked out. Xu hastily attempted to assassinate En Ming, the Governor, but was arrested and executed. A week later Qing government troops surrounded the Datong School, arrested Qiu Jin and threw her in prison. Beaten and tortured, she refused to divulge any secret. At the trial she proudly said: "There's no use for you to ask me about the Revolutionary League." On July 15 she was publicly executed in Shaoxing, her native city, at the age of 33.

Daring and progressive as she was, Qiu Jin had limitations due to her class origin and the times. Born into a wealthy family, she looked down upon the peasants as an ignorant mass and placed her hope for the eventual success of the revolution on individual heroes. She devoted all her energies to overthrowing the Qing government, but did not see that the entire social structure of old China required a revolutionary change as well.

Nevertheless, in view of her background, Qiu Jin can be considered as a great woman revolutionary who occupies an honorable place in modern Chinese history.

31. CHINA AND THE RUSSO-JAPANESE WAR (1904-1905)

The Russo-Japanese War of 1904-1905 was fought over the question as to which imperialist power should control Manchuria (China's northeastern provinces, the original home of the Qing rulers) and Korea. Even though both belligerents fought the war mainly on Chinese soil, thereby violating China's territorial sovereignty, the Qing government proclaimed its neutrality and remained an onlooker during the conflict. It was as if two robbers who had broken into the same house were fighting over the loot while the master of the house stood by to see which robber would win the prize.

During the Boxer Movement, Russia had dispatched thousands of troops to seize Manchuria. This directly threatened Japan's ambitions in both Manchuria and Korea. At the same time, Britain, having stopped Russian expansion through the Baltic and the Dardanelles, was looking for an ally to check the Russian advance in the Far East. Seeing that China was not going to be able to regain her strength, Britain looked to Japan to help maintain the "balance of power". On January 30, 1902, the two countries signed their first treaty of alliance. It provided that either power might take such action as was deemed necessary to protect its interests in China and Korea; that if, in taking such action, either power were attacked, the other would maintain a strict neutrality; but "if any other power should join in hostilities against that ally, the other power will come to its assistance, and will conduct the war in common, and make peace in mutual agreement with it". Protected against flank attacks by a third power, Japan now decided to go to war with Russia if necessary.

In negotiations with Russia, Japan asked for a complete withdrawal from Manchuria and Korea. Russia refused. In the opinion of her statesman Count Serge J. Witte, the essence of the Far Eastern problem was that each country wanted to "obtain as large a share as possible of the outlived Oriental states, especially of the Chinese Colossus. Russia, both geographically and historically, has the indisputable right to the lion's share of the expected prey." Negotiations broke off on February 5, 1904, without any agreement being reached. Three days later, the Russo-Japanese War began with a Japanese surprise attack on the Russian fleet off Lüshun. On April 13 the Russian flagship *Petropavlovsk* was blown up by a mine. Thereafter, the Russian squadron remained cautiously in port, and the Japanese fleet had nothing to do but keep guard. On May 30, the nearby port of Dalian was occupied by Japan.

On land the Russian army fared no better. In the first important battle along the Yalu River, one-third of the Russian forces were lost, while in another major battle, the Russian troops were forced to retreat to Shenyang. At the end of July the Japanese, having for months blocked Lüshun from the sea, began to besiege that fortified position with their land forces; on January 2, 1905, Lüshun surrendered to Japan, marking the turning point in the war. In the great battle of Shenyang that followed, 300,000 men were engaged on each side. Russia lost nearly 100,000 men, Japan about 50,000. The Russian troops were forced to withdraw to the north.

Meanwhile, determined to win the war at any cost, Tsar Nicholas II had dispatched his Baltic Fleet to the Far East in October 1904. Following the defeats at Lüshun and Shenyang, he ordered naval reinforcements to join the Baltic Fleet. The linkup was effected at Camranh Bay on the coast of Viet Nam. After many vicissitudes, they arrived in the Tsushima Strait on May 27, 1905. In the Battle of the Sea of Japan, the entire

Russian armada was practically wiped out. For the first time, a rising Asian power had defeated the Russian "Bear" from the north.

In Russia itself, revolution had broken out in January 1905. With disorder at home and defeat in the field, Nicholas II readily accepted U.S. President Theodore Roosevelt's offer of mediation. In August 1905, Russian and Japanese representatives met at Portsmouth, New Hampshire, and the Treaty of Portsmouth was signed there on September 5, 1905.

The treaty contained the following points:

• Russian recognition of Japan's "paramount political, military and economic interests in Korea".

• Evacuation by both powers of Manchuria, which was to be restored to the exclusive administration of China, with the exception of the Liaodong peninsula, the lease of which was to be transferred to Japan. China's sovereignty in Manchuria and the "open door" were expressly recognized.

• Russian cession to Japan of the railway from Lüshun as far north as Changchun (about 750 kilometers), with Russian retention of the railway north of that point.

• Restoration to Russia of the northern half of Sakhalin Island.

In the negotiations the United States acted as Japan's silent partner, hoping to enjoy equal opportunity with the other powers in the economic exploitation of Manchuria. It was soon clear, however, that Japan had no intention at all of respecting the "open door" in Manchuria. After 1907 Japan cooperated with Russia for the purpose of consolidating its own position vis-à-vis the other powers, and the "open door" in Manchuria was quietly and quickly closed. Japan's promise to respect China's sovereign rights in Manchuria proved worthless. A South Manchuria Railway Company was organized in 1906 by Japanese imperial ordinance. Far from being a mere railway organization, it exercised full control over the land and occupants of a "railway zone" extending for 25 kilometers on either side of the line. It controlled the supply of electricity, gas and water; managed schools, hospitals and hotels; operated steamship lines and managed the harbors; and worked the coalfields of Yantai and Fushun. While northern Manchuria remained within the Russian sphere of influence, southern Manchuria fell under Japanese military rule. China, the nominal master of the land, had virtually lost her rich northeastern provinces. What is more, a government proven unable to defend its sovereign rights in the face of foreign aggression could no longer command the respect and loyalty of its people. The clamor for reform became a veritable din, and more and more patriots joined the revolutionary movement.

32. THE QING GOVERNMENT'S ATTEMPTS TO SAVE ITSELF

To stem the tide of revolution, the Qing government tried to institute some of the reforms demanded by restless high-ranking Chinese officials. But the palliatives taken either failed to achieve their original aims or came too little and too late. The disappointment and disillusionment created among the promoters only hastened the downfall of the imperial regime.

The Empress Dowager's flight to Xi'an during the Boxer Movement in 1900 had taught her a bitter lesson. Even she began to see that only by instituting reforms could she hope to maintain the power of the imperial government and thus preserve the Qing dynasty. Following the advice of Zhang Zhidong, the powerful viceroy in the mid-Changjiang region, she abolished the old examination system based on the Confucian classics in September 1905. The new examinations would henceforth include the history of China and knowledge of foreign countries. The traditional academies were transformed into schools patterned after those of Japan, with many courses on modern subjects. A Ministry of Education was created in 1906. By 1909 the number of modern schools had grown to over 100,000 throughout the country. Many provinces sent their promising young men on scholarships to study abroad. Most of them chose Japan, which was nearer and less strange than the Western countries; the number of Chinese students there rose from 271 in 1902 to 15,000 in 1907. But this apparent success concealed future dangers, because far from remaining loyal to the old regime, the new intellectuals swelled the ranks of the opposition, many even becoming revolutionaries.

Military reforms were also emphasized. The traditional military examinations were abolished and new units were organized along Western lines, with modern equipment and Western methods of training. Military academies were opened in the provinces to train officers. It is questionable whether these measures really increased the military power of the imperial government itself, however. Yuan Shikai, Viceroy of Zhili (now Hebei) Province, who played a major role in the reforms, created a Northern (Beiyang) Army loyal only to himself. A similar modern army created by Zhang Zhidong in Hubei Province in central China was loyal to Zhang. The War Ministry established in 1906, although more specialized than the old, was able to impose only partial centralization in the absence of financial power.

Japan's victory over tsarist Russia in 1905 came as a great surprise to many Chinese. Powerful officials, including Zhang Zhidong and Yuan Shikai, saw the secret of Japan's success in the Meiji Reforms; they began to petition the Qing rulers to institute a constitutional monarchy as Japan had done and accelerate military reform. Responding to the pressure, the Empress Dowager Ci Xi sent five of her trusted officials to study the political systems in Europe, the United States and Japan in July 1905. Upon their return in 1906, they advised the Qing government to frame a constitution "in order to ward off a revolutionary crisis". Believing that actual implementation of a constitution could be delayed for several years, the Empress Dowager issued on September 1, 1906 an edict on preparations for a constitutional monarchy.

Meanwhile, members of the landlord and gentry class along the Changjiang River and the southeastern coast began to take action. They set up an Association for the Preparation of a Constitution in Shanghai and then established branches in their own provinces. The gentry associations sent delegations to Beijing to petition the Qing government to promulgate a constitution as soon as possible. Peasant uprisings and revolutionary outbreaks in various parts of the country further frightened the Manchu ruling class. On August 27, 1908, the Qing government issued its "Imperial-Approved Principles of the Constitution" and declared that the period of preparation was to be nine years.

The constitutional "Principles" consisted of two parts: (1) powers of the emperor, and (2) rights and duties of the subjects. In the first part, it was declared that the rule of the Qing dynasty would last forever, that the emperor's sacred rights were inviolable, that as supreme head of the executive, legislative and judicial branches of the government, he had the power to convene and dissolve parliament and proclaim laws and edicts. As commander-in-chief of the armed forces, he had the power to declare war and conclude peace, to confer honors and announce amnesties. In a word, the emperor would retain absolute authority, and the future parliament, if it was ever convened, would be merely a rubber stamp without any real power. As to the rights of the people, they would have freedom of speech, of press and of assembly as "permitted" by the law; their duties included the payment of taxes, military service and absolute obedience to the laws.

Shortly after the proclamation of these principles, Emperor Guang Xu and the Empress Dowager died one after the other, in November 1908. A three-year-old Puyi (1906-1967) ascended the throne, with his father Zaifeng (1883-1952) acting as regent. Wishing to concentrate power in the hands of the Manchus, Zaifeng dismissed Yuan Shikai from his position, asking him to "treat his sickness at home". Pretending to be in favor of a constitutional monarchy, he issued another edict in March 1909, ordering the establishment of a constitutional assembly in the capital and provincial assemblies throughout China "to actively prepare for constitutional rule". The members of these assemblies were carefully restricted to imperial clansmen, Manchu nobles, high-ranking officials and prominent gentry-scholars. The overwhelming majority of the people had no right to vote at all. In Shandong Province, for instance, only 119,000 inhabitants voted out of a total population of 38 million. Similar ratios were the rule for other provinces.

The "provincial assemblies" first met in October 1909. Despite their composition, they too became centers of opposition to the imperial government. In February 1910, the delegates asked that a parliament be convened immediately, but the government would only promise to call one in three years. As an interim measure, the regent in May 1911 appointed a "cabinet" of 13 members, nine of whom were imperial clansmen and Manchu aristocrats. Having lost faith in the professed sincerity of the Qing rulers to institute a constitutional government, the assemblies demanded the withdrawal of the "cabinet", but this demand too was rejected.

Without even the support of the constitutionalists, the only possible alternative to the revolutionaries, the Qing government became more isolated than ever among a dissatisfied and rebellious population.

33. THE 1911 REVOLUTION AND THE OVERTHROW OF THE MONARCHY

The Qing dynasty was overthrown by the Revolution of 1911. This memorable event opened a new chapter in Chinese history. The feudal monarchy which had ruled China for over 2,000 years was swept away, and China became the first republic in Asia.

Since the suppression of the "Boxers" in 1901, the situation had been deteriorating. To pay the huge indemnity imposed by the foreign powers and to maintain their extravagant court life, the Qing rulers increased taxes and levies, burdens which fell mainly on the shoulders of the peasants. The influx of foreign textiles and other machine-manufactured goods bankrupted many a rural domestic handicraft industry. Coupled with the sufferings of the people brought on by regional natural disasters, these new pressures were virtually unbearable. In 1904 rice riots broke out in the lower Changjiang region. Recorded popular uprisings numbered 113 in 1909, and rose to 290 in 1910. The whole country was like a volcano that might erupt at any time.

In the midst of mass misery and unrest, the revolutionaries intensified their activities. Between 1905 and 1910 they staged more than 10 revolutionary uprisings in various parts of south China. Despite their failures, they helped further revolutionary ideas among the people. At the beginning of 1911, Dr. Sun Yatsen and other leaders of the China Revolutionary League decided to stage a major uprising in Guangzhou, hoping to spark off a nationwide revolt and boost the morale of their followers. A headquarters was set up in Hongkong to make preparations and direct operations. A "dare-to-die" battalion of 800 volunteers was organized, and steps were taken to get the support of the local garrison, the New Army units, and secret societies. Dr. Sun himself went abroad to collect funds among the overseas Chinese patriots for the purchase of arms.

Toward the end of March 1911, a detachment of 100 "dare-to-die" volunteers, under the leadership of Huang Xing, attacked the governor-general's yamen in Guangzhou only to find that the official had fled. In the ensuing bloody encounter with government troops, 72 revolutionaries died. They were buried later at Huanghuagang (Yellow Flower Hill) outside the city; today the site has become a magnificent memorial for these early revolutionary martyrs.

China's reactionary rulers also faced trouble from another quarter. With foreign powers scrambling for railway and mining concessions, Chinese patriots, with the support of gentry-

Lin Zexu, opponent of the opium trade. (Contemporary painting)

Over 1,000 tons of opium being destroyed under Commissioner Lin's supervision in 1839. (Modern Chinese painting)

Hong Xiuquan, leader of the Taiping peasant revolution. (Modern sculpture)

Taiping forces defeating Qing government cavalry at Boyang Lake, 1859.

Empress Dowager Ci Xi (center).

Emperor Guang Xu.

Ruins of Yuan Ming Yuan (old Summer Palace) after
the firing by British-French troops in 1860.

Leaders of the Hundred Days' Reform in 1898, Kang Youwei (upper left), Liang Qichao (upper right) and Tan Sitong (lower center).

Sun Yat-sen (second from left) spreads revolutionary ideas among his schoolmates in Hongkong in 1888.

Eight foreign powers intervened to suppress the Boxer Movement in 1900. Among them were Russian troops (top) and British naval forces (bottom).

Yellow Flower Park in Guangzhou, where 72 revolutionary martyrs killed in April 1911 were buried.

Qiu Jin, woman revolutionary, executed at the age of 31.

merchants, had initiated a movement for the protection of railways and mines. In 1905 the people of Hubei, Hunan and Guangdong provinces had bought back the right to build a Guangzhou-Hankou Railway from a U.S. banking group which had already committed capital to the project. In Sichuan, a provincial railway company was organized to build a line to Hankou based on merchant and public shares, the latter bought with taxes, in particular a surtax on land. By 1907 a 15-kilometer section had been completed. Just as this patriotic movement was gaining strength, the Qing rulers declared a policy of "nationalization" of the railways in May 1911. This would pave the way for them to obtain loans by mortgaging Chinese railways to the foreign powers. Public indignation ran high, and a vigorous campaign against the Qing government's selling out of national interests swept south China. Popular resistance was at its greatest in Sichuan Province. A Railway Protection League was founded there, with branches in many cities. When its petitions and demonstrations produced no results, thousands of shareholders met in August in the provincial capital of Chengdu, and decided to close shops and schools, refuse to pay taxes, and form local militia units. On September 7, Governor-General Zhao Erfeng (?-1911) had the leaders arrested. When several thousand people demonstrated for their release, the police fired on them, killing about 40. This action of the Qing authorities antagonized the normally conservative gentry-merchants and agitation spread to many cities and towns in the province. Worried by the events in Sichuan, the Qing government ordered the New Army stationed in Wuhan to advance and quell the disturbances.

But the revolutionaries had already recruited thousands of secret followers in the New Army. Fearing that the march on Sichuan would weaken the revolutionary forces, the leaders decided on a pre-emptive strike on October 11, 1911. However, when an accidental explosion of a bomb in the Russian Concession on October 10 exposed the plan, the viceroy of the province began a large-scale search and arrest of revolutionaries.

At this critical moment, an engineering corps of the New Army rose up to capture the arsenal of the imperial troops at Hanyang (one of the three sister cities making up Wuhan along with Wuchang and Hankou), and the revolutionaries in other army units immediately rose in response, joining forces to attack the yamen of the governor-general who fled in panic to a gunboat anchored in the Changjiang River.   After a fierce night-long battle, the revolutionaries occupied the city of Wuchang, and within two days they were in control of the whole of Wuhan.

The victory of the revolution at Wuhan electrified the country.   One province after another declared independence from the central government.   Seeing that the Qing dynasty was a sinking ship, many constitutional reformers and dynastic officials also jumped aboard the revolution.   On December 10, 1911, a meeting of provincial representatives opened in Nanjing.   Dr. Sun Yat-sen, having just returned from abroad on December 25, was immediately elected Provisional President of a new Republic.   The once-powerful Qing dynasty, which had ruled China for 268 years, collapsed like a house of cards.

PART II
THE FAILURE OF THE REPUBLIC

34. THE RISE OF YUAN SHIKAI

The Provisional Government at Nanjing headed by Dr. Sun Yat-sen was short-lived. Yuan Shikai, who earlier had betrayed the "Hundred Days' Reform" of 1898, became the first President of the Republic of China in March 1912. This turn of events took place because of: (1) the fear in many quarters of social chaos; (2) the objective weakness of the revolutionaries; (3) Yuan's military power and political duplicity; and (4) the support given to Yuan by the foreign powers.

When the insurrection broke out at Wuchang on October 10, 1911, the Qing government, sensing the gravity of the situation, immediately appointed Yuan Shikai to head the Northern (Beiyang) Army with the authority of a viceroy to suppress the revolt. Not satisfied with this "lowly" post, Yuan declined on the pretext that his foot was still troubling him, which ironically had been the Imperial Regent Zaifeng's stated reason for dismissing Yuan from service in 1908. Only after being named Imperial Commissioner in charge of all the armed forces did he step forth and begin to fight the revolutionaries. His troops soon recaptured Hankou and Hanyang, and threatened the position of the revolutionary troops across the river at Wuchang.

However, the revolution was spreading rapidly; one province

after another in central-south China declared its independence. The imperial troops under Manchu commanders were suffering defeat after defeat in the field. In late October the revolutionary tide swept northward to Zhili Province where the seat of imperial power was located. In panic the Qing government dissolved its "cabinet of imperial clansmen" and appointed Yuan Shikai Premier, with full powers to negotiate a settlement with the revolutionaries. Entrusted with the task of saving the dynasty, Yuan was actually intent on his own rise to power.

In December 1911, representatives of the two sides to the conflict met in the International Settlement of Shanghai. The foreign powers, chiefly concerned with the preservation of their treaty rights and special privileges, frowned upon any revolution in China. Through their consular officials they warned the negotiators that the continuation of civil war would endanger their material interests and security, and a settlement should be reached as soon as possible. Beneath the surface, the foreign powers regarded Yuan Shikai as a "strong man" who could maintain "law and order" in their behalf, and gave him full support. They refused to turn over the revenue from China's Maritime Customs to the Nanjing republican government, thereby forcing it to make peace with Yuan Shikai.

The bourgeois revolutionaries, many of them closely linked through their social origins to the exploitation of the peasants in the countryside, were afraid to mobilize the masses and thus were in no position to wage an effective struggle against Yuan's forces. The old officials and constitutional reformers who had recently joined the ranks of the revolution for their own personal interests were also eager to come to terms with the northern military leader. Some members of the China Revolutionary League began to regard Dr. Sun Yat-sen's ideals as "too high-minded" for China and even advocated the dissolution of the organization. Attacked from without and sabotaged from within, Dr. Sun found himself in an untenable position. On January 22, he declared that should the Qing emperor agree to abdicate and Yuan Shikai come over to the

Republic, he would resign as Provisional President and nominate Yuan to the Nanjing parliament to take his place.

As soon as Dr. Sun gave his pledge to resign the presidency, Yuan Shikai "requested" the abdication of the Qing emperor. His loyal generals threatened to march on Beijing to force the issue. Dismayed by Yuan's betrayal, the Qing rulers had no way out. On February 12, 1912, Puyi, the last emperor of the Qing dynasty, formally stepped down from the throne.

Yuan Shikai telegraphed Dr. Sun Yat-sen, proclaiming himself a "defender of the Republic" who would see to it that the monarchical system would never return to China. Dr. Sun resigned his presidency and the Nanjing parliament immediately elected Yuan Shikai as his successor. Thus, the bourgeois revolutionaries handed political power to the self-seeking conspirator Yuan Shikai without a struggle.

To protect the fruits of the revolution, Dr. Sun Yat-sen had put forward three minor conditions for his resignation, the most important being that the government of the Republic should be established in Nanjing. His purpose, as a Chinese saying goes, was to "lure the tiger out of his lair". Yuan Shikai was of course reluctant to leave the citadel of his power. The foreign diplomatic corps, formerly the overlords of the Qing government and now Yuan Shikai's masters, were also unwilling to abandon their stronghold within the old capital.

On February 27, a delegation arrived in Beijing. It was sent by Dr. Sun Yat-sen to welcome Yuan Shikai on his assumption of the presidency in Nanjing. Yuan pretended to be willing, but secretly ordered his trusted generals to stage "mutinies" in Beijing and surrounding cities. Burning and looting became widespread. The foreign powers mobilized their troops to patrol the capital and protect the Legation Quarter. Yuan's generals issued a circular telegram, declaring that Beijing must remain the capital in order to maintain social peace and order. The helpless delegation bowed to this demand, and on March 10, 1912, Yuan Shikai took the oath as the first President of the Republic of China in Beijing. Yuan Shikai and his generals became the *de facto* masters of the infant Republic.

35. CHINA DURING WORLD WAR I

The outbreak of war in Europe in August 1914 touched off a new chain of events in China. Insofar as China was concerned, the three major developments of the war period were: (1) the expansion of Japan's influence on the continent; (2) Yuan Shikai's attempt to restore monarchical government; and (3) the rapid development of China's modern industry with the consequent growth of a national bourgeoisie and working class.

After the outbreak of the war, Japan joined the allied powers in declaring war on Germany and immediately sent troops to seize all German possessions — harbors, railways and mines — in China's Shandong Province. Japan regarded the titanic struggle among the European powers as a golden opportunity to expand its position in China. A memorandum issued by the Japanese militarist Black Dragon Society put the situation plainly: "Now is the most opportune time for Japan to quickly solve the Chinese question. Such an opportunity will not occur again for hundreds of years."

On January 18, 1915, in a secret visit to Yuan Shikai, the Japanese Minister presented the infamous "Twenty-one Demands". Without any attempt at subtlety, they called for China's recognition of Japanese predominance in Shandong, Inner Mongolia, Manchuria, the southeastern coastal provinces opposite the Japanese-occupied island of Taiwan and the Changjiang valley. One section of the document was particularly obnoxious. It demanded the appointment of Japanese "advisers" to the Chinese government administration, including the army and the police. It further required that China should purchase the bulk of its arms and munitions from Japan.

Negotiations over the demands dragged on for months, but on May 7 Japan delivered a 48-hour ultimatum to Yuan Shikai's government. Learning of the ultimatum through a "leak", intellectuals and students considered this a great national humiliation. They therefore initiated a movement to boycott Japanese goods. For his part, Yuan Shikai eventually yielded to most of the Japanese demands, hoping that he might thereby consolidate his personal power. For the next three decades until the end of World War II, the Chinese people regarded Japanese imperialism as their most bitter enemy.

The second major event was Yuan Shikai's attempt to assume the title of emperor. Although Yuan had sworn allegiance to a republican form of government when he took office as President, he wielded personal power in the only way he knew how — through political assassination, bribery and threats. By the end of 1913, he had become a virtual dictator ruling without parliament and had been empowered to designate his own successor. But Yuan's thirst for power was insatiable. His dream was to become emperor and founder of a new dynasty. To this end he had the support of an American political adviser, Dr. Frank J. Goodnow (1859-1939), a former professor of constitutional law at Columbia University and later President of Johns Hopkins University. In a memorandum circulated in August 1915, Goodnow argued that a republic did not suit China because "the intelligence of the people is not high". Many other foreign pundits agreed. Confident of the support of foreign powers, Yuan went ahead with his plans. He spent 2,000,000 Chinese dollars to organize a Peace Planning Association, which "urged" him to become the emperor. In November 1915 he convened a bogus National Congress which voted unanimously for the restoration of the monarchy. On January 1, 1916, Yuan ascended the throne and the fledgling Republic gave way to a dynastic empire.

But Yuan's imperial designs aroused tremendous opposition. Liang Qichao resigned the post of Minister of Justice and started a vigorous press campaign against Yuan. Cai E (Tsai Ao, 1882-1916), former governor of the southwestern province of Yunnan, secretly returned to his home base and declared independence. A National Protection Army was formed with the aim of ousting Yuan from power, and the rebellion quickly spread to other provinces. Seeing the widespread opposition to Yuan's schemes, the foreign powers, including Japan, withdrew their financial support. Finally, Yuan's trusted generals also deserted him. Dismayed, he decreed on March 22, 1916 the abolition of his reign. On June 6 Yuan died a broken-hearted man, deserted by his friends and condemned by public opinion as a traitor to the Republic.

The third major development of the war era was the rapid growth of modern industry due to the relaxation of foreign economic pressure. Compared with the 1913 level of China's imports, by 1918 goods from Britain had declined by almost a half, from France by more than two-thirds, and from Germany to nothing at all. With the European powers preoccupied with the war, Chinese industry benefited from the rise in the price of silver (on which the Chinese currency was based) and from the opening of new markets. Between 1914 and 1920 Chinese flour exports increased forty-fold. The number of spindles in Chinese-owned cotton mills rose from 484,000 in 1914 to 1,218,000 in 1921. And great progress was also registered in China's tobacco, carpet and silk industries. China's unfavorable balance of trade was reduced from 213 million taels of silver in 1914 to less than 20 million taels in 1919.

The rapid expansion in China's light industries entailed an equally rapid growth of the Chinese capitalist class and industrial proletariat. Bankers' and manufacturers' associations were formed in major cities like Shanghai and Beijing, and in many cities chambers of commerce were organized which began to play an important role in political and social life. The growth of the modern working class was even more impressive. Aside from the workers employed in Chinese-owned factories, there were many thousands more in foreign-owned, particularly Japanese, mills and works. Incomplete statistics put the number of industrial workers at 1,000,000 in 1914 and approximately 3,000,000 in 1919.

About 175,000 Chinese laborers were sent to France, Britain and other countries to work during the war. Many worked in or around factories, and their experience and contacts with the West broadened their horizons and awakened their class consciousness. Those who worked in Russia fell under the influence of the Bolsheviks, and some even fought in the Soviet

Red Army. Upon their return, they became active in the rising Chinese labor movement.

36. THE MAY FOURTH MOVEMENT

The May Fourth Movement, which was sparked by the indignation of Beijing students in 1919 against the Treaty of Versailles, was both a patriotic mass movement and a cultural revolution against Confucian ideas. It ushered in a new stage of the Chinese revolution in which the working class and radical intellectuals took over leadership from the weak bourgeoisie, paving the way for eventual political victory and a fundamental reconstruction of Chinese society.

In August 1917, China declared war on Germany and Austria-Hungary with the expectation that, after the Allied victory, it would be regarded as an equal member in the family of nations. This hope was strengthened when in January 1918, U.S. President Woodrow Wilson laid down his Fourteen Points, including the principle of national self-determination. Chinese intellectuals and students believed that once Germany was defeated the world would be made safe for democracy and international justice would prevail.

At the Paris Peace Conference, China asked as one of the "victors" for the return of the former German possessions and nullification of the special privileges enjoyed by German nationals in Shandong Province. Her delegation also demanded the abrogation of the Twenty-one Demands imposed by Japan on the Yuan Shikai regime, the withdrawal of foreign troops stationed on Chinese soil, abolition of foreign "spheres of influence", and restoration of Chinese authority over the Customs Administration. Public opinion in China believed that the victorious powers would give these just demands sympathetic consideration.

But these hopes were dashed when the news came that the

treaty settlement had transferred all former German possessions and privileges to Japan. The great powers had refused
even to discuss China's other demands. On May 4, over 3,000
angry university students marched to Beijing's Tian An Men
(the gateway to the Forbidden City) to voice their protest.
Calling for the return of Qingdao (the port formerly occupied
by Germany and later by Japan) and the abolition of the
Twenty-one Demands, they urged people to struggle to uphold
China's sovereignty and punish the traitors to that cause. Prevented from entering the Legation Quarter, they marched to
the house of Cao Rulin (Tsao Ju-lin, 1877-1966, the minister
who had signed the Twenty-one Demands), set it on fire, and
also beat up another official whom they considered to be a
traitor, Zhang Zongxiang (Chang Tsung-hsiang, 1879-1962,
China's Minister to Japan). Thirty-two students were arrested
that day and more were to be arrested later, but the patriotic
movement spread rapidly to other parts of the country.

In June the focus of the movement shifted to Shanghai, the
bastion of foreign imperialism and center of modern industry
in China. Thousands upon thousands of workers from textile
mills, machine shops, docks, bus and tram companies, and
government offices went on strike in protest against the actions
of the Beijing warlord government and Japanese imperialism.
Under the influence of students and shop assistants, businessmen closed the doors of their enterprises. Railroad workers
on China's major lines also went on strike. For the first time
in Chinese history, the working people themselves were involved in a political strike against foreign imperialists and their
Chinese lackeys. Student unions were organized in many cities,
where they led the movement to boycott Japanese goods.

Under tremendous popular pressure, the warlord government in Beijing was forced to dismiss the discredited officials
and release the imprisoned students. The Chinese delegation
at the Paris Peace Conference refused to sign the Treaty of
Versailles.

The May Fourth Movement brought an upsurge in the cultural revolution already under way. Criticism of China's tradi-

tional culture had started in 1915 with the appearance of *New Youth*, a leftist journal published by Chen Duxiu (Chen Tu-hsiu, 1880-1942) in Shanghai. In "Call to Youth", Chen had urged young people to make a complete break with the old traditions — to be independent instead of servile, progressive instead of conservative, scientific instead of indulging in fantasy. The magazine held that China under the bondage of Confucianism was gravely ill. To regain its health, China had to "smash the Confucian shop" and seek the advice of two gentlemen from the West — Mr. Science and Mr. Democracy.

Another writer who began to attract wide attention among the young readers was Lu Xun (Lu Hsun, 1881-1936), who later became the standard-bearer of China's new cultural movement. He described Chinese history as a record "scrawled all over each page with the words 'virtue and morality', but between the lines the whole book is filled with two words — 'man-eating'!"

A truly new feature of this cultural movement was that the leaflets, banners and pamphlets distributed by the militant students were written in the vernacular (*baihua*), the language of the common people. One of the most prominent advocates of the use of the vernacular in literature was Hu Shi (Hu Shih, 1891-1962), at that time a professor of literature at Peking University. Up to then, the classical language used for centuries had been the monopoly of scholars and the intelligentsia. Democracy, on the other hand, demanded that knowledge should be the common property of all the people. The adoption of the vernacular by the majority of publications was a great step forward for the dissemination of knowledge among the masses.

During the May Fourth Movement, publications and periodicals multiplied in China. Hundreds of magazines appeared. New ideas — socialism, communism, anarchism, trade-union syndicalism, pragmatism, humanism, women's emancipation, birth control, etc. — streamed into China. Out of this intellectual ferment came the new leaders who were to guide the Chinese revolution in the following decades.

37. CHRISTIAN MISSIONARIES AND THE CHINESE REVOLUTION

With a long tradition of tolerance, China is a country where Buddhism and Islam, originating in India and the Arab world respectively, have for centuries coexisted alongside the indigenous Confucianism and Taoism. In 1601 when the Italian Jesuit missionary Matteo Ricci (1552-1610) reached Beijing, then the capital of the Ming dynasty (1368-1644), he was welcomed at the imperial court as a man of great scientific learning and noble character. During the period of the early Qing dynasty, his successors, Johann Adam Schall von Bell (1591-1666) and Ferdinand Verbiest (1623-1688), were appointed directors of the Imperial Board of Astronomy and asked to apply their advanced knowledge of astronomy to the problem of devising an imperial calendar. Pursuing a policy of cultural adaptation, the Jesuits reconciled Confucian teachings with Christianity and regarded ancestor and heaven worship as social customs compatible with the Christian faith. Only toward the early part of the 18th century, when the Pope forbade Chinese Catholics to observe such traditional rites, did the then Emperor Kang Xi (reigned 1662-1722) proscribe Catholicism as a form of heterodox subversion.

Protestant missionaries first came to China in the early 19th century in the wake of foreign merchants, and did not confine their efforts merely to the religious sphere. Robert Morrison (1782-1834), a pioneer Protestant missionary from London who translated the Bible into the Chinese language, repeatedly urged the British government to set up its own courts of law in China to provide its citizens the privilege of immunity from Chinese law. Karl Gützlaff (1803-1851), a Pomeranian Lutheran missionary, worked closely with the opium merchants and served as interpreter for the British government in the negotiations of the Treaty of Nanjing, the first of the unequal treaties concluded between China and foreign powers. In fact, many Protestant missionaries even condoned "gunboat diplomacy" to force "Christ's way" into China. Thus, Christian missionaries came to be commonly regarded in China as the tools of economic and political imperialism.

As a result of unequal treaties signed after the Second Opium War (1856-1860), Christian missionaries acquired the right to reside and preach Christianity in the interior of China. The Catholic missionaries concentrated their main efforts in the small towns and the countryside. In many districts the Catholic church was the biggest landlord and the most astute moneylender. But the large cities were not neglected. In Shanghai, for instance, the Catholic church was the largest single real-estate owner. It also ran a number of orphanages which supplied child labor to the textile mills at an agreed sum per head.

The Protestant missionaries were largely concentrated in the urban and commercial centers. Besides their religious activities, quite a number were active in the cultural and medical fields. James Legge (1814-1897) translated Confucian classics into English, and Alexander Wylie (1815-1887) became a specialist in Chinese literature. Timothy Richard (1845-1919), for many years director of the Christian Literature Society in China, introduced Western bourgeois political thought, while W. A. P. Martin (1827-1916) translated a work of international law into Chinese. All these people and others played an active part in the promotion of cultural exchange between China and the West. In the field of education, by the 1920's there were thousands of missionary schools scattered across the land, and Christian colleges and universities had become the major centers for disseminating Western learning. The Peking Union Medical College, with endowments from the Rockefeller family, ran one of the best hospitals in Asia.

Politically, however, the interests of the missionaries as a whole lay in the maintenance of the status quo of old China. Rather than pursuing reforms which would undermine the power base of the ruling class, they tended to advocate those which thwarted the revolutionary struggles of the people.

During the Taiping Revolution in the mid-19th century, a few missionaries were at first sympathetic toward the revolutionaries, as they thought the success of a revolution at least partially inspired by Christian doctrines would help promote Christianity in China. However, as soon as Westerners obtained new privileges as a result of China's defeat in the Second Opium War, most missionaries joined their fellow countrymen in backing the Qing court and the reactionary landlords in crushing the Taiping Revolution.

During the 1911 Revolution that overthrew the Qing dynasty and established the Republic of China, most of the missionaries disdained Dr. Sun Yat-sen (known to all Chinese as the "father of the Chinese revolution") as an impractical dreamer, without political knowledge or experience. They welcomed Sun's yielding of the presidency to warlord Yuan Shikai, whom they considered "an experienced statesman" on whom they could depend for protection. James W. Bashford (1849-1919), a U.S. Methodist missionary, even defended Yuan Shikai's betrayal of the Republic in favor of a restored monarchy.

The roar of cannon during World War I and the salvoes of the October Revolution in Russia shook millions of Chinese people out of their lethargy. In 1919 the May Fourth Movement swept across the land. Many students and intellectuals felt that only democracy and science could cure China's ills. The Chinese Communist Party was born and the first Kuomintang-Communist revolutionary united front was formed to rid China of imperialist domination and feudal exploitation. But just as the revolution was surging ahead from victory to victory, Chiang Kai-shek suddenly turned against the Communists, and in 1927 instigated a massacre of the Front's militant workers and peasants (see p. 124 for details of Chiang Kai-shek's betrayal). The missionaries likewise abhorred the revolution. They praised Chiang Kai-shek's betrayal of the revolution and, with few exceptions, supported him to the end.

Two notable exceptions are worth mentioning. Episcopal Bishop Logan H. Roots (1870-1945) from the United States befriended Zhou Enlai and other Communist leaders as well as American progressive writers like Agnes Smedley and Anna Louise Strong. His home in Hankou once became the center for collecting medical and other supplies for the Communist Eighth Route Army and guerrilla fighters behind Japanese lines. Canadian missionary Dr. James G. Endicott (born in 1898) developed a deep sympathy for the awakened youth and peasant masses fighting against oppression in China. Disgusted at the fascist activities of the Kuomintang reactionaries, he cooperated with the Communists even though this brought clashes with his church and fellow missionaries. In 1946, after many inner conflicts, he decided to resign his missionary post to become a "rebel out of China". Both these men saw the crying need for fundamental change in old China and helped the revolutionaries in their own ways.

Since the Christian missionaries entered China under the protection of gunboats and their privileged position was based on the unequal treaties forced upon China by the Western powers, the Chinese Christians came to realize that, in order to be good citizens as well as good Christians, they must dissociate themselves from the past missionary activities in China. Motivated by patriotism and self-respect, the Chinese Christian community today has adopted the three principles of self-support, self-government and self-propagation, and has severed all strings of foreign control. Freedom of religious belief is guaranteed by the Constitution of new China. Just as Buddhists and Moslems who worship in their temples and mosques, Chinese Christians are free to congregate and hold religious services in the churches.

38. THE INTRODUCTION OF MARXISM TO CHINA

Marxism had its first significant impact on China as a result of the Russian Revolution of October 1917. Before the Russian success, Marx and Engels, the founders of scientific socialism, had been practically unknown to the Chinese people.

Mao Zedong in 1949 recalled: "It was through the Russians that the Chinese people found Marxism. . . . The salvoes of the October Revolution brought us Marxism-Leninism."

The first Chinese intellectual who grasped the meaning of the Russian Revolution was Li Dazhao (1888-1927), a professor of economics and chief librarian at Peking University. In November 1918 he published in *New Youth* two articles, "Victory of the Common People" and "Victory of Bolshevism", in which he hailed the October Revolution and predicted, "The world of the future will be that of the Red Flag." The progressive writer Lu Xun (1881-1936) saw in the October Revolution the "dawn of a new century". Chen Duxiu (1880-1942), dean of the Faculty of Liberal Arts at Peking University, also became an active protagonist for Marxism in China.

Marxism and the October Revolution attracted these intellectuals because like many others they were disappointed at the dismal failure of the Revolution of 1911. Great hopes had been aroused in the hearts of the Chinese people when the monarchy was overthrown and the Republic founded in 1912. Many had expected that the new form of government would give democratic rights to the people, promote the modernization of China's economy and culture, and help China win her rightful place among the nations. Despite such hopes, however, the Republic had soon been betrayed by its first President, Yuan Shikai, who after swearing allegiance to the Republic turned around and attempted to make himself emperor and the founder of a new dynasty.

After Yuan's death in 1916, China fell under the sway of unscrupulous warlords backed by various foreign powers who ruthlessly robbed the people and constantly fought among themselves, bringing chaos to the country and untold suffering to the people. The members of both national and provincial-level parliaments, elected from among the upper classes, a tiny minority of the population, did not represent the interests of the people at all, but were self-seeking politicians who voted according to the wishes of rich and powerful string-pullers behind the scene. China had become the "sick man of eastern Asia", and the patient's condition was deteriorating rather than improving. Bourgeois democracy of the Western type had obviously failed because mere change in the form of government could not reach the roots of China's troubles.

Progressive Chinese intellectuals saw the October Revolution as a social revolution as well as a political one. If tsarist Russia, according to Lenin, was like a prison in which the working people suffered terribly, all the more was this true of China. In the countryside where considerably more than 80 percent of the Chinese people lived, the landlords and rich peasants who constituted 10 percent of the population owned 70 to 80 percent of the arable land, while the poor peasants, the bulk of the population, owned only 20 to 30 percent of the land. The tenants, aside from being exploited and burdened down by heavy rent (amounting to 50 percent or more of the harvest), had to pay exorbitant rates of interest on loans and all sorts of taxes and levies. In Sichuan Province, for example, the agricultural tax was being collected 35 years in advance. All this plus the ravages of warlord soldiers, when piled up on top of famines caused by flood and drought, made life impossible in the villages. Many abandoned their homes to wander about as beggars or join bandit gangs.

In the cities, the workers in the factories, both Chinese- and foreign-owned, were treated like slaves. The working day, even for women and children, lasted 12 or more hours and included night work. Brutal working conditions, tyrannical foremen and the lack of sanitary facilities and safety provisions made life all but unbearable. Tuberculosis was widespread in the cities, and many workers died from a variety of other epidemics. Even small merchants and many professionals or other salary-earners found life hard and insecure. A university student often could find no work upon graduation. Unemployment was rife. In a large city like Shanghai, police would often pick up hundreds of dead bodies on a winter morning. The Chinese people, under the double yoke of foreign imperialist domination and domestic feudal oppression, were clearly even worse-off than the Russians under the Tsar. Some progressives concluded that, like Russia, China sorely needed a social revolution and that Marxism might well be the light that would lead the Chinese revolution to victory.

To keep things in perspective, however, it must be said that only a few Chinese intellectuals shared this radical view at the time. Others, like Dr. Hu Shi, advised the young people to discuss less "isms" but study more concrete problems, such as the life of a rickshaw coolie or prostitution. He in effect favored treating individual abscesses on the body instead of performing the major operation that would remove the root cause of the patient's sickness.

Marxism was regarded as "dangerous thought" by the authorities in China. Li Dazhao, one of the founders of the Chinese Communist Party, was strangled by order of warlord Zhang Zuolin (Chang Tso-lin, 1875-1928) in Beijing in the spring of 1927, the first martyr among the Communist leaders in the great revolution that was soon to sweep across China.

39. THE FOUNDING OF THE COMMUNIST PARTY OF CHINA

The Communist Party of China was officially founded in July 1921. Its First National Congress lasted five days, the first four days being spent in Shanghai, and the last on Nanhu Lake in nearby Jiaxing County of Zhejiang Province to evade police arrest. The 13 participants, representing 50 members scattered around the country, included Mao Zedong (Hunan), Dong Biwu (1885-1975, Hubei) and Zhang Guotao (Beijing). The delegates adopted the first Party constitution and elected Chen Duxiu as the Party's secretary-general.

The Party united Communist groups in Beijing, Shanghai, Guangzhou, Changsha, Wuhan and other cities. Marxism had aroused the interest of China's patriotic intellectuals because the Soviet Russian government, the first successful workers' government to be organized according to Marxist principles, had extended a friendly hand to the struggling Chinese people. In July 1919 the new Soviet government issued a manifesto proclaiming its intention to:

1.   Return to China territory seized by the former imperial Russian government;

2.   Restore, without compensation, to the sovereignty of China the Chinese Eastern Railway and the mines and forests appropriated by the former imperial Russian government;

3.   Refuse to accept further Boxer indemnity payments;

4.   Abolish all special privileges, including extraterritorial ones, of Russian subjects in China; and

5.   Consider null and void all unfair agreements made by the former imperial Russian government.

This manifesto was widely distributed in the Chinese language throughout China. In contrast with the greedy behavior of the other powers at the Paris Peace Conference, the new Russian workers' government regarded the Chinese people as equals and brothers. The manifesto sounded like a new gospel to the ears of patriotic intellectuals and students. If President Wilson's "self-determination of nations" did not extend to Asia, they thought perhaps Marxism, the theory of revolutionary socialism, might offer salvation for their oppressed country. Students in Beijing and Tianjin went into the streets to hail the victory of the October Revolution and joined Marxist study groups in their schools.

In March 1920, representatives of the Communist International came to China to help organize Communist groups in some major cities. Many Chinese students in Paris also took up the study of Marxism seriously. Among them were a number of future leaders, such as Zhou Enlai and Deng Xiaoping.

Some old Chinese intellectuals, like Liang Qichao, were opposed to the formation of a Communist Party. While willing to foresee the eventual victory of socialism over capitalism in the distant future, they maintained that China's immediate task, because of her economic backwardness, was to develop capitalism. In their view, industrial workers were too few in number and had too little education to lead China forward. For their part, the progressive intellectuals countered that capitalism could not possibly be developed under constant warlord extortion and foreign imperialist domination. The three million Chinese workers, although not numerous in proportion to China's huge population, were highly concentrated in a few industries — railways, mining, maritime transport, textiles and shipbuilding. They were under the triple oppression of capitalism, feudalism and foreign imperialism. This very concentration and extreme misery cemented their unity and made them determined to struggle against their oppressors. Furthermore, since most of them had but recently come from the countryside, they had close ties with the poor peasant masses, their natural allies in the revolutionary struggle. Representing China's new productive forces, the industrial proletariat was the most progressive class in modern China and was capable of playing the leading role in the revolutionary movement.

The founding of the Communist Party of China opened a new chapter in the annals of the Chinese revolution. In the past, all reforms, uprisings and revolutions had failed. Now a general staff of the leading class — the industrial proletariat — had been formed. This leadership was to guide the Chinese revolution from that time on and, after almost 30 years of tremendous battles waged by the whole people, achieve political victory.

40. EARLY ACTIVITIES OF THE CHINESE COMMUNIST PARTY

As a political party of the working class, the Chinese Communist Party concentrated its efforts in the first years on educating and organizing industrial workers and leading them in labor struggles for higher wages, better working conditions and other fundamental rights. To strengthen its leadership of the working-class movement, the Party established a "Chinese Trade Union Secretariat", which published the magazine *Labor*

Weekly and set up workers' schools and clubs in industrial and mining centers. Between January 1922 and February 1923, it led more than a hundred strikes in which 300,000 workers took part.

The first strike that challenged foreign interests took place in the British colony of Hongkong, where Chinese seamen were eking out only the most miserable existence. In January 1922, the Communist-influenced General Council of the Chinese Seamen's Federation called on its members to strike in order to back their demand for higher pay from the British shipowners. More than 30,000 seamen and dockers walked out, tying up all shipping. The British authorities tried every means to break the strike, but failed.

Near the end of February, a general strike was declared by Hongkong workers in support of the seamen's struggle. Sixty thousand responded, and the once prosperous colony almost became a dead city. To escape the brutal suppression in Hongkong, some strikers decided to leave for Guangzhou. Reaching Shatian near Kowloon, they were fired upon by British troops. Hundreds were killed or wounded. This massacre enraged the workers and widened the struggle.

At the call of the Chinese Communist Party, the railwaymen in north China organized solidarity committees to support the Hongkong strikers. Overseas Chinese, too, raised funds for the striking seamen, and a stream of letters of solidarity poured in from trade unions in other parts of the world.

The Hongkong seamen's strike lasted eight weeks. In the end, the British authorities were forced to yield to the strikers' demands. On March 6 they rescinded the order to close the Seamen's Union headquarters, released the jailed workers and promised to pay indemnities to the families of those killed at Shatian. The shipowners agreed to increase the workers' wages by 15 to 30 percent. This was the Chinese people's first victory in a century of anti-imperialist struggles, and it demonstrated the resolve of the working class to assert its rights.

To broaden the labor movement, the Trade Union Secretariat called the First All-China Labor Congress in Guangzhou on

May 1, 1922. A total of 162 delegates attended, representing 270,000 members in some 100 trade unions from 12 cities. Among the delegates were Communists, Kuomintang members, anarchists and non-party people. They agreed to oppose the forces of imperialism and the warlords as suggested by the Communist Party, passed resolutions for an eight-hour working day, for sympathy strikes and for making the Trade Union Secretariat an information clearing house in preparation for the formation of a national general trade union. The very fact that such resolutions were passed showed that the vast majority of the delegates recognized the leadership of the Chinese Communist Party in the labor movement.

The strike of the coal miners at Anyuan in Jiangxi Province in September 1922 once again demonstrated the power of the workers. The mines, a joint enterprise of Chinese and Japanese capital, produced 2,000 tons of coal a day to supply the Hanyang Iron Works in Hubei Province. The coal miners and associated railway workers totaled 20,000 men. Maltreated by haughty Japanese overseers and robbed by ruthless contract labor bosses, the workers were virtually beasts of burden.

The Communist Party of Hunan Province, then under the leadership of Mao Zedong, first set up workers' schools in the area to spread the idea of class struggle among the workers. A trade union was organized in May 1922, whose active members were recruited into the Communist Party. After careful planning, the union called a miners' strike on September 10 for higher wages, better working conditions and certain other rights.

When the miners set up picket lines around the mines, the provincial warlord sent troops to suppress the strike, but the soldiers refused to fire on the miners after listening to their grievances. This approach having failed, the mine owners plotted to have the key strike leader Liu Shaoqi (1898-1969) and his associates arrested during the negotiations, but thousands of miners surrounded the conference building and rescued their representatives. (Liu Shaoqi was later to become President of the People's Republic of China.) Stymied by the united strength of the workers, the mine owners were finally forced to give in to their demands.

This early strike wave reached its height in February 1923 when the Beijing-Hankou Railway workers stopped work in protest against a ban on the formation of a general trade union at Zhengzhou in Henan Province. All passenger, freight and military trains came to a stop amidst the strikers' shouts: "Fight for freedom and human rights!"

Under pressure from the diplomatic corps in Beijing, Wu Peifu (1873-1939), chief among the north China warlords at the time, sent troops to force the workers to return to work, but the workers refused. On February 7, Wu Peifu had his troops attack the unarmed pickets; large numbers of strikers were arrested and many were killed.

One of the strike leaders, Lin Xiangqian (Lin Hsiang-chien, 1889-1927) was arrested in Hankou and commanded to order his men to resume work, but he refused, saying, "I may lose my head, but I'll never call off the strike!" And thus he was killed.

After the "February 7 Massacre", the workers' movement ebbed temporarily, but this tragic event taught some thinking Chinese Communist leaders a bitter lesson. Given the small size of the working class in a basically non-industrialized country, the workers could not hope to achieve victory without allying themselves with other classes: the peasant masses in the rural areas, the small merchants and professionals in the cities, and even the democratic elements among the capitalist class who were opposed to both foreign imperialism and warlord feudalism.

41. THE FIRST KUOMINTANG-COMMUNIST UNITED FRONT

In August 1922, a frustrated Dr. Sun Yat-sen sought refuge in Shanghai following the overthrow of his revolutionary government in Guangzhou by a military *coup d'état*. His efforts of so many years had come to a dead end.

At this juncture, the Soviet Union and the Chinese Communist Party extended Dr. Sun a helping hand. They praised his persistent struggle for a democratic revolution, but pointed out his mistake of relying on various warlords instead of on the masses of the people to achieve his goal. The Soviet representative advised him to form a party uniting all progressive social strata, especially workers and peasants, and to set up a military academy to train cadres for a revolutionary army. This encouragement and advice helped Dr. Sun determine to give the Chinese revolution a new start.

In September Sun Yat-sen called a meeting to discuss the reorganization of the Kuomintang to which representatives of the Communist Party were also invited. On January 1, 1923, Sun publicized a Kuomintang document which advocated revision of the unequal treaties. Soon afterward, Adolph Joffe, the new Soviet envoy to China, met Sun in Shanghai. In a joint statement, both agreed that conditions in China were not yet ripe for the establishment of communism or a Soviet system. Joffe's expression of open support of the Chinese people's aspirations was in sharp contrast with the stand taken by the Western powers at the Washington Conference (November 1921-February 1922). There, under the banner of respect for China's "open door", they had pledged to support the existing warlord government in order that they might continue their joint exploitation of the Chinese people.

In February 1923, Sun Yat-sen returned to Guangzhou where he immediately set up a headquarters of a new revolutionary government. Soviet Russia sent Michael Borodin (1884-1951) and some military advisers to help him, and a provisional central committee of the Kuomintang which included a number of Communists was organized.

The Chinese Communist Party held its Third National Congress in Guangzhou in June 1923, and the question of forming a revolutionary united front with the Kuomintang was discussed. The congress affirmed Sun Yat-sen's contribution to the Chinese revolution and resolved to help him in reorganizing the Kuomintang and establishing cooperation between the two parties.

The gap between Sun Yat-sen and the West continued to widen. When he threatened in December to seize the customs revenues in the port of Guangzhou, the powers staged a naval demonstration to preserve the status quo. Thwarted, Sun angrily stated, "We no longer look to the Western powers. Our faces are turned toward Russia."

In January 1924, Sun Yat-sen called the First National Congress of the reorganized Kuomintang in Guangzhou. Among the Communists who attended were Li Dazhao, Mao Zedong and Qu Qiubai (Chu Chiu-pai, 1899-1935). The congress adopted the anti-imperialist, anti-feudal policy advanced by the Communists, agreed to absorb individual Communists and Socialist Youth League members into the Kuomintang, and decided to reorganize the Kuomintang into a revolutionary alliance of workers, peasants, the petty-bourgeoisie and national bourgeoisie. In this way, new blood was infused into the ranks of the Kuomintang and Sun Yat-sen became the leader of a revitalized revolutionary movement.

The congress adopted the "Manifesto of the First National Congress of the Kuomintang" in which Dr. Sun reinterpreted his Three People's Principles. The Principle of Nationalism no longer meant merely the replacement of the Manchu imperial rule by the rule of the Hans, China's majority nationality. Its aim was to liberate China from all forms of imperialist domination and give full equality to all nationalities within China. The Principle of Democracy was clarified as rule "shared by the common people", to distinguish it from the democracy in various other nations where it is "usually monopolized by the bourgeoisie and has become an instrument for oppressing the common people". As to the Principle of the People's Livelihood, Sun Yat-sen advocated equalization of land ownership and regulation of capital. Though not himself a Marxist, he regarded the Marxists as comrades-in-arms in the struggle for social justice.

Even more significant was Sun Yat-sen's linking of his revised Three People's Principles with three newly formulated
major policies: alliance with Soviet Russia, cooperation with
the Communists and support for workers' and peasants' movements. When some right-wing Kuomintang members objected
to cooperation with the Communists, he declared that rejection
of cooperation was equivalent to rejection of the revolution.
"If you don't want to cooperate with the Communists," he told
them, "I'll declare the Kuomintang dissolved and join the
Communist Party."

The new revolutionary government established the Huangpu
Military Academy near Guangzhou. Chiang Kai-shek, a
Kuomintang officer who had visited Soviet Russia to study the
organization of the Red Army, became president, Zhou Enlai
was the political director, and Ye Jianying and other Communists held leading positions. The Soviet advisers introduced
the military system and theories of the Red Army to the
academy whose cadets included many Communists and Socialist Youth League members. The academy became the training
center of officers for a revolutionary army.

For his audacity Sun Yat-sen earned the enmity of the imperialists. In October 1924, the British authorities in Hongkong attempted to overthrow the revolutionary government by
financing a group of Chinese comprador capitalists in an armed
uprising. This was quickly put down by the cadets of the military academy and a section of the army with the support of
workers and peasants.

The united front between the Kuomintang and the Communist Party brought new life to the Chinese revolutionary
movement, with Guangzhou becoming the center of attraction
for progressive patriotic youths from many parts of the country.

42.   THE DEATH OF DR. SUN YAT-SEN

Dr. Sun Yat-sen died in Beijing on March 12, 1925, his death
mourned by people throughout China.

In October 1924, the government in Beijing headed by warlords Cao Kun and Wu Peifu and backed by Britain and the United States had collapsed after the "Christian General" Feng Yuxiang (1882-1948) suddenly turned against them. A new government was formed by Duan Qirui (1865-1936) and Zhang Zuolin (1875-1928, Duan and Zhang were both backed by Japan) and General Feng Yuxiang (who had no foreign backing at the time) which then invited Dr. Sun to come to Beijing to discuss peaceful unification of the country.

At that time, many politically active people were demanding the convocation of a national congress, the framing of a constitution and the establishment of a truly democratic republic. Committees for this purpose had been formed in Shanghai and several southern provinces. In this context, Sun Yat-sen saw the warlord initiative as an opportunity to realize his long-cherished dream of a unified nation. With the support of the Communist Party, he accepted the invitation and left for Beijing in November.

Before starting out on his journey, Dr. Sun issued a statement in which he reiterated his stand against imperialism and feudalism and asked the people to support his struggle. Stopping in Shanghai, he was welcomed by the Chinese population, but the foreign authorities threatened to drive him out. At a news conference he stated that his mission to Beijing had a twofold purpose: to help convene a national assembly to put an end to warlordism and to abolish the unequal treaties, thus ridding China of imperialist control. "My mission is full of danger," he declared, "but as long as the people understand me, I have no fear."

When Dr. Sun arrived in Beijing, the warlord government tried to persuade him to abandon his revolutionary policies, but he stood firm. He insisted on the convening of a national congress which would include representatives of businessmen, industrialists, teachers and professors, workers and peasants. This proposal was supported only by Feng Yuxiang; for their part, Duan and Zhang wanted to hold a "rehabilitation conference" limited to military leaders and a few prominent civilians. Dr. Sun was faced with a long, hard battle.

But the battle was to be left for others. Exhausted from work and suffering from cancer of the liver, Dr. Sun had to be hospitalized. Knowing that he was on his deathbed, he dictated his testament to the Kuomintang:

> For 40 years I have devoted myself to the cause of the people's revolution with but one end in view: the elevation of China to a position of freedom and equality among the nations. My experience during these 40 years has convinced me that to attain this goal we must bring about an awakening of our own people and ally ourselves in common struggle with those people of the world who treat us as equals.

To the leaders of the U.S.S.R., he wrote a letter, which reads in part:

> I leave behind me a party which, as has always been my wish, will be bound up with you in the historic work of the final liberation of China and other exploited nations from the imperialist order. By the will of fate, I must leave my work unfinished and hand it over to those who, remaining true to the principles and teachings of the party, will show themselves to be my true followers. . . .

> Taking leave of you, dear comrades, I want to express the hope that the day will come when the U.S.S.R. will welcome a friend and ally in a mighty, free China, and that in the great struggle for the liberation of the oppressed peoples of the world, both these allies will go forward to victory hand in hand.

After Dr. Sun's death, his work was carried on by many people, chief among whom was his widow, Soong Ching Ling.

43. THE MAY 30 MOVEMENT

The mass movement popularly known as the "May 30 Movement" started in Shanghai in 1925. Triggered by the killing of a dozen Chinese citizens and the wounding of many others when British police in the International Settlement fired into a demonstrating crowd, it developed into a nationwide movement against imperialist brutality toward the Chinese people.

Foreign industry was expanding rapidly in China during the period after World War I. The number of spindles in Japanese-owned cotton mills, for example, had increased to 1,268,000 by 1925, some two-thirds of the number in Chinese-owned mills. To increase profits, the mill owners often replaced adult workers, whose wages were already very low, with still cheaper child labor. Chinese workers not only worked long hours under miserable conditions, but also had to face the threat of flogging or dismissal at any time. Chinese industrialists were also pushed to the wall. Many were on the verge of bankruptcy because foreign interests controlled the Chinese market through their preponderant political and economic power.

On May 14, 1925, Chinese workers in a Japanese-owned cotton mill in Shanghai went on strike to protest against the firing of some of their co-workers. On the second day of the strike, agents of the employers opened fire on the pickets, killing one striker and wounding a dozen others. This brutal action aroused the indignation of workers and students.

On May 30, over 2,000 students distributed leaflets in the International Settlement to protest the killing of the Chinese workers. The British authorities arrested hundreds of students, which only further angered people. By three o'clock in the afternoon, ten thousand people had flocked to the police station on Nanjing Road to demand the release of the arrested students. Shouts of "Down with imperialism!" and "People of China, unite!" filled the air. When the crowds refused to disperse, a British inspector ordered the police to fire; 11 demonstrators were killed outright and scores were wounded. This "May 30 Massacre" shocked the Chinese people. While the representatives of the foreign powers claimed the right to shoot and kill in order to maintain law and order, the Chinese people felt that it was a case of the "guests" killing the "masters of the house".

The Communist Party quickly formed an action committee to lead the anti-imperialist movement in Shanghai. On June 1, students stopped attending classes, workers left their factories and storekeepers shut their doors. A joint council of workers, merchants and students was organized which raised a number of demands: compensation and apologies to the families of the victims; the abolition of extraterritorial rights; the permanent withdrawal of foreign warships and troops from Shanghai; freedom of speech, press and assembly in the foreign concessions; and recognition of trade unions.

To suppress the popular upheaval, the imperialist powers sent warships up the Huangpu River, and their marines and troops killed and wounded more people. This action, however, only served to spread the struggle to other parts of the country, including those controlled by the warlords. In many cities, Committees to Wipe Out the National Humiliation were formed, which promoted sympathy strikes, mass demonstrations, boycotts of foreign goods, and the collection of money for the Shanghai strikers. In north China, for instance, strikes took place in the Japanese-owned cotton mills at Qingdao and the English-owned coal mines of the Kailuan Mining Administration at Tangshan.

The biggest sympathy strike took place in Hongkong on June 19, 1925; over 100,000 workers took part. The British authorities declared martial law and tried to break the strike. The strike spread to Guangzhou. On June 23, when a procession of demonstrators was passing through Shaji opposite the British and French concessions, they were fired upon by British and French guards and warships. Fifty-two people were killed and more than a hundred were seriously wounded. In retaliation, the workers' and people's organizations of Guangzhou broadened the strike to include 200,000 workers and started a boycott of the island. The strike-boycott was so effective that it cost the English in Hongkong millions of pounds sterling — even drinking water and vegetables had to be shipped in from the Philippines. The strike eventually lasted 16 months.

The May 30 Movement helped to strengthen the revolutionary movement against imperialism and feudalism throughout the country. In Guangzhou, the seat of the revolutionary government, it reinforced the left-wing of the Kuomintang in the tense period following Dr. Sun Yat-sen's death and helped to prepare the ground for a northern expedition against the warlords.

44.   CHINESE WOMEN AND THE REVOLUTION

Chinese women suffered a harsh lot in the old feudal society. According to the very early *Book of Songs* (*Shi Jing*), at birth a girl was given a roof tile to play with, and a boy was given a piece of jade. From early childhood a girl had to undergo the torture of foot-binding and was taught obedience — to the father before marriage, to the husband after marriage and to the son after the death of her husband. She had no right of inheritance, all land and other property being divided among the sons. Marriage was arranged by the parents, whose first concern was wealth and social status rather than the happiness of the would-be lifelong partners. As a rule, a bride never saw the groom before the wedding day.

The function of the wife was to bear sons for the family. If she failed to do so, the husband could take concubines in the hope of getting male offspring to continue the family line and perform the rites of ancestor worship. Chastity was expected of the female side only. After the death of her husband, she might be honored with a memorial arch if she committed suicide or remained unmarried for the rest of her life. A man, on the other hand, could take as many concubines as he could afford or patronize prostitutes if he so desired. In an ordinary peasant's or worker's family, the wife was merely the servant for the father- and mother-in-law and could be beaten by her husband at will. A girl, if not drowned at birth, might be sold as slave, maidservant, concubine or prostitute. All in all, a woman had many duties but no rights whatsoever.

Tragic though their condition was, Chinese women for centuries accepted it as they believed it to be the will of heaven and the natural order of things.

China's defeat in the Opium Wars around the mid-19th century gave a great shock to its rulers and people. Reformers and revolutionaries who wanted to make China a modern strong nation saw the necessity of improving women's lot. The Taiping peasant revolutionaries in the 1850's had women acting as commanders of army units and granted women the right to take examinations for official positions. Kang Youwei, leader of the "Hundred Days' Reform" in 1898, advocated the abolition of foot-binding for women and the introduction of girls' education. However, these early figures had no conception of equality between men and women; the Taiping leaders later had large harems and Kang Youwei took a number of concubines.

Dr. Sun Yat-sen recruited women as members of his China Revolutionary League formed in Japan at the turn of the century. Two noted figures were Qiu Jin, mentioned earlier, and He Xiangning (1878-1972, Madame Liao Zhongkai), a leader of the Kuomintang. The Three People's Principles aimed at giving equal political rights to men and women. During the May Fourth Movement in 1919, many girls' patriotic associations were formed in schools. These movements, however, were limited to students and a few educated women from upper-class families. It was the Communist Party which tried to organize women workers in the cities and peasant women in the countryside to free themselves of both feudal oppression and exploitation by foreign and domestic masters.

At its second congress in 1922, the Communist Party set up a women's department in the Central Committee, headed by Xiang Jingyu (1895-1928), a work-study student back from France. In her view, feminist rebellion was meaningless without political and social revolution. Only by uniting with the working class to overthrow the system of exploitation of man by man could women obtain real liberation. She went to workers' meetings in the silk, cotton and tobacco factories in Shanghai where most of the workers were women, and often visited their homes. In June 1924, she led a strike of 15,000 workers from 14 silk mills for higher wages, shorter hours and the right to form trade unions. After two weeks of stubborn struggle, the mill-owners were forced to yield. Later, she led a strike at the Shanghai Nanyang Tobacco Company. The workers' militancy and spirit of sacrifice convinced Xiang Jingyu that women factory workers would be the backbone of the women's liberation movement. On the other hand, the women workers saw in the Communist Party the leadership for their eventual liberation. International Women's Day (March 8) demonstrations became the focal point for mobilizing women to participate in political struggles.

The first Kuomintang-Communist united front in the early 1920's gave a great impetus to China's democratic revolution. Women in many provinces joined women's organizations. Young women Communists went into the countryside to urge peasant women to work toward overthrowing the landlord class, thereby gaining their own emancipation.

During the revolutionary upsurge in 1927 (see following topic) men and women in south China supported the revolutionary armies in their expedition against the northern warlords. While the men formed transport corps to bring ammunition and provisions to the front, women cooked and washed for the revolutionary soldiers and performed other services as well. The peasant movement was especially strong in Hunan Province; the womenfolk there began to assert their rights against the landlords, the patriarchs of the clans and their oppressive family elders and husbands. The Kuomintang reactionaries turned against the revolution in April 1927, and many Communists, including Xiang Jingyu and other women leaders, were shot in the ensuing White terror. Many women workers in the cities and peasant women in the countryside, however, continued to sympathize with the revolution. The Communist Party, on its part, regarded women as a great potential revolutionary force which could be mobilized to help achieve victory of the revolution.

45. THE NORTHERN EXPEDITION

In July 1926, the revolutionary Nationalist government at Guangzhou launched a military expedition against the northern warlords aimed at reuniting the country under its rule. Its armies made rapid progress across south China, winning battle after battle; within six months they took Wuhan and other major cities along the Changjiang River. Despite its initial successes, however, this phase of revolution failed due to betrayal by its leader, Chiang Kai-shek.

Kuomintang-Communist cooperation, with the aid of the Soviet Union, had greatly strengthened the revolutionary movement. In July 1925, a new kind of army — one in which the soldiers were fighting for a cause — was formed. Cadets trained by the Huangpu Military Academy became commanders and political directors at various levels of the army. By early the following year, this army had defeated all the warlords in Guangdong, turning that province into a revolutionary stronghold.

With the encouragement of the Nationalist government, trade unions grew by leaps and bounds. On May 1, 1926, the Third National Workers' Congress was held in Guangzhou, attended by 500 delegates representing 1,241,000 members. The congress pointed out that the industrial workers were the main driving force of the Chinese revolution and that the peasants were their natural allies. It called on the workers to cooperate with the peasants in giving wholehearted support to the revolutionary armies in a projected northern expedition.

Meanwhile, peasant associations were springing up in rural areas. As early as 1923, the peasants in Haifeng County in Guangdong had formed such associations under the leadership of Peng Pai (1896-1929), a Communist student who had turned against the landlord class from which he came. These associations had demanded reduction of rent, abolition of usury and exorbitant levies, and had formed self-defense corps to protect themselves against the attacks by the landlords' private forces. Subsequently, peasant associations were set up in many parts of the country. By May 1926, when a peasant congress was held in Guangzhou, it was attended by delegates from 11 provinces, representing a total of nearly 1,000,000 members. In an open letter to the peasants, the Communist Party pointed out that the fundamental solution to their problem lay in carrying out a program of "land to the tillers", and that in order to achieve this goal they must unite with the workers in the overthrow of warlord governments.

With the spread of revolutionary sentiment, the rift between the left and right elements in the Kuomintang came into the open. The rightists, whose spokesman was Dai Jitao (Tai Chi-tao, 1890-1949), were opposed to cooperation with the Communists. Chiang Kai-shek, while secretly in league with the rightists, pretended to be a true disciple of Dr. Sun Yat-sen and a faithful follower of his three major policies. On the basis of this apparently "left" stand, he was trusted by Borodin and Chen Duxiu, the Communist Party leader. Although Chiang organized an attack against the Communists and the Soviet advisers in March 1926, and ousted Communists from leadership in the revolution, the young and inexperienced Communist Party continued to support Chiang Kai-shek. In this misplaced trust lay hidden the seeds of the eventual failure of the Northern Expedition and the end of the first revolutionary civil war in China.

The Northern Expedition began as a three-pronged drive. The western or main wing was spearheaded by a regiment led by the Communist Ye Ting; its objective was to reach the provinces of Hunan and Hubei to confront the forces of the British- and U.S.-backed Wu Peifu, the strongest of the warlord armies. Composed largely of Communists and supported by workers and peasants serving as carriers and propagandists, the regiment stormed its way northward. They reached Wuhan in October, and before the year was out, the whole province of Hubei fell under their control. The Nationalist government then moved from Guangzhou to Wuhan, a strategic city on the mid-Changjiang River.

The second and third prongs were composed of Chiang Kai-shek's troops; their attack was directed against the warlord Sun Chuanfang (1885-1935, also backed by Britain and the United States) in the rich lower Changjiang valley and the coastal province of Fujian. Here, too, the workers and peasants wholeheartedly supported the revolutionary armies, which quickly occupied the capital cities of Fujian, Zhejiang, Jiangxi and Anhui provinces.

On January 3, 1927, a mass rally was held in Wuhan to celebrate the victory of the Northern Expedition and the transfer of the Nationalist government to that city. British marines stationed in Wuhan took up bayonets against the masses, killing one seaman and wounding scores of demonstrators. Infuriated, a huge crowd rushed into the British Concession in Hankou on January 5, and demanded its return to China. The following day a large number of people in the river port of Jiujiang occupied the British Concession there following the killing of some Chinese workers by British troops in yet another incident. In the face of such popular pressure, the British government thought it wise to yield to these demands and formally returned both concessions to China. For the first time since the First Opium War, the Chinese people had through their own united efforts restored their sovereignty over a portion of territory that had previously been taken from them.

46. CHIANG KAI-SHEK TURNS AGAINST THE REVOLUTION

Chiang Kai-shek maintained secret ties with Dai Jitao and other members of the Kuomintang's right wing at a time when he was still shouting revolutionary slogans. At the same time, the enemies of the revolution — the feudal landlord class, Chinese capitalists and foreign imperialists — were looking for an ally within the revolutionary camp. They began looking to Chiang Kai-shek, now chief commander of the revolutionary armies but also a former stockbroker with Shanghai underworld connections.

As the Northern Expedition rolled forward in late 1926 and early 1927, landlords had good reason to abhor the revolution. Wherever a revolutionary army set foot, the poor peasants flocked to join peasant associations, which then seized political power from the landlords. In Hunan Province, the peasant masses often arrested the most hated landlords, put high paper-hats on their heads, and paraded them through the villages. They demanded the reduction of rent and interest, and sometimes invaded the landlords' houses, slaughtering their pigs and distributing their grain to the poor. Some big landlords who had committed particularly heinous crimes were brought before mass accusation meetings and publicly executed. As a result, the top local bullies and evil gentry fled to Shanghai, while those of lesser ranks ran to other major cities and county towns, where they spread horror stories about the peasant movement. At the height of this movement, the young Mao Zedong conducted his own investigation and concluded: "In a few months the peasants have accomplished what Dr. Sun Yat-sen wanted, but failed, to accomplish in the forty years he devoted to the national revolution. This is a marvelous feat never before achieved, not just in forty but in thousands of years."

No less alarmed were the industrialists whose factories were now being regularly shut down by workers' strikes for higher wages and the right to form trade unions. In Shanghai, China's largest industrial center, the workers organized the General Trade Union and revolted against the warlord Sun Chuanfang, fighting his troops in the streets. Although the first two uprisings failed, a third one led by Zhou Enlai and other Communists on March 21, 1927 routed the warlord's troops after more than two days of hard fighting. A popular provisional government was set up to welcome the approaching revolutionary army.

The foreign powers, mainly concerned with the perpetuation of their dominant position in China, took a hostile attitude toward the revolution from the beginning. At first they attempted to smother it by force. In September 1926, British gunboats bombarded Wanxian City on the upper Changjiang River in Sichuan Province, destroying numerous stores and houses and killing and wounding several thousand soldiers and civilians. Again, in March 1927, under the pretext that foreign consulates and nationals in Nanjing had been assaulted by Chinese "mobs", American, British and other foreign warships opened fire on the city from the Changjiang River, causing a great loss of lives and property among the Chinese population. Failing to achieve their objective by force, the foreign powers then adopted the traditional policy of "divide and rule" in attempting to split the revolutionary ranks.

After setting up his military headquarters at Nanchang, the capital of Jiangxi Province, Chiang Kai-shek considered himself strong enough to defy the authority of the revolutionary Nationalist government at Wuhan, which was then dominated by Kuomintang left-wingers (including Mme. Sun Yat-sen) and Communists. In January 1927, he demanded that the government be moved from Wuhan to Nanchang, where he was in complete control. In reply, the central committee of the Kuomintang at Wuhan took away his leading positions in the party, government and army in an attempt to prevent him from seizing all power.

Bankers from Shanghai, politicians representing various warlord governments and the agents of foreign imperialists all converged on Nanchang to offer Chiang their help. In secret talks he was promised a loan of 60,000,000 Chinese dollars if he would break with the Communists and the Soviet Union and suppress the peasants and workers. Chiang quickly agreed.

In the early hours of April 12, 1927, thousands of thugs from the underworld Green Gang came out of the International

Settlement disguised as workers to attack the workers' armed militia. Pretending to oppose "internal dissension among the workers", Chiang Kai-shek ordered his troops to disarm the workers and occupy the headquarters of the General Trade Union, where a spurious union composed of underworld figures was immediately set up. Next day the Shanghai workers called a mass rally and demanded the return of their weapons. Unaware that Chiang Kai-shek had turned against the revolution, they went to the General Headquarters of the Northern Expeditionary Army to present their petition, only to be mowed down by machine-gun fire. The blood of hundreds of workers stained the rain-washed streets of Shanghai red.

The Shanghai massacre ushered in a large-scale slaughter of many revolutionary workers, peasants, Communists, progressive intellectuals and students throughout the country. In Beijing, warlord Zhang Zuolin's police force broke into the Soviet embassy; there they seized approximately 30 Communists, including Professor Li Dazhao, who was immediately murdered.

Having emerged as the new "strong man" of China, Chiang Kai-shek set up his own government at Nanjing in opposition to the Nationalist government at Wuhan. Although Chiang continued to pay lip service to Dr. Sun Yat-sen's Three People's Principles, his actual backing consisted of Chinese capitalists and rural gentry on the one hand and the foreign powers on the other.

47.   THE SOVIET UNION'S ROLE IN THE REVOLUTION OF 1925-1927

In order to rouse the masses to revolutionary action, the Comintern (Communist International), under the leadership first of Lenin and then of Stalin, aided in the founding of the Chinese Communist Party; helped in the reorganization of the

Kuomintang into a revolutionary party (consisting of workers, peasants, small and big patriotic capitalists); and gave valuable advice in the formation of a united front between the Kuomintang and the Communist Party. This led to the rapid growth of revolutionary trade unions and peasant associations, and the establishment of a revolutionary army.

Of course, Stalin's conception of the united front between the masses of workers and peasants (represented by the Communist Party) and the national bourgeoisie (represented by the Kuomintang) was not unconditional. In May 1925 he stated: "Such a dual party is necessary and expedient, provided it does not restrict the freedom of the Communist Party to conduct agitation and propaganda work, provided it does not hinder the rallying of the proletarians around the Communist Party, and provided it facilitates the actual leadership of the revolutionary movement by the Communist Party." In other words, in China the Communists within the Kuomintang must have the freedom to spread revolutionary ideas, organize the workers and peasants, and prepare to assume the actual leadership of the coming revolutionary upsurge.

Unfortunately, in practice, too much confidence was placed on Chiang Kai-shek, who was mistakenly seen as a true follower of Dr. Sun Yat-sen and the "man of the hour" who would lead the revolution to victory. For his part, Chiang Kai-shek played his role cleverly. After removing prominent Communists from leading positions in the spring of 1926, he put on a show at the Third All-China Labor Congress in Guangzhou at the end of May. As commander-in-chief of the revolutionary army, he clenched his fist and shouted, "Long live the world revolution" to thunderous applause by the worker delegates. As a result, Chen Duxiu and many other leaders of the Communist Party were completely hoodwinked and willingly abdicated leadership of the united front and the Chinese revolution.

After Chiang Kai-shek's counter-revolutionary coup d'etat in Shanghai in April 1927, the Comintern representatives in China mistakenly shifted their trust to Wang Jingwei (1883-1944),

Revolutionary Military Government set up at Wuchang in 1911.

Qing officials fleeing from Hankou after the outbreak of the Revolution of 1911.

Revolutionary soldiers patrolling the streets in Hankou.

Revolutionary army ready for action at Hankou in 1911.

Yuan Shikai worships Heaven in Beijing in December 1915 after announcing his decision to become emperor of China.

Sun Yat-sen with his followers and friends in Tokyo, 1916.

Beijing students demonstrating on May 4, 1919 against the Versailles Treaty, which transferred former German possessions in Shandong Province to Japan.

Nanhu Lake not far from Shanghai. The boat is where the First Congress of the Chinese Communist Party held its last day session to elude police arrest in July 1921.

Mao Zedong, a young delegate from Hunan Province to the First Congress of the CCP.

Li Dazhao (1889-1927), Peking University professor who became a founder of the Chinese Communist Party and died a martyr in Beijing in 1927.

Opening ceremony of the Whampoa Military Academy in May 1924. (From left to right) Liao Zhongkai, Chiang Kai-shek, Dr. and Mme. Sun Yat-sen.

Sun Yat-sen (center) and Li Dazhao coming out of the First National Congress of the Kuomintang in January 1924.

Dr. and Mme. Sun Yat-sen (center front) at a Lenin memorial meeting in Guangzhou, February 1924.

Dr. and Mme. Sun Yat-sen at the army and navy headquarters on New Year's day, 1924.

leader of the left-wing Kuomintang, who was already in covert contact with Chiang Kai-shek in Nanjing. When a secret Comintern telegram came, advising the Chinese Communists on how to take the leadership of the revolution by raising an army of workers and peasants, the Comintern representative in China, M. N. Roy, showed it to Wang Jingwei. Knowledge of this document gave Wang an excuse to clamp down on the Communists. Soon afterward, the Wuhan government which he headed also started to disarm and slaughter workers and peasants, joining hands with the Nanjing government.

One of the lessons of the defeat of the Chinese revolution of 1925-1927 was that it demonstrated that a revolution with its many sudden twists and turns could not be directed from thousands of miles away through reliance on reports and telegrams. The Chinese revolution had to develop its own leaders who could solve problems immediately and independently in response to an ever changing situation.

48. THE COMMUNISTS' EFFORTS TO RESIST THE COUNTER-REVOLUTION

During the white terror unleashed by the Nanjing and Wuhan Kuomintang governments in 1927 as many as 380,000 Communists and their supporters were massacred. However, it failed to eliminate all the Communists and other revolutionaries. Those who survived the mass slaughter fought on with renewed determination.

The first decisive step to fashion a counter-attack came on August 1, 1927 at Nanchang, the capital of Jiangxi Province. Under the leadership of Zhou Enlai, Zhu De (1886-1976), He Long (1896-1969), Ye Ting (1896-1946) and others, 30,000 insurgent troops rose against the Kuomintang authority early that morning, and within five hours the revolutionaries held the whole city. Later, when Chiang Kai-shek rushed large-scale reinforcements by land and water to recapture this strategic point, the Communists, greatly outnumbered, withdrew and marched southward. This bold action marked the beginning of the second revolutionary civil war — a new stage in which the revolution was carried on under the exclusive leadership of the Communist Party and with its own armed forces. In the People's Republic of China today, "August 1" is celebrated as Army Day — the day on which the People's Liberation Army was born.

On August 7, an emergency meeting of the Central Committee of the Chinese Communist Party was held in Hankou. It condemned Chen Duxiu's capitulationist policy, dismissed him from the post of secretary-general and formulated a policy of armed struggle against the Kuomintang. To promote the agrarian revolution, the committee decided to stage uprisings during the autumn harvest in the four provinces of Hunan, Hubei, Jiangxi and Guangdong, where the revolution had strong peasant support. However, there was a failure to recognize that the revolution was temporarily on the ebb, and this failure opened the way for the "leftist" errors of adventurist attacks on cities and calls to workers to initiate strikes even when there was no hope of success.

The "Autumn Harvest Uprising" began in early September and ended in October 1927. In Hunan Province, Mao Zedong gathered a motley army of miners from Anyuan, peasant self-defense corps from Pingxiang and Liling, as well as some Nationalist army soldiers and officers, students, peasant cadres and sympathizers. After an unsuccessful attempt to take the provincial capital Changsha, Mao Zedong and his forces withdrew to the Jinggang Mountains on the border between Hunan and Jiangxi provinces. Here in a region remote from warlord control, they set up a rural base where they could recoup their strength, train and prepare for a new upsurge of the revolution.

At Guangzhou, the "home-base" of the Northern Expedition, the local Communist forces staged an uprising on December 11, 1927. At three o'clock in the morning, the Officers

Training Regiment under Ye Jianying, together with those garrison troops sympathetic to the revolution and some workers' militia units, suddenly attacked the counter-revolutionary troops in the city. Within two hours all major strategic positions had fallen into the hands of the insurgents. The Guangzhou Commune — the first real organ of workers' political power — was set up immediately. Tens of thousands of workers flocked to the revolutionary headquarters to receive arms and be directed to battle posts. The rapid victory of the insurrection startled the reactionaries, but soon, under the protection of foreign warships, Kuomintang reinforcements converged on the scene. After three days of bitter fighting, the defenders of the Guangzhou Commune were defeated. The painful lesson which the Communists derived from this defeat was that they must build up their own armed forces in order to achieve military victory and not commit them to battle prematurely.

In April 1928, Zhu De and Chen Yi (1901-1972) led the remainder of the troops which had taken part in the Nanchang Uprising and some peasant contingents to link up with Mao Zedong's forces near the Jinggang Mountains in Jiangxi Province. This merger gave them greater strength, and the revolutionary base was expanded to include several counties. The establishment of a base area in the inaccessible Jinggang Mountain area not only saved the hungry and ragged revolutionary troops in the short term, but could even be said to have paved the way for the eventual nationwide victory of the revolution some 20 years later.

49. CHIANG KAI-SHEK CONSOLIDATES HIS POLITICAL POWER

To extend his political power, Chiang Kai-shek launched a second "northern expedition" in February 1928. In May when his troops were marching through Shandong Province, Japan moved to occupy Jinan, the provincial capital, under the pretext of protecting Japanese citizens residing in that city. Instead of resisting this foreign interference, Chiang went to Tokyo and humbly explained that his government posed no threat to Japanese interests in China.

The Kuomintang armies occupied Beijing in June, changing its name to Beiping (Northern Peace) to emphasize the fact that Nanjing (Southern Capital) was the new national capital. Soon afterward, the "Young Marshal" Zhang Xueliang, warlord of the Northeast, became allied with the Kuomintang. For a time it seemed that Chiang Kai-shek had truly unified the country; the Nanjing government came to be recognized as the central government of China. October 10, 1928 (the anniversary of the 1911 Revolution) was celebrated as marking the victory of the national revolution as well as the end of the warlord era and civil war.

China, however, was unified in name only. War broke out the following year, first between Chiang Kai-shek and the Guangxi warlords over control of central China, and then between Chiang Kai-shek on one side and Feng Yuxiang and Yan Xishan (1883-1960, "local emperor" of Shanxi Province) on the other over the control of the North. Minor warlords in the southwestern provinces of Yunnan, Guizhou and Sichuan continued to fight among themselves. Unable to subdue them all, Chiang Kai-shek made compromises with many local warlords, allowing each to manage his own affairs as long as lip-service was paid to the central government.

The unstable political unification resulted in increased burdens on the people. China's huge army had grown to 2,500,000 men from 1,200,000 five years earlier (the maximum under the Qing dynasty was 400,000), thus creating a great drain on central government funds. Mounting taxes, conscription for military service and looting by underpaid and undisciplined soldiers were the inevitable by-products.

The Nanjing government had been set up after the suppression of the workers' and peasants' movements. To consolidate his power, Chiang Kai-shek intensified repression against the opposition. In addition to "yellow" trade unions which collaborated with the Kuomintang, "black" unions were created by the police and special services to hound Communists or other "subversive" elements. The workers' plight became worse: low wages, long working hours under unsanitary conditions, oppression by labor bosses and gangsters, miserable housing and unstable employment. In the countryside, the landlord-gentry or their agents resumed their oppression of the peasants with a vengeance. The old feudal order was bolstered by a *baojia* system, by which families were grouped in units which were held jointly responsible for any "unlawful" incident. Driven into destitution and despair, many peasants joined secret societies such as the Red Spears, Big Swords, Sacred Soldiers of the Buddhist Way, and bandit gangs.

With regard to the unequal treaties between China and the foreign powers, the Nanjing regime adopted a conciliatory policy in place of mass struggle. The foreign powers in turn made some minor concessions in order to assuage the nationalist fervor of the people and enhance Chiang Kai-shek's prestige. They returned to China 20 out of 33 concessions, but kept the important ones like those in Shanghai. Britain gave up the leased territory Weihaiwei on the Shandong coast. A few secondary powers (such as Denmark and Belgium) gave up their extraterritorial rights completely. China recovered full customs autonomy in 1933, but foreign trade remained colonial in character and had an unfavorable balance. Foreign financial domination due to payments on indemnities and debts remained, as did Western control over many important mines, railroads, factories and even public services in major cities. Britain, France and Japan continued to enjoy such privileges as extraterritoriality, concessions and military rights. The system of unequal treaties remained largely intact; China was still a semi-colony exploited by competing foreign powers.

As Chiang Kai-shek was regarded as the "strong man" of China, the West supported him with military supplies and technical assistance. Chiang's personal armies had French tanks,

Italian airplanes and British artillery.   A 70-man German military mission directed by Generals von Seeckt and von Falkenhausen was attached to Chiang's headquarters.   The purpose
of this aid was to help Chiang suppress the Communist
"bandits" rather than to assist China in achieving prosperity
and full independence.

The great majority of Western-trained intellectuals — teachers, engineers, doctors, lawyers and journalists — backed
Chiang Kai-shek and his national government.   They cherished
the false hope that the Kuomintang would unify the country
and bring about China's modernization.   Divorced from the
masses of the people, they lived in a world of comforts and
privileges.   People like Madame Chiang Kai-shek, T. V.
Soong (1894-1971), H. H. Kung (1880-1967) and others constituted what the economist Samir Amin has called a new elite
whose life-style was much more tied to the West than to the
old feudal habits and customs.   Only a few refused to go
along.   Soong Ching Ling (Madame Sun Yat-sen), one of the
20th century's most outstanding and courageous women, stood
firm on the side of the revolution.   Lu Xun (1881-1936),
Mao Dun (Shen Yanbing) and other leftist writers continued
the struggle against the right with their sharp pens.   Unfortunately, these few voices were too weak to shake Chiang's
power at the time.   For the moment Chiang Kai-shek seemed
to be undefeatable.

50.   GROWTH OF THE REVOLUTIONARY
BASE AREAS

Relatively small, isolated revolutionary base areas could be
established because of the specific conditions in China at that
time.   The main features consisted of the following:

1.   China was a predominantly semi-feudal agricultural
country with many localities practically self-sufficient economi-

cally.   The peasants worked in the fields and gave a half or more of their produce to the landlords as rent.   The women stayed at home weaving cloth, raising pigs and chickens, and making various handicraft articles such as baskets and straw mats.   The town and county fairs gave them the opportunity to sell their wares and buy what they needed for work and for use at home.   The self-sufficiency of the local economy enabled the revolutionaries to establish bases which could exist for a long time without getting supplies from elsewhere.

2.   China had a very poorly developed communications network.   Aside from a few railways and steamship lines linking the major cities in the eastern part of the country, the vast rural areas had only bumpy roads and footpaths, many of which were difficult to negotiate even on foot.   The inaccessible mountainous areas between two or three provinces were often the strongholds of bandit gangs or rebel groups who were able to defy government authority for years.   Under these circumstances, it was not so difficult for revolutionaries to set up their own bases.

3.   China was a semi-colonial country; the rivalry among the different imperialist powers led to disunity among the ruling groups in China.   Constant wars among the warlords for supremacy and the lack of a strong central government enabled the revolutionaries to set up, maintain and expand their revolutionary bases.

4.   China had already gone through a great revolution between 1925 and 1927.   Many workers and peasants had become ardent supporters of the revolution.   This provided the seeds from which the Red Army grew.

5.   The correct policies of the Communist Party were also an important factor in the continued existence and expansion of the revolutionary base areas.   Politically, the Party carried out a policy of land distribution to the land-hungry peasants and farm laborers, thus winning their wholehearted support. Militarily, the Party trained a disciplined Red Army using guerrilla tactics and helped form people's militia units to serve as effective auxiliaries of the regular armed forces.

However, not many people understood that correct policies must be based on a scientific analysis of concrete situations. When the revolutionary base in the Jinggang Mountains was repeatedly attacked by Chiang Kai-shek's troops, some Communists at first wondered how long they could "keep the red flag flying". For a long time many Party leaders, including those in the Central Committee, continued to think that the Chinese revolution had to follow the path of the Russian October Revolution — seizure of large cities first and expansion to the rural areas later. They did not understand that, in a predominantly semi-feudal society like China, the peasants were the natural allies of the urban working class, and that when reaction was strong in the cities, it was necessary to set up revolutionary bases first in the rural areas, to consolidate and expand the revolutionary bases gradually and then to surround and capture the cities. It was to Mao Zedong's credit that he saw the feasibility of setting up autonomous revolutionary bases in the countryside.

Mao Zedong predicted that "if the Red Army does not move away (as advocated by some Communist leaders), building on the foundations we already have, we shall be able gradually to expand to surrounding areas and our prospects will be very bright." What he foresaw came to pass. Furthermore, his example in setting up base areas was followed by others. By 1930 the Red Army had grown to 100,000 men. Fifteen revolutionary base areas had been established in various parts of the country in defiance of the authority of Chiang Kai-shek's reactionary government.

51. LIFE IN THE EARLY REVOLUTIONARY BASE AREAS

Life in the revolutionary bases was as exhilarating as it was hard. Each day brought new physical and intellectual challenges, and the revolutionaries took pride in living up to these challenges.   Food, clothing and medical supplies in the base areas were extremely scarce because of the tight blockade by Chiang Kai-shek's military forces.   Writing about the Jinggang Mountain base in the winter of 1928, Mao Zedong said:

> In addition to grain, each man receives only five cents a day for cooking oil, salt, firewood and vegetables, and even this is hard to keep up. . . . Cold as the weather is, many of our men are still wearing only two layers of thin clothing. Fortunately we are inured to hardships.   What is more, all of us share the same hardships; from the commander of the army to the cook everyone lives on the daily food allowance of five cents, apart from grain. . . . Consequently the soldiers have no complaints against anyone. . . . Our hospitals up in the mountains give both Chinese and Western treatment, but are short of doctors and medicines.

In spite of such privations, the morale of the soldiers was very high.   This was due to the introduction of democracy — something entirely new — into the army ranks.   Officers were not allowed to beat the men; soldiers were free to hold meetings and speak their minds; and the accounts were open for all to see.   Newly captured soldiers in particular felt that the Kuomintang army and the Red Army were as different as night and day.   Many prisoners of war were quickly transformed under the changed conditions.   They felt spiritually liberated, even though material conditions were unusually hard.   The very soldiers who only recently had had no courage in the Kuomintang or warlord armies became valiant fighters after joining the ranks of the Red Army.

The intellectual atmosphere of the revolutionary bases was democratic, vital and intense.   From the leadership to the lowest ranks, men were encouraged to think creatively, discuss ideas freely, and experiment with new solutions to the problems involved in building an army and gaining the support of the masses.   For example, in the agrarian revolution, the policy had at first been confiscation and redistribution of all land. Every inhabitant, man or woman, old or young, received an equal share. This drastic measure drove a sizeable number of middle peasants (who derived their income wholly or mainly from their own labor without exploiting others) to make common cause with the landlords against the revolutionaries. After the results were known, the policy was changed to one of confiscation of public land and landlord-owned land only. Under the changed policy, the middle peasants no longer sided with the landlords, and the latter were rendered weak and ineffective in their opposition.

A similar process took place with regard to intermediate classes in the towns, where an ultra-left policy of almost indiscriminate killing and burning had at first been adopted. To win over such intermediate classes so as to isolate the main enemy, Mao Zedong proposed the protection of the interests of the middle and small merchants.

The Red Army was composed of heterogeneous elements — workers, miners, peasants, students and intellectuals, peddlers and even some bandits. To weld them together into an effective and disciplined fighting force, an educational program was worked out to supplement purely military training. The men were taught that they were not mercenaries fighting for personal gain or the selfish ambitions of a warlord, but for the liberation of the poor and the oppressed and the creation of a new and just society. To counter the enemy propaganda that "the Red bandits kill everyone on sight", the fighters were taught to regard captured Kuomintang soldiers as class brothers. The wounded were given medical treatment, and those who wanted to stay were welcomed into the ranks, while those who preferred to leave were given traveling money.

A local people's militia was organized to supplement the army. While the army was concentrated to combat the enemy's own concentrated forces, the militia was dispersed as guerrilla units to harass the enemy's rear and cut its transportation lines.

People's governments were established at county, district and township levels, though largely in name only at first. The feudal practice of arbitrary rule by superiors was so deeply rooted in the minds of the people — including Party members — that it could not be swept away all at once. A detailed organic law providing for people's councils at all levels was worked out in an attempt to introduce democracy into political life. Other laws limited land tax to 20 percent or less of the crops and stipulated that in areas where the peasants were poverty-stricken no tax should be levied at all.

Life in the early revolutionary base areas was so full of hardships that the situation might have been regarded as hopeless. The determined revolutionaries, however, did not despair. Doggedly they tried not only to survive and build an army, but to free the peasants from the shackles of centuries-old feudal exploitation and create a new democratic life for the masses.

52. THE RED ARMY'S CLOSE TIES WITH THE PEOPLE

The Kuomintang and warlord armies were regarded by the people as "uniformed bandits". Their officers and men often forced their way into stores and homes, carrying away anything of value and abusing women. In their efforts to suppress the revolution, they adopted the slogan, "Rather kill a hundred innocent people by mistake than let a single Communist get away!" A common saying among the people which reflected their traditional attitude toward the military stated, "As good iron is not used to make nails, so a good fellow never becomes a soldier."

In sharp contrast, the Red Army was regarded by the poor people as their own. A Red Armyman helped the peasants in their farm work and organized them to fight the ruthless exploitation of the landlords and moneylenders. He was honest in his dealings and his behavior was exemplary. How did he become such a type of a soldier? It was because a new recruit in the Red Army was taught to see the errors of old ideas and habits and was instilled with a new revolutionary spirit.

First, persistent educational work was carried on. Some officers and men, for instance, at first believed that the task of the Red Army was merely to fight and win battles. They did not understand that the Red Army was an arm of the revolution. Besides destroying the enemy's military strength, it had to shoulder such political tasks as educational work among the masses and organizing the people to help in the establishment of revolutionary political power.

Some members of the Red Army lacked discipline and were reluctant to carry out majority decisions or even to obey orders. Others wanted to spread Red political influence through adventurist roving guerrilla actions rather than patient work in building up the base areas. To overcome these and other weaknesses in political understanding, the leadership instituted the study of Marxism-Leninism and a scientific approach to problems in the basic units of the army.

Organizationally, the Red Army adopted the principle that "the Party commands the gun and the gun must never command the Party". Party groups were established at every level. This system of Party organization ensured implementation of the educational program and gradually unified the disparate elements into an effective fighting force. Furthermore, it guaranteed working-class leadership, prevented a reversion to warlordism, or the control of the army and political decision-making by one man, as was the case in Kuomintang and warlord-controlled areas.

The Red Army leaders worked out certain rules and regulations governing the relations between the army and the people. From the earliest days of the Red Army, the soldiers were taught to speak politely to the masses, pay fairly for all purchases, and never to force people to perform labor services, hit or swear at people. Gradually these rules of behavior evolved into what became known as the "Three Main Rules of Discipline" and "Eight Points for Attention", which were observed by all units of the Red Army.

The Three Main Rules of Discipline:
1. Obey orders in all actions.
2. Don't take a single needle or piece of thread from the masses.
3. Turn in everything captured.

The Eight Points for Attention:
1. Speak politely.
2. Pay fairly for what is bought.
3. Return everything borrowed.
4. Pay for everything damaged.
5. Don't hit or swear at people.
6. Don't damage crops.
7. Don't take liberties with women.
8. Don't ill-treat captives.

To help the soldiers remember these rules, they were turned into a simple tune which they could sing while marching.

That these rules were in fact observed by the great majority of the Red Armymen has been attested by many eyewitnesses, both Chinese and foreign. The rapid growth of the Red Army into a force capable of facing the numerically stronger and better equipped troops of the Kuomintang came about primarily because they were accepted and supported by the peasants as a genuine people's army.

53. CHIANG KAI-SHEK'S EFFORTS TO WIPE OUT THE BASE AREAS

In January 1929, the main forces of the Red Army, under the command of Mao Zedong and Zhu De, broke out of the blockade enforced by Chiang Kai-shek's troops around the Jinggang Mountains and started to open up new Red areas in southern Jiangxi and western Fujian provinces.

Everywhere they went, they carried out the agrarian revolution. On the basis of their previous experience, they adopted a policy of relying on the poor peasants and farm laborers; uniting with the middle peasants and restricting the rich peasants; protecting the medium and small businessmen; and eliminating the landlords as a class. The landlord's land was confiscated and distributed to the land-hungry poor peasants and farm laborers, who became the mainstay of the new democratic government. Many middle peasants who got additional land also became supporters of the revolution. Debts at usurious rates of interest were canceled. Middle and small businessmen were relieved of the heavy tax burden. Even former landlords were allotted equal shares of land so that they too could live on their own labor rather than becoming lawless elements. This moderate policy won the support of the masses and aroused their enthusiasm for production. By the fall of 1931, the Red areas in southern Jiangxi Province and the adjacent regions had grown to include 21 counties with 2,500,000 inhabitants. In November a provisional central government of a "Chinese Soviet Republic" was established at Ruijin, with Mao Zedong as chairman.

Chiang Kai-shek regarded the growth of the Red areas as a serious threat to his power. Toward the end of 1930, at the conclusion of his war against Feng Yuxiang and Yan Xishan in the North, he ordered 100,000 troops to launch an "encirclement and suppression" campaign against the central Red area. At the time, the Red Army troops there numbered only 40,000 men. In the face of this much stronger force, the Red commanders adopted the tactics which involved luring the enemy deep into the base area where favorable terrain and strong popular support could turn the balance. In a five-day running battle, the Red Army smashed the enemy offensive, seized 13,000 rifles and captured the commander himself.

In April 1931, Chiang Kai-shek amassed 200,000 troops for a second "encirclement and suppression" campaign. The Red commanders decided to defeat the enemy using mobile warfare tactics. In the latter part of May, the Red Army scored five successive victories in a 400-kilometer eastward sweep stretching from southern Jiangxi to western Fujian, wiping out 30,000 enemy troops and capturing 20,000 weapons.

But the fighting had also taken its toll of the Red forces, now reduced to 30,000 men. Before they could gain respite and get replacements, Chiang Kai-shek in the beginning of July launched a third "encirclement and suppression" campaign with 300,000 troops; he acted himself as commander-in-chief. The Red Army dispatched part of its forces to the rear of Chiang Kai-shek's troops and fell upon the weaker units. In five days it scored three victories, annihilating five enemy divisions. The rest of the enemy fled in panic and Chiang Kai-shek was forced to return to Nanjing in defeat.

The Red Army gradually perfected the guerrilla tactics which they had originally learned in their battles against Kuomintang troops in the Jinggang Mountains. These tactics were described in a 16-character Chinese phrase: The enemy advances, we retreat; the enemy camps, we harass; the enemy tires, we attack; the enemy retreats, we pursue. In the course of fighting Chiang Kai-shek's "encirclement and suppression" campaigns, the Red Army learned how to spring surprise attacks on the enemy by making feinting movements, how to fight mobile warfare with fluid battle lines, and how to fight battles of quick decision in which the enemy was wiped out before reinforcements could arrive. With such techniques the Red Army was able to defeat the enemy bit by bit, piece by piece, replenish its arms and ammunition by capturing them from the enemy side, and grow steadily stronger in the protracted revolutionary war.

54. THE CULTURAL FRONT IN THE EARLY 1930S

The League of Left-Wing Writers, which existed from 1930 to 1936, played a significant part in promoting a new revolutionary literature and art in China. On the basis of the Marxist-Leninist conception that literature and art should serve the interests of the working class and the oppressed colonial and semi-colonial peoples, its members used their writings to struggle against supporters of the old order. The league was formed in Shanghai in March 1930. Its leader was Lu Xun, who had first become famous during the May Fourth Movement for his short stories such as "A Madman's Diary" and "The True Story of Ah Q". With satire, vivid imagery and irony, he exposed the evils of the old society. At the beginning, the approximately 50 members of the league were drawn from the Creation Society (founded by the poet and historian Guo Moruo) and the Sun Society (founded by the writer Jiang Guangci), both organizations of revolutionary writers. The league's aim was to help bring about the liberation of the working class and to oppose repression from all quarters. Aside from disseminating Marxist-Leninist theories on art and criticism, its members studied foreign progressive and revolutionary literature, trained young writers, particularly those from the ranks of workers and peasants, and published progressive books and periodicals.

At the league's inaugural meeting, Lu Xun warned the members that if they remained "parlor socialists" without contacts with real life, they might easily shift from left- to right-wing writers. He called on them to be resolute in struggle against the old society and to hold fast to the common aim of serving the workers and peasants rather than pursuing personal ambitions.

The establishment of the league marked a new stage in the development of China's revolutionary literature, and Chiang Kai-shek was determined to crush it. In reaction, certain literary figures allied with Chiang Kai-shek started in June 1930 a "nationalist literature and art movement" which advocated fascist culture in China. In September, the Kuomintang outlawed the League of Left-Wing Writers and ordered the arrest of Lu Xun and other well-known members. Many young writers were jailed and Lu Xun himself had to go into hiding.

In January of the following year, the Kuomintang issued emergency laws directed against those who "threatened national security"; under this pretext 18 promising writers, members of the league, were executed, and several bookstores were closed down for selling what the Kuomintang called "reactionary publications".

Despite Chiang Kai-shek's attempt to crush the league, its members continued to criticize popular writers and intellectuals who opposed the idea of a proletarian literature. Among them were members of the Crescent Group, such as Hu Shi and Liang Shiqiu, who took the position that literature should reflect a class-free human nature. With his sharp pen, Lu Xun pointed out that since everybody in a class society belonged to a definite class, it was ridiculous to write about individuals as if they were apart from or above classes. The thoughts and emotions of a wealthy oil tycoon could only be very different from those of a poor old woman picking unburned coal balls from a pile of cinders.

Another group represented by Lin Yutang advocated that literature should entertain the leisured classes with humor. Lu Xun referred to them sarcastically as literary hacks who would inevitably sink to supporting the "butchers of the people". He insisted that at a time when "tigers and wolves" were roaming around killing people, every piece of writing should be a dagger or a spear aimed at the enemy.

In 1934, under the slogan of the "New Life Movement", Chiang Kai-shek began to propagate the study of the Confucian classics and a return to feudal morals. Lu Xun pointed out that it was the rich and powerful who had made Confucius a sage and that in reality he had nothing to do with the common people.

The League of Left-Wing Writers wielded a substantial influence among students. Branches were set up in many major cities, and the league's numerous magazines, such as *The Pioneer* and *The Tatler*, had a wide circulation. In novels (such as Mao Dun's *Midnight* and *Spring Silkworms*), short stories (such as Lu Xun's *Call to Arms* and *Wandering*), plays and films, the darkness of the old society was exposed and the necessity for revolution stressed. Contacts were maintained with foreign progressive and anti-fascist writers, and their best-known works were translated into Chinese.

Through its publications, the league supported the struggles of the Chinese Communist Party. When the Red Army reached northern Shaanxi in October 1935 after the Long March carried it over 5,000 kilometers across the mountains and rivers of south and west China, Lu Xun sent a message to Mao Zedong, telling him that China's hope for a bright future lay in him and the Red Army. After the league was voluntarily dissolved in 1936 to open the way for a broader anti-Japanese cultural organization, many of its members went to work or study in Yan'an, then the capital of the Central Liberated Area under Communist control.

55. PROBLEMS IN THE URBAN LABOR MOVEMENT

The Chinese labor movement developed from the beginning under the leadership of the Communist Party. When Chiang Kai-shek turned against the revolution in 1927, he tried to suppress the labor movement, too. In spite of the Kuomintang White terror, however, the workers' movement in the cities came to life again as a result of the patient and persistent efforts of Communist organizers. By 1930 the number of underground Party branches among industrial workers had grown to 229 from less than 100 the year before. The revived trade unions actively defended workers' rights and led the struggle against the Kuomintang.

In May 1930, Chiang Kai-shek became involved in a war with the "Christian General" Feng Yuxiang and warlord Yan Xishan over control of north China. The war lasted seven months, resulting in 300,000 killed and wounded among more than 1,000,000 troops on both sides. Chiang's preoccupation with the struggle for power against the warlords provided a favorable condition for the revival and development of the labor movement.

At this time, however, the Party Central Committee located in Shanghai fell under the control of a leftist trade union leader, Li Lisan (1899-1967). Failing to understand that the Chinese revolution was at a low ebb following Chiang Kai-shek's ruthless suppression of the masses, Li believed a new revolutionary upsurge was close at hand and began to organize workers' uprisings in the cities to be supported by Red Army assaults from the outside. Instead of consolidating the revolutionary bases in the rural areas, he ordered the Red Army to attack the large cities in central China, to "converge our forces on Wuhan and water our horses in the Changjiang River". In his opinion, the occupation of the strategic city of Wuhan would lead to the setting up of a Soviet government for all China.

In the summer of 1930, Li Lisan ordered the Red Army under Mao Zedong and Zhu De to leave the base area and attack Nanchang, the capital of Jiangxi Province. The city was strongly defended by Kuomintang troops, and Mao Zedong and Zhu De realized that the attack would simply destroy their own forces. Instead they headed west and joined with another Red force under Peng Dehuai (1898-1974) recently dislodged from Changsha. The combined forces then marched toward southern Jiangxi Province, where they liberated more areas and expanded the revolutionary base. In later years Zhu De was to tell the American journalist Agnes Smedley, "For the first time we had openly disobeyed the orders of the Central Committee." In October Li Lisan was called to Moscow and asked to examine his own errors.

In January 1931, the "28 Bolsheviks" headed by Wang Ming (Chen Shaoyu, 1904-1974) came to control the Party Central Committee at Shanghai. Instead of learning from the leftist mistakes committed by Li Lisan, they maintained that the Chinese Communist Party was not revolutionary enough. In a country where the peasants constituted over 80 percent of the population and winning them over was absolutely essential for the eventual victory of the revolution, Wang Ming insisted that the main danger lay in the "right opportunist" line as represented by Mao Zedong's "peasant mentality".

In the labor movement, they also adopted a leftist policy. They called on the workers to stage uprisings to overthrow all capitalists, including small shopkeepers, instead of concentrating on the urgent task of mobilizing the masses to struggle against imperialist domination and feudal exploitation. This ultra-leftist policy of immediate socialist revolution without taking into account the actual Chinese conditions at the time antagonized large sections of city dwellers, and the Communist activists were easily caught by Chiang Kai-shek's dragnet of secret agents in cooperation with foreign police in the International Settlement, the French and other concessions.

In the latter part of 1931, the Communist headquarters in Shanghai was discovered by the Kuomintang with information from some defectors. Hundreds were arrested and shot at an execution ground specially reserved for such spectacles. The labor movement in the cities collapsed, and Wang Ming and other Communist leaders fled to the southern Jiangxi Soviet area created by Mao Zedong and his followers.

The Kuomintang then tried to control the workers through its own trade unions. No elections were held, and all trade union officials were Kuomintang appointees who were agents of the secret police. Their main duties were to spy on militant workers and suspected Communists. No worker dared present demands of any sort for fear of arrest and imprisonment. The trade unions served as mere window-dressing for the Kuomintang government.

56.   JAPAN'S INVASION OF NORTHEAST CHINA

Taking advantage of China's national disunity and the other foreign powers' preoccupation with economic troubles at home,

Japanese troops suddenly attacked Shenyang in China's Northeast (Manchuria) on September 18, 1931, on the pretext that the Japanese-operated railroad there had been dynamited by Chinese troops. The "Young Marshal" Zhang Xueliang of Manchuria, then in Beijing, asked Chiang Kai-shek for orders. Chiang's answer: "In order to avoid any enlargement of the incident, it is necessary to resolutely maintain the principle of non-resistance." Even a direct seizure of Chinese territory by an obviously expansionist power could not shake Chiang from his preoccupation with the destruction of all Communist forces. A few days later Chiang announced that he was appealing for help to the League of Nations, which was then recognized as powerless. The League twice solemnly set time limits for the withdrawal of Japanese troops, which Tokyo simply ignored.

The Japanese government continued its army's advance into China's Northeast; on March 1, 1932, the puppet state of "Manchukuo" was established with the hapless Puyi, the emperor who had been overthrown in the 1911 Revolution, as figurehead Chief Executive. In September of that year, a protocol of alliance was signed between Japan and "Manchukuo" for the joint suppression of communism and the safeguarding of "national security".

The League of Nations had appointed a commission of inquiry — the Lytton Commission — to go to Manchuria and delve into the rights and wrongs of the case. After months of investigations, it reached the surprising conclusion that both aggressor and victim were guilty and proposed a compromise settlement. Disillusioned by the impotence of the League of Nations, Chiang Kai-shek's Nanjing government resumed regular diplomatic relations with the Soviet Union in December 1932, ending a break of five years. For her part, Japan withdrew from the League of Nations in March 1933.

Confident that Chiang Kai-shek would continue his non-resistance policy and that no outside powers would interfere, Japanese troops advanced on Jehol Province, occupying its capital, Chengde. Having annexed Manchuria (almost 10 times the size of the American New England states), they then prepared to invade Mongolia to the west and the territory south of the Great Wall. With Japanese troops driving ever deeper into China, the inaction of the central government became more and more difficult for the Chinese people to countenance. Chiang Kai-shek's policy of fighting the Communists while appeasing the Japanese aggressors became a scandal among all patriotic Chinese.

57. KUOMINTANG GENERALS WHO RESISTED JAPAN

On January 28, 1932, Japanese troops attacked Shanghai, China's largest industrial and commercial center on the southeastern coast. This action further aroused the patriotic indignation of the Chinese people and shocked the Western powers, which had important economic interests in the city. Ignoring Chiang Kai-shek's orders not to resist, General Cai Tingkai (1892-1968) and other officers of the 19th Route Army, then garrisoning the city, decided to fight.

The heroic stand of the 19th Route Army exhilarated the citizens of Shanghai. Over 60,000 Chinese workers in Japanese-owned factories walked out, and Chinese employees in all Japanese stores and other establishments quit their jobs. Students and young workers created corps of anti-Japanese volunteers which fought on the front, gave medical care to wounded soldiers, or collected food and other supplies in the rear. Encouraged by the support of the whole population, the soldiers fought tenaciously and inflicted heavy casualties on the enemy. They held off the invaders for more than a month, forcing the Japanese army to change its command three times.

Far from aiding the 19th Route Army, Chiang Kai-shek actually sabotaged its efforts. He refused to send reinforcements and cut off all munitions and supplies. His action aroused enormous public indignation. He Xiangning (Madame Liao Zhongkai), wife of one of Dr. Sun Yat-sen's close comrades-in-arms, sent Chiang an outfit of women's clothes, chiding him for "not acting like a man".

On March 3, additional Japanese troops landed at Liuhe, northwest of Shanghai. Outflanked, the 19th Route Army was forced to withdraw from the city. Later, Chiang shifted it to Fujian Province to fight the Communists.

Exasperated by Chiang's policy of "first pacification, then resistance", Cai Tingkai joined with Li Jishen (1886-1959), another Kuomintang general, in setting up a "People's Revolutionary Government" in Fujian Province in November 1933. This coincided with Chiang Kai-shek's fifth "encirclement and suppression" campaign against the central Red area in Jiangxi. Had the Red Army launched a sudden attack on Chiang's forces in coordination with the 19th Route Army, it might have saved the Fujian government and smashed Chiang's anti-Red campaign. Unfortunately, the Red area had by that time fallen under the control of "leftist" leaders who condemned the Fujian government for "seeking a third road" and refused to launch such an attack. Subjected to heavy assault by Chiang Kai-shek's superior forces, the Fujian people's government collapsed in January 1934.

Another Kuomintang leader who fought the Japanese invaders was the "Christian General" Feng Yuxiang. When the Japanese forces occupied Duolun in eastern Chahar (today's eastern Inner Mongolia) on May 1, 1933, Feng emerged from retirement to organize a People's Federated Anti-Japanese Army. In July Feng's army actually cleared the enemy out of Chahar and took over military and political control. But Feng's patriotic activities displeased Chiang Kai-shek, whose cohorts claimed that Chahar had turned Communist. In August Feng was forced to return to retirement on Taishan Mountain in Shandong Province. The Japanese occupied Duolun, gateway to Inner Mongolia.

58. THE CHINESE COMMUNISTS' POLICY TOWARD JAPANESE AGGRESSION

In contrast with Chiang Kai-shek's non-resistance policy toward Japanese aggression, the Central Worker-Peasant Democratic Government of China, set up in November 1931 at Ruijin in Jiangxi Province, declared war against Japan the following spring. It called on the people to rise up and drive the Japanese invaders out of China. In January 1933, it declared its willingness to cooperate with any army units in fighting the Japanese aggressors under three conditions: (1) immediate cessation of attacks on the Red areas; (2) guarantee of democratic rights (freedom of speech, press, assembly, etc.) for the people; and (3) arming of the masses and the creation of volunteer units.

At the same time, guerrilla units were organized in China's Northeast under the leadership of the Communist Yang Jingyu (1905-1940). His forces grew from a few hundred to 10,000 men. Under the banner of the Northeast Anti-Japanese Allied Army, they fought bitter battles against the Japanese for years around the Changbai Mountains in southern Manchuria. Many Koreans living in Manchuria also took part in the struggle against the Japanese, who had seized Korea as a colony in 1895.

In July 1934, the Communist government ordered the 10th Corps of the Red Army under the leadership of Fang Zhimin (1900-1935) to march northward as a vanguard unit to fight against the Japanese invaders. The 10th Corps, about 10,000 strong, broke through the Kuomintang lines in northeastern Jiangxi Province and reached south-central Anhui Province later in the year. It suffered heavy losses, however, and Fang Zhimin was captured by Kuomintang troops in January 1935. Chiang Kai-shek tried every means to persuade this talented military leader to join the Kuomintang forces, but Fang stood firm.

In a secret letter from jail to his friends, he urged them not to despair but to continue the struggle for national salvation with all their talent and intelligence. Then he added: "Should I die, a lovely flower may grow out from where I'll be killed or buried. Please regard it as the embodiment of my spirit. When it nods its head in the breeze, you may think I am paying respects to all patriots who are struggling for the liberation of the Chinese nation. When it sways its body you may think I am singing a song encouraging the fighters to march on!"

Fang Zhimin was publicly exhibited in a cage and then secretly put to death in Nanchang on Chiang Kai-shek's orders on August 6, 1935.

59. THE LONG MARCH BEGINS

In June of 1932, Chiang Kai-shek, instead of mobilizing the army and people to resist Japanese aggression, had thrown 500,000 Kuomintang troops into his fourth "encirclement and suppression" campaign against the central revolutionary base in Jiangxi Province. Thanks to sound strategy and the support of the masses, the Red Army, as in the previous campaigns, smashed this attack in eight months of hard fighting. But Chiang Kai-shek would not give up his plans despite the growing demands of patriotic elements throughout the country to resist the Japanese aggressors. With a loan of $50,000,000 from the United States, ostensibly for the purchase of cotton and wheat, and a large loan from Japan, he bought war planes and armaments and engaged military advisers from Germany and elsewhere. In October 1933, he launched the fifth "encirclement and suppression" campaign with a million soldiers and 200 airplanes. Following the advice of the German adviser Hans von Seeckt, the Kuomintang troops adopted a strategy of consolidating their positions with blockhouses and pillboxes as they advanced instead of pressing headlong, as in earlier campaigns. By January 1934, almost 3,000 such strongpoints surrounded the Red area in Jiangxi Province.

The central Red area at that time had come under the control of "leftist" leaders — Russian-trained students headed by Wang Ming and Bo Gu (Qin Bangxian, 1907-1946), who were members of the Party Central Committee. Having lost mass support in Shanghai and other cities through recklessly adventurist policies, they had moved their headquarters to the central Red area at the beginning of 1933. They removed Mao Zedong from his leadership position and criticized his tactics as "guerrillaism". Li De (the Austrian Otto Braun), military representative of the Comintern, rejected the well-tested tactics of deploying forces where the enemy least expected them in favor of defending fixed positions. Under the slogan "we'll not yield one inch of territory to the enemy", the Red Army waged positional warfare against a much stronger and better equipped foe. The result: after 12 months of pitched battles, the Red Army had suffered heavy losses and had failed to break the blockade.

Mao Zedong proposed that the Red Army break out of the encirclement and march toward central Hunan Province, where no enemy strongpoints existed and where mass support was strong, but the other leaders ignored his advice. By spring of 1934 the revolutionary base had been squeezed into an area of only five or six counties. The Red forces were in imminent danger of complete destruction. Only then did the Party leadership decide to evacuate southern Jiangxi and to try to establish a new revolutionary base.

In October 1934, the Party Central Committee ordered the First Front Red Army and Communist cadres, about 80,000 strong, to set out from Jiangxi and Fujian, leaving 30,000 troops behind to continue guerrilla warfare in the area. Without adequate preparation or clear understanding of the new objective, the main Red forces withdrew in great disorder. Loaded down with heavy equipment, including even printing presses and sewing machines, they moved slowly. Pursued from behind, blocked in front, and pounded from the air, they lost more than half of their men within three months. At this juncture, Mao Zedong advised the Red Army to move into the southwestern province of Guizhou, away from Chiang Kai-shek's main forces. At the beginning of 1935, they crossed the Wujiang River and captured the city of Zunyi in northern Guizhou.

An enlarged meeting of the Political Bureau of the Party was held in the city; Mao Zedong criticized the mistaken military strategy which had led to their current predicament. Both Zhou Enlai and Zhu De supported his position, and backed the proposal to make him leader of the Party. The meeting reorganized the Central Committee and set up a military command group with Mao Zedong as chairman.

The Zunyi meeting marked a decisive turning point in the history of the Chinese Communist Party, establishing a collective leadership headed by Mao Zedong, Zhou Enlai, Zhu De and others. This leadership was able to turn a tortuous and disheartening retreat into an epic victory, thus saving the Red Army and the Chinese Communist Party, and laying the foundation for the eventual victory of the Chinese revolution.

60. THE LONG MARCH — SOME MAJOR EVENTS

The route of the Long March totaled 12,000 kilometers (about 8,000 miles), more than twice the width of the American continent. In a year's time, the fighters passed through 11 provinces on foot over some of the most difficult terrain on earth. They crossed 24 dangerous rivers and 18 mountain ranges, five of which are snow-capped all year round. On their way, they defeated, eluded or outmaneuvered an array of central government forces and broke through the intercepting armies of provincial warlords. They successfully crossed the areas of six different minority nationalities, through which no Chinese army had gone for many years, because of long-standing friction between the majority Han Chinese and many minority nationalities.

The Long March is one of the great exploits of military history; Hannibal's march over the Alps "looks like a holiday excursion beside it", in the words of the American correspondent Edgar Snow. Had it failed, it would have meant the demise of the Red Army and the indefinite postponement of the Chinese revolution.

After the Zunyi meeting, the Red Army reorganized its forces and returned to the old guerrilla tactics, but this time on a much larger scale which pitted their whole army against the opposing forces in a deadly game of escape and pursuit. During a short respite its ranks were replenished and Party leadership was strengthened. The new leadership gave the rank and file a clear goal, reaching northwest China, and a rationale for the move, namely, to fight the Japanese aggressors and save the nation. Perhaps most important was the confidence that they could achieve these goals despite the overwhelming odds.

Heavy, unnecessary equipment was abandoned, giving them increased mobility. Instead of the old straight-line marches which had made them easy targets for Chiang Kai-shek's far more numerous and better equipped troops, they moved in zigzags and circles, playing "hide and seek" with the enemy. Through sudden night marches, they avoided pitched battles with a much stronger foe.

By the end of January 1935, the Red Army was on the move again, having by clever feints misled the enemy as to the line of march. In April, leaving the enemy forces far behind near Kunming in Yunnan Province, it suddenly veered northward and crossed the Jinsha River (the upper reaches of the Changjiang) into Sikang, now in western Sichuan Province. This maneuver enabled the Red Army to break through Chiang Kai-shek's encirclement and opened the way toward northwest China.

After crossing the Jinsha River, the Red Army entered the mountain area inhabited by the Yi nationality. Thinking that the hated Kuomintang troops had come again to plunder them, these minority people rushed out with swords and spears to block the way. Liu Bocheng, commander of the army's vanguard corps, went to meet the Yi chieftain. Explaining through an interpreter the Red Army's relationship to the Kuomintang troops, he further described the Communist Party's nationalities policy, which was to treat all nationalities in China as equals. The Red Army's aim was to liberate the whole people, including the Yis, and to save the nation from Japanese aggression. Then, following the custom of the Yi people, Liu and the chieftain swore brotherhood by drinking the blood of a freshly killed chicken. The Yi people thereafter provided guides to lead the Red forces through their territory.

Toward the end of May, the Red Army reached the turbulent Dadu River, flanked by precipitous cliffs, in western Sichuan Province. Here, some 70 years before, the Taiping troops under General Shi Dakai had been trapped and wiped out by Qing government forces. Chiang Kai-shek expected the Red Army to meet the same doom. But one army unit crossed the river at Anshunchang, a small town by the riverside, and another, conquering hunger and cold, raced 150 kilometers westward to Luding, the last possible crossing near the Tibetan border. Kuomintang troops had removed the planks of the suspension bridge, leaving only iron chains swinging over the raging torrent below. Braving the bullets from the opposite shore, some 20 Red soldiers dashed forward and began to crawl over the chains, all the while tossing hand grenades at the enemy and replacing the missing planks. Unable to stop their advance, the enemy set fire to the bridgehead on the opposite bank. Undaunted, the Red soldiers dashed through the flames and captured the position, thus seizing the opening the Red Army needed to cross the river.

Their hardships, however, were not yet over. In June 1935, the marchers climbed doggedly over the Great Snow Mountains of Sichuan Province. In the rarefied air and bitter cold, many poorly clad soldiers perished from exposure. On one peak, the fighters had to cut down long bamboos to lay a path through a long stretch of waist-deep mud. Even then one army corps lost two-thirds of its transport animals; hundreds of men fell down and never got up. On July 20, they entered the Maogong area in northwest Sichuan Province, where they met with the Fourth Front Army under the command of Zhang Guotao (Chang Kuo-tao). Here they paused for a rest, took assessment of their losses and reorganized their ranks.

Differences of opinion on the correct course came to the surface at this point. Zhang Guotao maintained that for the Red forces to survive they should cease marching northward and establish base areas in the remote frontier regions of southwest China. Rejecting this pessimistic view, the majority of the Central Committee members were determined to continue into the Northwest in order to be able eventually to fight the Japanese. In August, the First Front Army, under the leadership of Mao Zedong and Zhou Enlai, began marching toward the Great Grasslands on the Sichuan-Tibet border. In the midst of this deserted swampland of perpetual rain, the fighters could find neither food nor shelter. More men and animals were lost. But those who survived managed to reach the Gansu border on October 19, 1935, entering northern Shaanxi Province just below the Great Wall. A year later, the Second and Fourth Front Armies arrived via different routes and joined forces with the First Front Army. Only one-tenth of the original army and Party personnel who had set out reached Shaanxi. The rest had either died or stayed behind as guerrilla fighters. The epic Long March was thus triumphantly concluded.

The Long March was also a highly successful propaganda tour. The Red Army passed through a vast area populated by 200 million people. Wherever they went, they called mass meetings, gave theatrical performances and inscribed slogans on walls, calling on the people to fight the local landlords, warlords and Kuomintang reactionaries. They explained that their aim was to fight the Japanese aggressors and save the whole nation, including the national minorities as well. For the first time many millions came face to face with the Red fighters and saw how differently they behaved from the warlord and Kuomintang troops. Many began to see that the

Red soldiers were not "bandits" as claimed by Kuomintang propaganda, but real friends of the people.

The Long March is replete with true stories of heroism and self-sacrifice. Its success brought legitimacy to the Communist Party and gave hope to Chinese progressives everywhere that the revolutionaries would eventually play an important role in the liberation of China.

61. THE DECEMBER NINTH MOVEMENT

The military occupation of China's Northeast and the establishment of the puppet regime of "Manchukuo" was by no means the Japanese government's final goal. Reaching into Inner Mongolia and north China, the Japanese bought raw materials at extremely low prices, intensified the exploitation of cheap Chinese labor in their factories and mines, and flooded the market with products imported in open evasion of China's customs tariffs. These actions pushed Chinese industrialists and businessmen to the wall and even threatened European and United States interests in China. Japan aimed to set up local "autonomous governments" and to make all of northern China their exclusive sphere of influence.

In face of this open expansion, Chiang Kai-shek and his Nationalist government continued to do nothing. In June 1935, it signed the infamous Ho-Umezu agreement, which promised the withdrawal of all Chinese troops from north China, the disbanding of Chinese organizations there, and the banning of all anti-Japanese activities throughout the country. In October, the Japanese government made further demands, including: (1) the complete independence of the five northern provinces (Hebei, Shandong, Shanxi, Chahar and Suiyuan); (2) the establishment of a demilitarized zone in all the coastal provinces; and (3) China's withdrawal from the League of Nations and cooperation with Japan and "Manchukuo" in the establishment of a Far Eastern politico-economic bloc. In November, Yin Rugeng (1885-1947), a Japanese puppet, set up the "East Hebei Anti-Communist Autonomous Government" near Beijing. All north China and eastern Inner Mongolia were on the verge of being torn away from Chinese sovereignty by the Japanese imperialists.

At the same time, the Chinese Red Army, astonishing the world, had arrived in north Shaanxi at the end of the Long March. On August 1, 1935, while still on the march, it issued a new statement entitled "Appeal to Fellow Countrymen Concerning Resistance to Japan and National Salvation". It called once again for the cessation of internecine strife and concentration of all forces (military, financial, human and material) to resist Japanese aggression. It advocated the formation of a national defense government and a united anti-Japanese army, of which the Red Army would become a part. Later, in a ten-point manifesto for national salvation, it called for the confiscation of all Japanese property in China, the release of all political prisoners and the unity of all the Chinese people, irrespective of political beliefs, in order to resist Japanese aggression. More noteworthy was the fact that it now pinpointed Japanese imperialism as the sole enemy and advocated the establishment of friendly relations with those countries which sympathized with the Chinese people's struggle against Japan.

This clear call for national resistance sparked an immediate response. On December 9, 1935, thousands of Beijing students took to the streets. Defying police batons, bayonets and water hoses, they shouted: "Down with Japanese imperialism", "Oppose the 'autonomous' movement", and "Stop all civil war and unite against Japanese aggression". Although scores were arrested and over 100 wounded, the students were not intimidated.

On December 16, the day a so-called "Hebei-Chahar Political Affairs Council" was to be set up under Japanese pressure, 30,000 students from various schools in Beijing broke through the police blockade around their campuses and marched through the streets. Students in the suburbs broke open the city gates and joined the ranks of the demonstrators. At a huge open-air rally in which tens of thousands of citizens took part, a resolution was passed opposing the "autonomous" organizations and demanding the release of the jailed students and the lifting of the ban on the patriotic movement. The Kuomintang authorities mobilized the city police and two regiments of their army to suppress the students, but from early morning until late at night the bare-handed students fought back. Under public pressure, the Kuomintang authorities were forced to postpone the establishment of the Hebei-Chahar Political Affairs Council.

These student demonstrations, later known as the December Ninth Movement (because the demonstrations started on that date), shook the whole country out of its lethargy. Student demonstrations took place throughout China, and national salvation associations were formed among intellectuals, industrialists, merchants, women and workers. But Chiang Kai-shek persisted in his policy of non-resistance, becoming increasingly isolated from the people. A great political storm was brewing.

62. THE XI'AN INCIDENT —
THE ABDUCTION OF CHIANG KAI-SHEK

On December 13, 1936, headlines around the world carried the extraordinary news that Chiang Kai-shek had been abducted by two of his own generals in the northwestern Chinese city of Xi'an. What did it mean? How would it end? At home and abroad his supporters and enemies alike anxiously awaited further details of what came to be known as the "Xi'an Incident".

The immediate events leading up to the abduction have to be seen against the larger background of Japan's occupation of more and more Chinese territory, the rising outrage of the Chinese people, and Chiang's stubborn insistence on fighting the Communists instead of the Japanese invaders. Chiang seemed determined, moreover, to silence those who disagreed with him by whatever means necessary. In May 1936, a number of prominent democrats, including Soong Ching Ling, established in Shanghai the All-China Federation of National Salvation Associations to coordinate patriotic activities throughout the country. Chiang paid no attention to their urgent appeal for national unity against a foreign foe, and instead jailed seven of the group's leaders. Chiang's high-handed treatment of respected patriots and flagrant disregard of public opinion only increased their indignation.

Chiang arrived in Xi'an on December 4. Convinced that the armies of the northwest were not fighting Communist forces with sufficient energy and determination, he had come to confront the armies' commanders. He set up his headquarters at the Lintong resort east of Xi'an, summoned Zhang Xueliang (the "Young Marshal") of the Northeastern Army and General Yang Hucheng (1892-1949) of the Northwestern Army, and harangued them about the necessity of fighting Communists. Both generals reported to him that his policy was causing great unrest among their officers and men, who were convinced they were fighting the wrong enemy. They urged Chiang to change his policies; only a union of all patriotic forces against the Japanese invaders could save the nation. Chiang flew into a rage and declared that he would not change his stand.

On December 9, 1936, the first anniversary of the student demonstrations against Japanese aggression, over 10,000 Xi'an students took to the streets once more. They shouted: "Stop the civil war!" "Unite against Japan!" "Northeastern Army brothers, fight for your homeland!" Angered by the Kuomintang governor's evasive answer, the students decided to brave the bitter winter winds in a march to Chiang's headquarters at Lintong, some 25 kilometers away. Hearing this, Chiang ordered the police and army to stop the unarmed students at all costs. Machine-guns were placed along the roadway and mounted troops stood ready for action.

At this juncture, General Zhang Xueliang rushed to the scene, anxious to avert what he knew might easily become a hideous slaughter. He pleaded tearfully with the students to give him more time to talk to Chiang Kai-shek. He promised he would have an answer for them within a week. As he talked, hundreds of rickshaw pullers arrived on the scene, their carts laden with food for the demonstrators donated by Xi'an citizens. Convinced by this evidence of mass support that their cause would ultimately be won, the students agreed to give the general another week. The meeting ended in an outpouring of emotion with the singing of patriotic anti-Japanese songs.

Realizing that Chiang could not easily be brought to change his mind, Zhang Xueliang and Yang Hucheng decided on drastic measures. In the early hours of December 12, Zhang's troops suddenly surrounded Chiang's residence and overpowered his bodyguards. Alerted by the sound of gunshots, Chiang jumped out of bed, leaped out the window in his night clothes, climbed over a wall and fell into a ditch. Though slightly injured, he ran for his life. Hours later a search party discovered China's "strong man" shivering in his pajamas, trying to hide behind a boulder on the hillside. He was immediately taken back to Xi'an.

News of Chiang's seizure threw the Kuomintang authorities at Nanjing into turmoil. The pro-Japanese clique headed by He Yingqin had no concern for Chiang personally; on the contrary, his death or long-term imprisonment might well open the way for them to seize power. But the pro-British and American faction headed by the Soong family — Soong Mei-ling (Chiang's wife), her brother T. V. Soong and H. H. Kung (married to Soong Ai-ling) — were deeply concerned. Aside from their family feelings, Chiang's removal would seriously weaken their own grasp on power. They agreed that a peaceful settlement was essential, even if it meant making concessions to Chiang's captors.

The captive, meanwhile, was refusing even to talk with his abductors. Uncertain what to do next, the two generals asked Communist leaders, whose judgment they respected from earlier contacts, to send a delegation to parley with Chiang. Many rank-and-file Communists, when they heard that their leaders would have some say in Chiang's fate, thought first of revenge. No punishment seemed too dire for this tyrant who had slaughtered and tortured tens of thousands of Communists and other patriots. But the Party leadership was more farsighted. The long-term interests of the Chinese people had to be placed above personal feelings. Chiang's removal at this juncture would only play into the hands of the Japanese imperialists and further divide the Chinese nation. At the same time, the incident provided a vital opportunity to forge a national united front, if the negotiations were handled correctly.

As soon as they arrived in Xi'an, Zhou Enlai and the other representatives explained all of this to the two generals. At about the same time, T. V. Soong and Madame Chiang Kai-shek arrived in Xi'an to take part in the talks. After prolonged and delicate negotiations, an agreement was reached on December 23. For his part, Chiang agreed to cooperate with the Red Army in resisting Japanese aggression; release the seven patriotic leaders of the All-China Federation of National Salvation Associations as well as other political prisoners; reorganize the national government to include anti-Japanese elements; and call a conference of all parties and military leaders to discuss a strategy for saving the nation. Zhou Enlai and Chiang Kai-shek met face to face for the first time in ten years. Chiang reiterated his promise to stop the civil war and invited Zhou Enlai to Nanjing for further negotiations. On December 25, Chiang and Zhang Xueliang flew back to Nanjing. Chiang Kai-shek never forgave his captors. He kept Zhang Xueliang prisoner and under house arrest for more than 40 years and had General Yang Hucheng, his wife and son murdered in a prison camp in Chongqing on the eve of its liberation in 1949.

The peaceful settlement of the Xi'an Incident marked a turning point in modern Chinese history. It ended the 10-year civil war between Communist and Kuomintang forces and ushered in a new period of unity against the Japanese aggressors.

63.   THE SECOND KUOMINTANG-COMMUNIST UNITED FRONT

The "Xi'an Incident" had forced Chiang Kai-shek to change his earlier steadfast refusal to resist the Japanese until he had succeeded in his aim to eliminate the Communists. With his life in danger, however, he agreed to heed the appeals for national unity of some of his own generals and soldiers, as well as many ordinary people throughout China.

The second Kuomintang-Communist united front came in 1937 at a time when China's very existence as an independent nation was threatened by Japanese aggression.

The idea of a national united front against Japanese aggression had first been put forward by the Red Army on August 1, 1935, during the course of the Long March. In an appeal to the Chinese nation, it proposed the cessation of civil war and concentration of all human and material resources on resistance to the Japanese invasion. After the Red Army reached its new base in northwest China, it put out a ten-point program which attracted wide support among all sectors of the population. It called for the confiscation of Japanese property in China to finance the war of resistance, release of political prisoners, granting of democratic rights to the people and improvement of their livelihood through the reduction of taxes. It pinpointed Japanese imperialism as the main enemy of the Chinese people and advocated the establishment of friendly relations with nations sympathetic or neutral toward the Chinese people's struggle against the Japanese invaders.

To strengthen the tenuous peace thus obtained, the Communist Party on February 10, 1937 sent a telegram to the Kuomintang Central Executive Committee stating that if the Kuomintang would end the civil war, introduce democratic reforms and take immediate steps to prepare for resistance to Japan, the Communist Party, on its part, would pledge: (1) to cease all efforts to overthrow the Kuomintang government; (2) to convert the Red Army into a unit of the National Revolutionary Army; (3) to change its independent regime into a special region of the Republic of China; and (4) to stop confiscation of the landlords' land. More than a dozen prominent Kuomintang members, including Soong Ching Ling, He Xiangning and the "Christian General" Feng Yuxiang, advocated the restoration of Dr. Sun Yat-sen's Three Major Policies — alliance with the Soviet Union, cooperation with the Communists and support of the interests of the workers and peasants. After heated debates with the pro-Japanese clique, the committee passed a resolution which substantially accepted the Communist proposals.

Negotiations between the Communists and the Kuomintang began. Zhou Enlai shuttled between Yan'an, Xi'an, Hangzhou and Lushan Mountain to talk with Kuomintang leaders and Chiang Kai-shek himself. In June Chiang suddenly proposed that the two parties form a National Revolutionary League, with himself holding full powers as chairman. In the name of national unity, he demanded not only that the Red Army be essentially dissolved and its members join the Kuomintang forces as individuals, but also that Mao Zedong and Zhu De should leave the Red Army and the country. Zhou Enlai responded that the major issue at hand was how the two political parties could work together to resist Japanese aggression, not Communist surrender to the Kuomintang or the subjugation of the Red forces by the Kuomintang armies.

The negotiations dragged on without definite results. Although the Communists repeatedly offered to cooperate with the Kuomintang in resisting Japanese aggression, Chiang Kai-shek still harbored hopes for a negotiated peace with Japan. Only after Japan's sudden attack on Shanghai on August 13, which threatened his own base of power, did Chiang Kai-shek come out for national defense against Japanese aggression.

On August 22, the Red Army was renamed the Eighth Route Army, with Zhu De as commander. A month later, the Kuomintang government made public the Communist Party's "Manifesto on Kuomintang-Communist Cooperation", and Chiang announced the legalization of the Communist Party and the promulgation of an official policy of cooperation. This inaugurated the second Kuomintang-Communist united front, this time against Japanese aggression. On October 12, the Kuomintang government officially designated Communist guerrilla fighters in south China, some 12,000 strong, as the New Fourth Army.

64. JAPANESE MASSIVE INVASION OF CHINA AND WORLD POWERS' REACTIONS

On July 7, 1937, Japanese soldiers suddenly attacked the Chinese troops near Lugouqiao, southwest of Beijing, in an attempt to seize all north China as a step to convert the whole of China into an exclusive Japanese colony. This act aroused the indignation of the Chinese people, who were determined now to stand up and resist Japanese aggression in order to save their country from extinction.

The axis powers — Germany, Italy and Japan — were bent on redividing the world through military aggression. The major Western democracies, including Britain, France and the United States, attempted to protect their own interests in the Pacific by appeasing Japan and persuading it to turn north and attack the Soviet Union. The Soviet Union, threatened by the German-Japanese Anti-Comintern Pact which had been signed on November 25, 1936, gave active support to the Chinese people's resistance to Japanese aggression.

For years relations between Chiang Kai-shek's government and Nazi Germany had been quite close. A German military mission under General von Falkenhausen was stationed in China. It helped train Kuomintang troops and gave advice on how to fight the Communist Red Army in Chiang's "encirclement and suppression" campaigns. When Japan started its large-scale invasion of China, Hitler's government endeavored to mediate between the two "friendly" countries through its ambassador in China. However, a compromise settlement could not easily be arranged. In the spring of 1938, the German military mission was withdrawn under Japanese pressure.

Britain, Japan's long-time ally in the Far East, was quite willing to sacrifice Chinese interests as long as the Japanese did not tread on Britain's own interests. When Japanese troops occupied China's coastal cities, British officials turned over the revenues of the Chinese Maritime Customs Administration to the Japanese invaders. In north China, the British-dominated Kailuan mines readily supplied the invaders with coal. On November 1, 1938, Prime Minister Chamberlain declared that when the Sino-Japanese war ended Japan alone could probably not supply all the capital needed to develop conquered Chinese territories, and that British capital would certainly have a part to play.

Already pursuing a policy of appeasement in Europe through the Munich Pact, the British government did not hesitate to give in to Japanese demands in China. In 1936 it agreed that in the British Concession in Tianjin, Japanese forces had the right to "suppress or remove any such acts or causes as will obstruct them (the Japanese) or benefit their enemy". Thus the British authorities handed quite a number of Chinese patriots over to the Japanese for execution. In 1940, under Japanese pressure, Britain closed the Burma Road through which China had been receiving some supplies from the West. France likewise closed the Haiphong-Yunnan Railway. Both were willing to offer their services in arranging a Sino-Japanese "settlement" at China's expense.

The United States, reacting in much the same manner as it had when Japan had invaded China's Northeast in 1931, again proclaimed high-sounding principles but refused to take effective steps to check Japanese aggression. On October 5, 1937, President Roosevelt made a speech recommending a "quarantine" to halt the spreading "epidemic of world lawlessness". The following day the State Department announced that it considered Japan's action in China to be contrary to the Nine-

Power Treaty of 1922 and the Kellogg-Briand Pact of 1928. But it took no steps to implement any "quarantine" nor did it impose sanctions against Japan. In spite of the fact that wide sections of the American public were sympathetic to the Chinese people, American businessmen continued to buy large quantities of raw silk from Japan and to sell shiploads of scrap steel which fed Japan's war industry. Congress followed a policy of "non-intervention" by passing the Neutrality Acts of 1935 and 1937. Up to the eve of Pearl Harbor, the State Department attempted to negotiate a Far Eastern version of the Munich Pact with Japan.

The only power which gave China any real help in her hour of need was the Soviet Union. On August 21, 1937, immediately after Japan's July 7 attack on the Lugouqiao Bridge, (which marked the beginning of China's war of resistance against Japanese aggression), the Soviet Union signed a treaty of non-aggression with the Nanjing government. It also extended credits of U.S. $100-million in 1938 and $150 million in 1939 for China's purchase of war materials.

As a result, China received tens of thousands of tons of needed munitions from the U.S.S.R. through Xinjiang in the Northwest. In addition, Moscow dispatched 1,000 airplanes and 2,000 aviators to aid China's defense. Soviet planes and fliers played an important role in helping protect such major cities as Hankou, Chongqing, Chengdu and Lanzhou against Japanese air raids. Moscow also sent a military mission of some 500 men to take the place of the withdrawn German military advisers to Chiang Kai-shek at Nanjing. So great was the contrast between American inaction and Soviet help that even the anti-Communist Madame Chiang Kai-shek wrote in January 1939 in the U.S. mass-circulation *Liberty Magazine*:

> Eighty percent of Japan's war supplies come from America ... and 95 percent of the aviation gasoline which was used by Japan in her ruthless bombing was American. Throughout the first three years of resistance Soviet Russia extended to China for the actual purchase of war supplies

and other necessities, credits several times larger than the credits given by either Great Britain or America. . . .

I may point out that Russian help has been unconditional throughout.

In retaliation for Soviet military aid to China, Japan attacked Lake Khassan (Zhanggufeng) not far from Vladivostok in 1937 and Khalkin-Gol in Outer Mongolia (a Soviet ally) in 1939, but was defeated in both battles. In the latter case alone, 660 planes and large numbers of Japanese tanks were destroyed, while 25,000 soldiers were killed. Rebuffed in its attempt to move into Soviet territory, an attempt which had the tacit blessing of the Western powers, Japan chose to follow what it considered the "line of least resistance" in the Pacific and southeastern Asia.

65. CHIANG KAI-SHEK DURING THE SECOND UNITED FRONT

The formation of the second Kuomintang-Communist united front gave Chiang Kai-shek the opportunity to become the great leader of a national war against the Japanese aggressors. His call on August 13, 1937 to fight the Japanese invaders to the bitter end had the support of the whole Chinese people.

In the first stage of the war, which lasted from July 1937 to October 1938, Japanese troops launched assaults on many fronts. In face of the powerful Japanese war machine, some Kuomintang armies fought tenaciously to the surprise and admiration of foreign journalists and observers. The battle of Taierzhuang in southern Shandong Province in April 1938, in which a crack Japanese division was destroyed, gave confidence to the Chinese people that they could win the war with united efforts. However, the lack of modern weapons and experienced officers made the Chinese soldiers, though brave, no match for an overwhelmingly superior foe. In a little over a year, the Japanese invaders occupied practically all the major cities in the more developed part of the country — Beijing and Tianjin in the north, Shanghai and Nanjing in the lower Changjiang valley — and drove from Guangzhou in the south to Wuhan in central China. Chiang Kai-shek adopted the strategy of "trading space for time", moving his capital westward to Chongqing on the upper Changjiang in Sichuan Province.

The Chinese government, entirely cut off from the seacoast, was in a perilous situation. The Japanese thought Chiang Kai-shek would be compelled to accept their peace terms. They sent Wang Jingwei (1883-1944), a veteran Kuomintang leader who believed that the axis powers would eventually win the war, to Chongqing to persuade Chiang to cooperate with Japan in the creation of the "Greater Asia Co-prosperity Sphere". To his credit, Chiang rejected the Japanese proposals. He declared: "The aim of the Japanese is to control China militarily under the pretext of anti-communism, to eliminate Chinese culture under the cloak of protection of Oriental culture, and to expel European and American influences from the Far East under the pretext of breaking down economic walls."

Wang Jingwei later set up a Japanese puppet government at Nanjing, but Chiang wasn't ready for outright capitulation. In March 1938, a quasi-representative People's Political Conference was set up. Although the one-party Kuomintang dictatorship remained, there was a glimmer of hope for more democracy to come. In April the Kuomintang Congress formulated a "Program of Armed Resistance and National Reconstruction", which was accepted by the Communists as a common wartime platform to resist Japan. Meanwhile, Soviet aid continued to be shipped in through the Northwest. Toward the end of 1938, therefore, the situation looked relatively favorable.

During the second stage of the war, which began in the spring of 1939 and lasted for six years, the Japanese invaders undertook no major military operations against Kuomintang troops. As the Japanese already controlled China's major cities and industrial areas, the Kuomintang forces were no real threat; more importantly, Japan was heavily involved during the latter part of this period in fighting American and other Allied forces

in the Pacific. While continuing diplomatic maneuvers to in-
duce Chiang Kai-shek to surrender, the Japanese directed their
main military efforts at the guerrilla bases in the rear.

As the Japanese eased their military pressure on the Kuomintang areas, Chiang Kai-shek, too, adopted a passive policy in
fighting the invaders. He now regarded the growing number
of Communist-controlled liberated areas behind Japanese lines
as a serious threat to his personal power, and began to mount
one anti-Communist campaign after another. In late 1939
and early 1940, he ordered attacks on the Eighth Route Army
in the Shaanxi-Gansu-Ningxia Border Region in northwest
China. The attacks were quickly repulsed by alert Red forces.
A more serious assault took place at the beginning of 1941.
Chiang set up a trap by ordering the New Fourth Army to move
from its position south of the Huanghe River to a new one
north of the river. While the New Fourth Army's headquarters personnel and rear echelon of 9,000 men were passing
through a confined mountainous area, they were ambushed
by Kuomintang troops nine times their number. The
"Southern Anhui Incident", as it came to be known, strained
the Kuomintang-Communist united front to the breaking point.
Accusing the New Fourth Army of "disobedience", Chiang ordered its disbandment and stopped all financial support to
the Communist-controlled areas.

When the United States entered the Pacific War after
Japan's attack on Pearl Harbor in December 1941, President
Roosevelt sent increasing quantities of Lend-Lease material to
Chiang Kai-shek's government and appointed General Joseph
Stilwell (1883-1946) commander of the China-Burma-India
theater of operations. Although Chiang then declared war on
Japan, he nonetheless sent his best troops to blockade Yan'an
in the Northwest. Meanwhile, under the slogan of "saving
the nation by a winding path", he directed scores of his
generals and other high-ranking officers to defect to the Japanese
side, taking with them 500,000 men. By so doing he shifted
onto the shoulders of his Japanese adversaries the burden of
feeding and equipping these troops which Chiang hoped to

use as "reserves" for fighting the Communists in the post-war period.

As Chiang Kai-shek ceased all efforts at fighting the Japanese invaders, the morale of his troops sagged rapidly. Corruption became increasingly widespread among his officers. Generals reported inflated figures for divisions under their control in order to pocket salaries and supplies. Thus a division often had only 2,000 to 6,000 men instead of the official figure of 10,000. Supplies, equipment and rations were resold for private profit, and an elaborate black-market network involving a number of civilian and military officials stretched from Chongqing to enemy-controlled Shanghai on the coast. While many officers were getting rich from the war, the common soldiers suffered from malnutrition and lack of medical care for such ravaging diseases as malaria, tuberculosis and dysentery. Forced conscripts were often chained together to prevent them from escaping. Starved and maltreated, many died or deserted on the way to the front.

The miserable plight of the Chinese soldiers and Chiang Kai-shek's non-resistance policy toward Japan shocked many foreign well-wishers' sense of common decency, including General Stilwell. In a letter to his wife in September 1944, he wrote that Chiang Kai-shek "wants to finish the war by coasting, with a big supply of material, so as to perpetuate his regime. He has blocked us for three years, and continues to do so. He has failed to keep his agreements." Chiang Kai-shek was well aware of this criticism. In October 1944, he forced the recall of General Stilwell by President Roosevelt and continued to wait for the United States and the Soviet Union to win the war.

66. THE CHINESE COMMUNIST PARTY AND THE UNITED FRONT

As the initiator and organizer of the anti-Japanese national united front, the Chinese Communist Party tried to maintain

it, strengthen it and enlarge it throughout the war. The purpose of the alliance was to mobilize the masses for a people's
war — the only road to victory. Despite Chiang Kai-shek's
repeated sabotage and disruption, the Chinese Communist
Party stayed within the united front until the war was won.

Although Chiang Kai-shek was forced to agree to the
establishment of the second united front, he had no faith in
the people or the Communists. In his opinion, the war should
have been fought — if fought at all — by a regular army alone,
and that the people as a whole had no role to play. He also
hoped the Red forces would be decimated or wiped out by the
powerful Japanese armies, thus paving the way for the perpetuation of his personal dictatorship in the post-war period.

The Communist Party, on the other hand, believed that only
by mobilizing the masses could China hope to win the war
against such a powerful enemy. To this end, democratic rights
— freedom of speech, assembly and organization, as well as
the people's right to arm themselves — had to be guaranteed.
Thus, from the very beginning two diametrically opposite lines
of strategy existed within the two-party united front.

Within the Chinese Communist Party itself, however, not all
leaders agreed on the Party's role in the united front. Wang
Ming, a longtime Party representative to the Comintern in
Moscow and a member of its executive committee, returned to
China toward the end of 1937. Following the Comintern line
of trying to win Chiang Kai-shek over to an anti-fascist stand,
despite the many pro-fascists among his supporters, Wang Ming
proposed to make the renewed Kuomintang-Communist
cooperation a solid united front with Chiang Kai-shek as
supreme commander. The Red forces should be incorporated
into the Kuomintang armies, and every proposal and action
should first be submitted to and approved by the Kuomintang
headquarters. He raised the slogan that "everything must go
through the united front". In his view, Chiang Kai-shek, with
his large armies, was the only person who could lead China to
win the war against Japan.

A meeting of the Central Committee of the Communist Party

was held in October-November 1938. Mao Zedong pointed out that in effect the united front in China had not led to a broadening of the central government to include democratic elements and that Chiang Kai-shek was holding fast to his personal dictatorship. Therefore, if everything had to go through the united front (i.e., the Kuomintang), it would be tantamount to one-sided submission on the part of the Communists. Remembering the bitter experience of the first Kuomintang-Communist cooperation in 1924-1927, Mao Zedong voiced the view that to give Chiang Kai-shek absolute control of the Red Army would enable him to butcher the Communists again. Having learned that "without a people's army the people have nothing", he would not allow the Red forces to be absorbed by Chiang's armies. "Our policy," he stated, "is one of independence and initiative within the united front, a policy of unity and independence." The session repudiated Wang Ming's line.

What happened soon afterward bore out Mao Zedong's words. When Xiang Ying, one of the leaders of the New Fourth Army, delayed the transfer of his troops northward, he fell into a trap laid by Chiang Kai-shek and was killed in the "Southern Anhui Incident" in the spring of 1941.

This incident almost destroyed the united front. Within the Communist Party a leftist tendency appeared. Some thought that the breakup of the united front was imminent. To combat this trend, the Communist leaders pointed out that Japanese imperialism still remained the main enemy of the Chinese people as long as its troops continued to occupy Chinese territory. Under such circumstances, internal disputes had to be subordinated to the struggle for national survival against a foreign foe. The Communist Party thus stuck to its policy of unity as long as Chiang remained, even if in name only, within the camp of resistance to Japanese aggression. Instead of regarding all Kuomintang soldiers with hostility, it tried to win over many of them as friends to continue the war against Japan. It adopted the policy of developing the progressive forces (peasants and workers), winning over the intermediate elements (the middle bourgeoisie and enlightened gentry), and directing its attacks only against die-hard reactionaries. By so doing, it shattered the attacks mounted by the reactionaries, won over many fair-minded democratic elements (the Democratic League was formed at this time), and lessened the danger of capitulation to the Japanese by the reactionary cliques.

The Communist Eighth Route Army had scored the first Chinese victory against the Japanese invaders at the strategic Pingxingguan Pass in Shanxi Province, north China, in September 1937, giving the Chinese people faith in eventual victory. Now the Party decided that its main task was to penetrate to the rear of Japanese troops and develop guerrilla warfare there. Guerrilla bases and liberated areas were set up one after another behind Japanese lines. By July 1940, the Communist-led Eighth Route and New Fourth armies had grown from 40,000 to 500,000 men. The people's militia, now 200,000 strong, devised many effective means to harass enemy troops, such as planting land mines and waging tunnel warfare. The liberated areas, with a total population of 100 million, had become the main battlefields against the Japanese invaders.

To consolidate the liberated areas (which existed in various stages of development, from north China down to Hainan Island in the extreme south), the Party carried out an agrarian policy of reduced rents and interest on loans. This policy greatly raised the enthusiasm for production of the poor peasants while preserving the basis for united opposition to Japan among all sections of the population. In the local governments, the Party introduced a "three-thirds system", which meant that the Communists, the other progressives, and middle elements each made up one-third of the total number of members. Hard as conditions were in the Japanese rear, the Communists set up primary schools for the children, introduced part-time study (night and winter schools) for adults, and conducted literacy drives in the army and among the peasants. Newspaper reading groups were organized to enlighten the masses on current events at home and abroad. This implementation of an enlightened united-front policy improved the material and cultural life of the people and heightened their determination to fight on. The consolidation and expansion of liberated areas in the rear of the Japanese troops created what was in effect a vast stronghold manned by people united and ready to combat any Japanese army unit at any time, and base-area guerrilla actions contributed greatly to the Chinese people's eventual victory.

67. WRITERS AND ARTISTS JOIN THE ANTI-JAPANESE STRUGGLE

Japanese aggression in China aroused the patriotic indignation of many Chinese writers and artists who then used their talents to rouse the people to greater efforts of resistance. Following the Japanese invasion of northeast China in 1931, Xiao Jun (Hsiao Chun, born in 1907), a young writer, joined a guerrilla detachment that fought the Japanese aggressors in that region. In his novel, *Village in August* (published in 1935), he described the beauty and grandeur of the mountains and rivers of northeast China and the dauntless spirit of the ragged and hungry fighters against a ruthless foreign foe. This aroused the patriotism of the readers and intensified their hatred toward the enemy. Qu Qiubai (Chu Chiupai, 1899-1935), a leader of the Left-Wing Writers League, pointed out that the urgent task of literature and art was to arouse the masses to stand up and resist foreign imperialist aggression. Xia Yan (born in 1900), an outstanding playwright, completed in 1935 the film scenario *Sons and Daughters of the Storm*, based on a synopsis written by Tian Han (1898-1968). The film's theme song *March of the Volunteers*, words by Tian Han and set to music by the composer Nie Er (1912-1935), became an immensely popular song of resistance:

> *Arise, ye who refuse to be slaves,*
> *With our flesh and blood, let us build our new Great*
> *Wall. . . .*

This song became the national anthem when the People's Republic was founded in 1949.

In early 1936 the Left-Wing Writers League decided to dissolve itself in order to pave the way for a broader organization that would include all writers and artists who stood against Japanese aggression and for national salvation.

The Japanese attack at Lugouqiao near Beijing in 1937 and the attempt to reduce China to a Japanese colony awakened more Chinese writers and artists to the seriousness of the national crisis. Guo Moruo (Kuo Mo-jo, 1892-1978), well-known Chinese poet and historian (who later became president of the Chinese Academy of Sciences), returned to Shanghai from Japan and started the *National Salvation Daily* to arouse the masses to fight the invaders.

After the fall of Shanghai and Nanjing, many writers and artists fled to Wuhan during the spring of 1938. They formed the All-China Writers' and Artists' Anti-Japanese Association, with Guo Moruo, Ba Jin, Lao She (1899-1966) and some 40 others as council members and Zhou Enlai as an honorary member. The association set up branches and correspondence networks in various parts of the country, published the magazine *Anti-Japanese Literature and Art* throughout the war, and organized groups of writers and artists to visit the battlefronts. The All-China Dramatists' Anti-Japanese Association dispatched ten groups of players to various battle areas to perform for the fighters.

To arouse the people to fight a foreign invader, the writers and artists devoted their talent to popular forms easily understood by the mostly illiterate masses. Lao She, later author of the well-known novel *Camel Xiangzi* (*Rickshaw Boy*), wrote anti-Japanese ballads and children's rhymes. "Living newspaper" plays and street-corner skits appeared.

Beginning in 1939 after the Kuomintang government had reestablished a capital in Chongqing, a city perched in the mountainous upper reaches of the Changjiang, the Japanese imperialists slowed their advance and began trying to neutralize the Kuomintang through political pressure and threats. Reactionaries in the government saw this as a good excuse to drop any pretense of fighting the Japanese and resume anti-Communist campaigns. In early 1941, Kuomintang forces launched a surprise attack on the Communist-led New Fourth Army in southern Anhui Province. Over 9,000 anti-Japanese fighters were killed. The government also applied strict censorship to all manuscripts and publications, banning scores of progressive newspapers and magazines, and closing down many bookstores. Numerous left-wing writers and artists were persecuted or jailed. "Chongqing became a large concentration camp," Guo Moruo later recalled.

Under the circumstances, many progressive writers and artists sought refuge in Hongkong, or in the Communist-controlled liberated areas. Those who remained in Chongqing followed the leadership of Zhou Enlai (then Communist representative in Chongqing) and Guo Moruo, director of the government's Cultural Affairs Committee. Guo wrote a historical play *Qu Yuan* that spoke directly to the situation at the time. In the play set during the Warring States period (475-221 B.C.) the patriotic poet Qu Yuan fought against the reactionaries of his time. Vilified as a lunatic at a local tyrant's court, the outraged Qu Yuan exclaims at the end:

> Wind! Roar, roar! Roar with all your might! In this pitchy darkness without the light of day everything is asleep, wrapped in deep slumber or dead; it is time for you to roar, roar with all your might!

The staging of the play created a furor in the wartime capital. Its lines struck a responsive chord in students and intellectuals. They were repeated on campuses, in the streets, and public squares. The Kuomintang authorities branded the play a distortion of history and tried to prevent further performance. But Guo Moruo was protected by his position as a Kuomintang official. The play gave courage to progressive writers and artists. Soon more works exposing the dark rule of the Kuomintang appeared.

Some artists and writers living under Japanese occupation also showed their unyielding spirit. One outstanding example was the famed Beijing Opera star Mei Lanfang (1894-1961). When the Japanese troops attacked Hongkong where he was residing in December 1941, he decided to retire from the stage altogether. After his return to Shanghai, he lived in isolation and earned his livelihood by selling his own paintings and pawning his valuables collected through the years. A Japanese puppet official one day came and asked him to lead an opera group on a performance tour in celebration of the Japanese victory. Sarcastically he retorted, "You should lead such a group as I've heard that you are a good opera singer, too." The official left in great embarrassment.

68.   THE YAN'AN FORUM ON LITERATURE AND ART

As Japanese armies overran China's major cities, a number of patriotic students and intellectuals went to the liberated areas in order to play their part in the war efforts. But they had different ideas on how to do this. Some remained in their cave dwellings, their heads buried in foreign classics, thinking they should absorb international standards in order to "uplift" the standards of the masses. Some, feeling that the artist's duty was to expose "the dark side of life", proceeded to do so, taking their materials from both the Kuomintang-controlled as well as the base areas. Some felt a conflict between their duties as dedicated revolutionaries and as artists. Art, they thought, should exist for art's sake only, and should be divorced from politics. Many genuinely wanted to write about the struggles of the ordinary workers and peasants, but knowing only intellectuals, their descriptions of ordinary people were stereotyped and false.

To help artists and writers find some answers, the Communist Party in May 1942 held a forum on literature and art in Yan'an. Mao Zedong spoke twice at this historic meeting, in part summing up the thinking of the most progressive artists and setting forth conclusions reached through discussion and argument. He reminded artists that they had a very important role to play in the ongoing struggle. The revolution needed armed forces to fight the battle of the sword, but that was not enough. The revolution also needed a cultural army — fighters armed with pens — to educate and unite the people and promote the liberation of the country.

To accomplish this task, writers and artists must first shift their class stand and become one with the masses, seeing things from their viewpoint. No artist can write convincingly of what he doesn't know. "China's revolutionary writers and artists, writers and artists of promise," he said, "must go among the masses . . . in order to observe, experience, study and analyze all the different kinds of people, all the classes, all the masses, all the vivid patterns of life and struggle, all the raw materials of literature and art." They must also learn the language of the masses. Only then can they proceed to do creative work.

Mao also criticized various erroneous conceptions of literature and art. He argued that "art for art's sake" is really a myth, that there is no art which does not ultimately serve one class interest or another. Writers cannot fall back on the idea of portraying "love and beauty" or "human nature". Human nature, he maintained, inevitably assumes a class character in a class society. "Classes have split society into many antagonistic groupings," he observed. "There will be love of all humanity when classes are eliminated, but not now." "It is good to learn from the best of foreign literature, but slavish imitation is ridiculous; we must master our own national style."

As to the assumption that the task of literature and art has always been to expose the dark side of life, Mao stressed the difference between exposing our enemies in order to condemn them and exposing the faults of the masses in order to educate them. It is necessary to criticize the shortcomings of the people, but in doing so one must take the stand of the people and speak out of wholehearted eagerness to protect and educate them. Artists must be equally willing to criticize their own shortcomings with the utmost candor, learn from their mistakes and resolve to correct them.

Mao Zedong called upon artists and writers to take up the great and exciting task of creating a new type of culture, and warned them that it would not be easy:

> Intellectuals who want to integrate themselves with the masses, who want to serve the masses, must go through a process in which they and the masses come to know each other well. This process may, and certainly will, involve much pain and friction; but if you have the determination, you will be able to fulfill these requirements.

The forum had a great impact on writers and artists in the liberated areas. Many of them went to live in the villages and tried to create works depicting the peasants' life and struggles. And it wasn't long before the lessons of the forum began to bear fruit. Perhaps the first of these fruits was *Brother and Sister Reclaiming Wasteland*, a skit in the form of a folk dance. It describes how a young peasant and his sister, inspired by the great production drive then going on, work hard to reclaim a plot on a hillside in order to grow more grain. Its humor and popular style won immediate acclaim among the peasants. Zhao Shuli (1906-1970), the first well-known writer depicting village life, then came out with a number of short stories. His *Xiao Erhei's Marriage* describes how a peasant youth married a village girl whom he truly loved over the objections of their superstitious parents. *The Rhymes of Li Youcai* (a village songster) and *Changes in Li Village* both portrayed the struggles of the poor peasants against the feudal landlords over village elections, reduction of land rent and interest. These fresh themes in Chinese literature were written in the vivid and living language of the ordinary people. In 1945 the opera *The White-Haired Girl* (written jointly by He Jingzhi and Ding

Yi) was staged, portraying a peasant girl who has run away to the mountains to escape from a landlord's oppression, later to be rescued by the Communist army. Woodcuts, sketches and paintings began to appear recording the details of the life and work of the common people. A new trend was under way in Chinese literature and art.

69.   THE RECTIFICATION MOVEMENT IN THE LIBERATED AREAS

In the course of the anti-Japanese war, young people from many parts of the country had flocked to join the Communist Party. By 1941 its ranks had swollen from 100,000 to 800,000 members. They were filled with patriotic fervor and revolutionary enthusiasm but lacked revolutionary theory, 65 to 70 percent of peasant origin and 15 to 20 percent students and other people of petty-bourgeois background from the cities and Kuomintang-controlled areas. To raise their political understanding so as to consolidate their ranks and strengthen their unity with the people became an urgent task. Thus, while conducting a war against a powerful foreign enemy and trying to maintain the delicate united front with the Kuomintang, the Party Central Committee decided to launch a rectification movement — an educational campaign among all Party members.

The rectification movement started in the Shaanxi-Gansu-Ningxia Border Region in the Northwest, and from 1941 to 1944 it spread to other liberated areas scattered around the country. It emphasized three major aspects: the style of study, Party relations and writing. "Style" here denoted far more than personal preference or manner; it involved the sum total of individual and collective Party orientation and action.

In May 1941 Mao Zedong gave the talk "Reform Our Study" at a cadre meeting, and the following February he gave the lecture "Rectify the Party Style of Work" at the opening of the Central Party School in Yan'an.   On both occasions he pointed out the need to unify theory and practice.   Study, he said, does not just mean memorizing and repeating Marxist-Leninist principles or phrases, but using these principles to analyze and guide the revolutionary struggle.   In order to study properly, one has to overcome subjectivism.   There are two kinds of subjectivism: dogmatism usually associated with intellectuals and empiricism with men of action.   Those with book-learning must develop in the direction of practice; only then will they stop being content with books and avoid committing dogmatic errors.   Those experienced in work must take up the study of theory seriously; only then will they not mistake their partial experience for universal truth and not commit empiricist errors.

As to the style of Party relations, members must guard against sectarianism, whether inside or outside the Party.   To do so, one must get rid of the old habits of extreme individualism and anti-organizational attitudes.   All Party members must take the interests of the Party into account, and should respect one another and learn from one another.   Toward those outside the Party, Communists must learn how to cooperate with all progressive forces and form close ties with the masses.

On the style of writing, Mao Zedong bitterly criticized Party jargon and emphasized the need to study language.   First, one should learn from the masses, as the people's vocabulary is rich, vigorous, vivid and expressive of real life.   Secondly, one should absorb fresh things from abroad, not only progressive ideas but new expressions as well.   Thirdly, one should learn whatever is alive in the classical Chinese literature.   If stereotyped writing was not eliminated, he warned, it would poison the whole Party and jeopardize the revolution.

The rectification movement started with the study of over 20 documents, including speeches by Mao Zedong and Liu Shaoqi (*How to Be a Good Communist* and *Inner-Party Struggle*), writings by Lenin, Stalin and Dimitrov (Bulgarian Communist and leader of the Comintern), and relevant decisions of the Party Central Committee. Toward the end of June 1943, Zhou Enlai returned from Chongqing to Yan'an. Completely devoted to the revolution without regard for personal interests, he took the lead in criticizing his own "leftist" errors committed in the past. This set a fine example for others at criticism and self-criticism meetings, where the principle of "curing the sickness to save the patient" was adopted. Another example was Ding Ling, a leading woman writer at the time. Her article "Thoughts on International Women's Day" in the *Liberation Daily* in 1942 was severely criticized by General He Long. But as she knew the purpose was to achieve unity through criticism, she didn't mind and the two became very good friends later on.

The rectification movement strengthened the collective leadership of the Party. A political bureau meeting in March 1943 decided to establish a central secretariat in charge of daily work. It also set up commissions for propaganda and for organization, with many leading Communists as members. This collective leadership ensured free discussions of burning problems and helped keep revolutionary actions along the correct line.

In addition to its positive aspect of consolidation, the rectification movement also had a negative thrust: to purge the ranks of enemy agents infiltrated into the Party to collect information or to undermine it from within. In the course of the cadre-screening drive, real enemy agents were indeed uncovered, but in the urgencies of the moment, errors were made as well. In some cases false confessions were extracted by coercion, though this method was in no way sanctioned by the Party leadership. Still, the great majority of the cadres came through the rectification movement as better revolutionaries than before.

The movement concluded with a critical review of the history of the Party, clarifying especially the "leftist" errors committed by Wang Ming and his followers. This review strengthened Mao Zedong's leadership in the Party.

In sum, the movement greatly improved the Party's style of

work in terms of a closer integration of Marxist-Leninist theory with actual Chinese conditions; strengthened ties with the masses; and promoted the spirit of criticism and self-criticism, or "unity — struggle — unity" in intra-Party life.

70.   LIFE IN COMMUNIST-CONTROLLED AREAS

In 1940 and 1941 the Communist-controlled base areas faced tremendous economic difficulties. Japanese troops, concentrating their attacks on the liberated areas in an attempt to consolidate their rear, adopted a policy of widespread burning, killing and looting.   In this scorched-earth drive, it is estimated that 30 million civilians lost their lives and vast tracts of land were left covered only with rubble and charred cinders. At the same time, Chiang Kai-shek tightened the blockade of the Border Region and stopped all subsidies to its government and armed forces.   For a period of time the Red soldiers faced dire shortages of daily necessities, such as clothes, shoes, vegetables, cooking oil, paper and bedding.

In this critical situation, Communist leaders decided to promote production and ensure supplies by creating a self-sufficient economy.   To rouse the production enthusiasm of the peasants, they launched a campaign to reduce rent and interest. Peasant associations and other organizations were urged to demand and enforce a 25 percent rent reduction, with a rent ceiling set at 37.5 percent of the crops.   The interest rate on loans was limited to 1.5 percent a month, or 18 percent a year, much lower than the usurious rates formerly charged by the moneylenders.   This benefited the poor peasants economically and challenged the political supremacy of the landlords in the rural areas.

While adopting a policy of "better troops and simpler administration" to cut down on political personnel and military expenditures, the government of the Border Region called upon all cadres to take part in productive labor in a mass production movement. Party Central Committee members planted their own vegetables and learned the native method of spinning. All government organizations, schools, and military units were encouraged to grow as much of their own food as possible. By 1943 all army units were extensively engaged in agriculture, and some were operating small-scale industrial or commercial enterprises as well.

An outstanding example was the 359th Brigade under General Wang Zhen, which undertook the reclamation of Nanniwan, a barren hilly area southeast of Yan'an. When they first arrived, there were no caves or houses to live in nor tools to work with. The Border Region was so poor that the soldiers could not bring enough food with them. From the very beginning they had to provide almost everything they needed with their own hands. They cut wood for primitive shelters and dug caves in the hillsides. They each reclaimed a bit of land to grow food crops. By 1943 they had reclaimed over 10,000 hectares of farmland, which yielded more grain than they needed. Meanwhile, the soldiers learned to make practically everything, such as clothes, blankets, shoes, tables and chairs, paper and charcoal. They became completely self-supporting, receiving no subsidy from the government. The "spirit of Nanniwan" inspired many other army units at the time and has become a virtue treasured by the Chinese people.

The government encouraged the voluntary formation of mutual aid teams and cooperatives. Remuneration was based on the amount of labor and investment (land, draft animals and farm tools) each member contributed, a system which benefited the prosperous as well as the poor. By 1943 fully 80 percent of the peasants had joined these organizations. Over 130,000 hectares had been reclaimed and many areas produced a surplus of grain as well as some cotton.

At the beginning, the Border Region had had no industry or handicrafts to speak of. To achieve self-sufficiency, the government set up iron-smelting and oil-refining works, machine shops, arsenals, pottery and porcelain kilns, and small factories making cloth, blankets, shoes, paper and soap. By the end of 1942, the number of factories had grown to 84, with almost 4,000 workers. This represented a remarkable achievement under severe war conditions.

To provide the textiles needed for clothing, the government revived traditional home weaving. By the end of 1943 the number of women weaving at home had risen dramatically; their output far outstripped the local factory production. In this and other ways, Chinese peasant women contributed significantly to the economic as well as political and military life of the base areas, thereby gaining higher social and economic status in a predominantly feudal China.

Through the mass production drive, the Communist Party converted the once poor and backward loess region of north Shaanxi and the encircled guerrilla bases behind Japanese lines into relatively prosperous and progressive areas of China. It instituted elections and other democratic practices, thus giving power to those who formerly were powerless. It thus won the confidence of the peasant masses, laid the material foundation for a protracted war against the Japanese invaders, and pointed the way to a cooperative approach to China's eventual modernization.

71. LIFE IN KUOMINTANG-CONTROLLED AREAS

As the war dragged on, conditions in "Free China" became steadily worse. Instead of introducing democratic reforms as the Communists demanded, the national government became more authoritarian under Chiang Kai-shek. Real power was in the hands of the "big four families" led by Chiang Kai-shek, T. V. Soong, H. H. Kung (both Chiang's brothers-in-law) and the Chen brothers, and the political cliques under their control. The government consistently defended the established order and the interests of the privileged classes.

To finance its war economy, the government simply printed more and more money, leading to ruinous inflation. The following table tells the story:

Year	Paper money issued (in million yuan)	Price index	Ratio between yuan and U.S. dollar
1937	2,060	100	3:1
1941	15,810	1,980	30:1
1945	1,031,900	249,100	3,250:1

Thus, in the eight years of the anti-Japanese war, the amount of paper currency in circulation increased over 500-fold, while commodity prices jumped almost 2,500 times. While bringing misery to the common people, runaway inflation meant enormous profits for the major capitalists headed by the "big four families". H. H. Kung became the richest man in China, with huge deposits of U.S. dollars in American banks.

Aside from controlling China's currency through the state banks, these four families monopolized most of China's commerce and industry. They robbed the peasants by paying extremely low prices for commodities such as cotton, tea, tobacco leaves, tung oil and hog bristles, and gouged consumers by charging extortionate prices for such daily necessities as salt, sugar, soap and matches. They also controlled China's exports of coal, tungsten and antimony, and imports of grain, cotton and manufactured goods like automobiles, machinery and equipment. The large capitalists controlled over 70 percent of all capital investments in China. This overwhelming concentration of economic and political power in the hands of a few families threatened the very existence of thousands of small industrialists and businessmen.

In 1941, the government re-established the tax in kind in the countryside, demonstrating its lack of faith in its own currency. This further increased the burden on the peasants, who had to hand over 50 percent or more of their produce. The Central

Agricultural Bank, instead of giving financial aid to those who tilled the soil, worked hand in glove with village usurers, who seized land from the impoverished peasants by foreclosing on loans. This was even true in famine-stricken areas. In Henan Province, for instance, many peasants in the 1943 famine were reduced to subsisting on elm bark and dried leaves.

Eyewitness accounts of the situation were recorded by U.S. correspondents Theodore A. White and Annalee Jacoby in their book *Thunder Out of China*:

> Peasants who could not pay were forced to the wall: they sold their cattle, their furniture, and even their land to raise money to buy grain to meet the tax quotas. . . . One of the most macabre touches of all was the flurry of land spec-ulation. Merchants from Xi'an and Zhengzhou, small government officials, army officers, and rich landlords who still had food were engaged in purchasing the peasants' an-cestral acres at criminally low figures. Concentration and dispossession were proceeding hand in hand, in direct pro-portion to the intensity of hunger.

As economic conditions deteriorated, the government inten-sified its political repression. Concentration camps were set up in large cities like Lanzhou, Xi'an and Chongqing. Secret agents combed the country for "subversive elements". Stu-dents and progressive people were arrested, imprisoned or simply murdered. All newspapers and publications were sub-jected to tight censorship. In 1939-1940, nearly all the branches of the progressive Life Bookstore run by the well-known writer and publisher Zou Taofen (1895-1944) were closed down.

In 1944 the Japanese sea lanes in the Pacific were seriously threatened by the U.S. naval victories. Japan began a new offensive in China in order to open up a land route to supply the troops in Southeast Asia. In a few months, the corrupt and demoralized Kuomintang troops suffered 500,000 casualties and lost large parts of north, central and south China. Japanese armies of only 60,000 men succeeded in opening up supply lines from northeast China straight down to Viet Nam. The ineptitude of the Kuomintang government and armies was thus fully exposed to the Chinese people.

In short, wartime conditions in "Free China" under Kuomintang control presented a sharp contrast to those in the Communist-led Border Region and other liberated areas. Though favored with voluminous U.S. aid, the Kuomintang-controlled regions sank deeper into the economic and political chaos of a decadent, oppressive society. People throughout China had lost faith in this government.

72. TWO VISIONS OF CHINA'S FUTURE

The historic battle of Stalingrad in the autumn of 1942 turned the tide of war against the Nazi invaders in the European theater. At the same time, the Allied naval offensive in the Pacific was relentlessly pushing Japanese forces westward. The Chinese people were hopeful that their nation would emerge victorious in the protracted anti-Japanese war.

Anticipating China's eventual victory, Chiang Kai-shek in March 1943 published a book called *China's Destiny*. It was his opinion that the old Confucian virtues, which had "made the nation great in remote times", could again be pressed into service to uplift China from the abyss of misery and disunity. Chief among these virtues was obedience — a son's obedience to his father, a wife's to her husband and the people's to their ruler, in this case, Chiang Kai-shek. In favor of feudal exploitation and oppression in the countryside and bureaucrat-capitalist control of modern industry and commerce in the cities, he blamed the unequal treaties for all of China's misfortunes. He condemned the May Fourth Movement for having introduced alien ideas of liberalism, socialism and Marxism in China and alleged that the Chinese Communist Party was a sort of new warlord. He exhorted the people to turn back to the past and to patiently await "a fuller enjoyment of life".

To counter these reactionary ideas, the Chinese Communist Party proposed the early reorganization of the Kuomintang regime into a democratic coalition government. This had been advocated by Mao Zedong as early as January 1940 in his article *On New Democracy*. After analyzing Chinese conditions, he maintained that the Chinese revolution had to go through two stages, a bourgeois democratic revolution and a socialist revolution.

While the ultimate aim of the Communist Party was to build a socialist society and eventually a communist one, its goal in the first stage was to rid China of imperialist and feudal oppression and to transform China into an independent, democratic republic. As the Chinese bourgeoisie was too weak to shoulder this responsibility alone, the future republic had to be of a new type — the joint rule of the proletariat, the peasantry, the intellectuals and sections of the bourgeoisie. This new democratic republic would be different from the old European-American form of bourgeois capitalist republic and also different from the working-class-led socialist republic as existed in the Soviet Union.

Mao also outlined the economic and cultural policies of the new democratic republic. Economically, the state enterprises would be of a socialist character and constitute the leading force in the whole economy, but "the republic will neither confiscate capitalist private property in general nor forbid the development of such capitalist production as does not 'dominate the livelihood of the people', for China's economy is still very backward". However, it would confiscate land from landlords for distribution to those peasants having little or no land and abolish feudal relations in the rural areas. The better-off peasants' land and property would not be affected, and various types of cooperative enterprises encouraged as a transition to socialism.

Mao Zedong maintained that the culture of the new democratic republic would have three distinctive features. First, it is national. It opposes imperialist oppression and upholds the dignity and independence of the Chinese nation. Secondly, it is scientific. Opposed as it is to all feudal and superstitious ideas, it stands for seeking truth from facts and for the unity of theory and practice. Thirdly, it belongs to the broad masses and is therefore democratic. It should mainly serve the workers and peasants who make up more than 90 percent of the nation's population and should gradually become their very own.

Mao said, "Combine the politics, the economy and the culture of New Democracy, and you have the new democratic republic, the Republic of China both in name and in reality, the new China we want to create."

In the spring of 1945, two congresses were held simultaneously in China — the Sixth National Congress of the Kuomintang and the Seventh National Congress of the Communist Party. At the former, Chiang Kai-shek had the ideas in his *China's Destiny* adopted, ensuring that Kuomintang rule would continue under his personal dictatorship. At the latter, Mao Zedong repeated his demand for the formation of a democratic coalition government.

"These two lines," Mao Zedong declared, "are in conflict with each other. We firmly believe that, led by the Chinese Communist Party and guided by the line of its Seventh Congress, the Chinese people will achieve complete victory, while the Kuomintang's counter-revolutionary line will inevitably fail."

73. ATTEMPTS TO AVOID CIVIL WAR AFTER WORLD WAR II

The end of World War II did not bring peace or unity to the war-weary Chinese people. The democratic coalition government demanded by the Chinese Communist Party was still but a hope when the long struggle against the Japanese aggressors came to an end on V-J Day (August 15, 1945). The Communists had become stronger than ever, with a regular army of 915,000, a militia of 2,200,000, and a population of 95,500,000 in 19 liberated areas scattered over many parts of the country. Chiang Kai-shek, backed by the United States, was determined to wipe out the Communists.

On August 11, soon after the Japanese government announced its readiness to surrender, Chiang Kai-shek sent a cable to Zhu De, commander of the Red armies, ordering him not to move his troops and not to accept the surrender of any Japanese units. This order ran counter to the Potsdam Declaration, since the united front was still in existence; the Red armies had as much right to disarm enemy forces and accept Japanese surrenders as any other force. On the same day, Chiang ordered his own officers to "step up the war effort . . . push forward without the slightest relaxation". On August 13, the Communist leadership rejected Chiang's order.

On the same day, Mao Zedong spoke at a meeting of cadres in Yan'an. He pointed out: "In the past eight years we have changed places with Chiang Kai-shek — formerly we were on the mountain and he was by the river; during the War of Resistance we were behind the enemy lines and he went up to the mountain. Now he is coming down from the mountain, coming down to seize the fruits of victory." As the victory had been won by the people with bloodshed and sacrifice, it was to the people that the fruits of victory should go. But Chiang Kai-shek was planning for civil war.

The U.S. government under President Truman adopted a policy of exclusive support for Chiang Kai-shek and the Kuomintang, despite the advice of many Americans who knew the situation in China firsthand. At the same time, however, it proclaimed its willingness to play the role of "honest broker" to avert civil war in China. Chiang Kai-shek had invited Mao Zedong to come to Chongqing for talks. On August 19 American Ambassador Patrick Hurley (1883-1963) flew to

Yan'an to "negotiate" as a third party. On August 26 Mao Zedong flew with Hurley to Chongqing.

In view of the almost universal desire for peace among the Chinese people, the Communist Party preferred to avoid fighting if a peaceful way could be found to transform the Kuomintang one-party regime into a democratic coalition government. There was the possibility that Chiang Kai-shek would be realistic enough to heed world public opinion and seek a peaceful solution to the Chinese problem. And, should negotiations fail and civil war break out again, the people would see clearly who the real culprit was. As Mao Zedong later said, "We did well to go this time, for we exploded the rumor spread by the Kuomintang that the Communist Party did not want peace and unity."

The negotiations lasted 43 days. On October 10, a "summary of conversations", also known as the "October 10th agreement", was issued. On the positive side, Chiang Kai-shek was forced to agree to the basic policy of peace and national reconstruction put forward by the Communist Party, and accept "long-term cooperation" for building a democratic new China. He also promised to put an end to the Kuomintang's political "tutelage" and to convene a political consultative conference with representatives of all political parties as well as prominent non-party leaders. However, he stubbornly refused to recognize the legal status of the Red Army and the popularly elected governments in the liberated areas. As a result, no agreements were reached on the latter points. Further negotiations were decided upon to reach a final settlement.

The Communist side showed a great deal of flexibility and willingness to compromise in the talks. It agreed to withdraw from eight liberated areas in south China, which the Kuomintang leaders regarded as thorns in their sides. It first proposed cutting the Red strength to 48 divisions against the Kuomintang's 263 divisions. When the Kuomintang said that it would reduce its troops to 120 divisions, the Communists replied that they were willing to reduce by the same proportion to 24 or even 20 divisions. These concessions for the sake of averting civil war and achieving national unity won the sympathy of numerous middle-of-the-roaders.

However, when the fundamental interests of the people were involved, the Communists refused to yield an inch. They insisted that the liberated areas' continued existence had to be protected, and that the Red forces must keep their weapons. Mao Zedong declared, "The arms of the people, every gun and every bullet, must all be kept, must not be handed over" to the Kuomintang.

While in Chongqing, Mao Zedong and Zhou Enlai took time out to meet with leaders of democratic parties, youth groups, women's organizations, trade unions and newsmen. They explained the Communist Party's desire for peace and unity and their hopes of reconstructing China into a democratic, progressive, prosperous and modern nation. As many Chinese were already disillusioned with the Kuomintang, more and more came to place their hopes in the Communist Party.

While the Communists were winning more friends and supporters, the Kuomintang was alienating millions in the areas recovered from the Japanese. Taking over Japanese enterprises and properties as their own, the capitalists headed by the "big four families" became richer than ever. Uncontrolled inflation, food shortages and official corruption drove many middle-class families into bankruptcy and destroyed their confidence in the Kuomintang. Confiscations, robberies, rapes, wanton murders and widespread terrorism by the Kuomintang troops and secret agents turned the people's jubilation at victory over Japan into disappointment and anger.

74.   U.S. ROLE IN EARLY POST-WAR PERIOD

In July 1945, the protracted anti-Japanese war was on the threshold of victory. Mao Zedong, speaking on behalf of the Chinese Communist Party, warned the United States government not to support Chiang Kai-shek's policy of fomenting civil war in China. In his article "On the Danger of the Hurley Policy", he wrote:

> It has become increasingly obvious that the policy of the United States toward China as represented by its ambassador Patrick J. Hurley is creating a civil war crisis in China. . . . If the Hurley policy of aiding and abetting the reactionary forces in China and antagonizing the Chinese people in their immense numbers continues unchanged, it will place a crushing burden on the government and people of the United States and plunge them into endless trouble.

Nonetheless, the Truman administration continued to give massive support to Chiang Kai-shek. On August 10, 1945, one day after the second atomic bomb had been dropped on Nagasaki and two days after the U.S.S.R. had entered the war against Japan, General Wedemeyer, Stilwell's successor as commander of U.S. forces in the China theater and Chiang's chief of staff, was instructed to aid the Kuomintang government in accepting the Japanese surrender and reoccupying all areas held by the Japanese troops. Four days later, General Douglas MacArthur, the Supreme Commander of the Allied Powers (SCAP) in the Pacific, issued an order designating Chiang Kai-shek's government as the sole agency qualified to accept the Japanese surrender in China (excluding Manchuria), Taiwan and Indochina north of the 16th parallel. Even as the Chongqing negotiations proceeded, U.S. air and naval forces were transporting some 500,000 Kuomintang troops to take over major cities and communications lines in north and east China still under Japanese control. In addition, 53,000 U.S. marines landed at Tanggu and Qingdao on the north China coast to occupy Beijing, Tianjin, the Kailuan coal mines and the Beijing-Shanhaiguan Railway. These places were then turned over to the Kuomintang.

Emboldened by American support, Chiang Kai-shek deployed six armies along the Great Wall. He broke his promise to avoid civil war, ordering Kuomintang troops to attack the

Communist forces.   No longer able to play the role of an
"honest broker" because of Chiang's open abrogation of earlier
agreements, Hurley resigned as ambassador to China.   President Truman immediately appointed General George C. Marshall to be his special representative to China.   U.S. policy remained the same, however.

General Marshall arrived in China toward the end of 1945
as a mediator in the conflict between the Kuomintang and the
Communist Party.   This was, however, in reality an attempt
to soften up the Communists, deceive the Chinese people and
thus gain control of all China without fighting.   Under pressure of the cries for peace, both domestic and abroad, Chiang
Kai-shek on January 10, 1946 signed a cease-fire agreement
with the Communist Party.   A Political Consultative Conference which included some representatives of the democratic
parties was convened.   In a session lasting for three weeks,
the conference called for the peaceful reconstruction of China
and the reorganization of the Kuomintang government along
democratic principles.

The cease-fire proved to be shortlived, however. The cease-
fire agreement was soon broken by Chiang Kai-shek on January
13, and a Kuomintang central executive committee meeting in
March rejected the resolutions of the Political Consultative
Conference and insisted on prolonging the Kuomintang's one-
party dictatorship.   General Marshall admitted that his
"mediation" was a failure.   The United States continued to
transport additional Kuomintang forces to major cities and
other strategic positions in preparation for civil war against the
liberated areas.   A U.S. Military Advisory Group was set up
to assist the Kuomintang government in strengthening its armed
forces.   The Export-Import Bank had extended a loan of
$82,800,000 to the Kuomintang government after V-J Day.   In
April 1946, it earmarked an additional $500,000,000.   On
June 14, the U.S. government extended $51,700,000 in long-
term credit, covering the delivery of "civilian type" equipment
and supplies such as machinery, motor vehicles and communications equipment, which could easily be used by the

Kuomintang in the civil war against the Communists. On August 30, the U.S. sold the Kuomintang government a huge amount of war surplus at bargain prices. In September, Zhou Enlai complained to General Marshall that since Chiang first broke the cease-fire, he had moved 1,740,000 soldiers against the liberated areas, all with U.S. support.

When all of his preparations had been completed in July 1946, Chiang Kai-shek started an all-out offensive against the liberated areas in northeast, north, central and east China. At this critical juncture, the Communist Party adopted the policy of "land to the tillers" rather than reducing rents and interest on loans as had been practiced during the anti-Japanese war. The confiscation of the landlords' land and its distribution to the land-hungry poor peasants greatly heightened their enthusiasm for the revolution. They either enlisted in the people's army or gave active support to the Communist forces. The Communist Party renamed its troops the Chinese People's Liberation Army, and the War of Liberation began.

On July 7, 1946 (the anniversary of the outbreak of the anti-Japanese war), the Central Committee of the Chinese Communist Party issued a statement bitterly attacking American policy. The Communists charged that American military, economic and financial aid to the Kuomintang government was designed to support the reactionary group in dictatorship and civil war and called upon the United States to "cease armed intervention in our country's internal affairs".

It is important to note that the Communists' bitter remarks were directed against the American government and not the American people. On a previous occasion, at the concluding session of the Seventh National Congress of the Chinese Communist Party in June 1945, Mao Zedong had declared:

We oppose the U.S. government's policy of supporting Chiang Kai-shek against the Communists. But we must draw a distinction, firstly, between the people of the United States and their government and, secondly, within the U.S.

government between the policy-makers and their subordinates.

The Chinese people remember with gratitude the many fair-minded Americans who voiced their opposition to the U.S. government's policy of supporting the Chiang Kai-shek government.

75. THE CIVIL WAR RESUMES

With military and economic superiority clearly on his side, Chiang Kai-shek in July 1946 launched an all-out civil war. The Kuomintang troops at that time numbered 4,300,000 men against Communist forces of only 1,200,000. Chiang's armies had a practical monopoly of heavy equipment and modern transport and an unopposed air arm, while the Communist forces had only "millet plus rifles". The Kuomintang controlled the large cities with their modern industrial plants and commercial establishments, while Communist bases were located in the economically backward countryside. Furthermore, Chiang Kai-shek could count on the support of the United States, while the Communists had no significant foreign aid. Chiang bragged that "the Communist problem can be settled by military means within five months".

With American assistance in transporting troops, the Kuomintang registered impressive-looking initial advances. In north China, they extended their control over major cities and the strategic Longhai Railway stretching from the seacoast westward along the Huanghe River. In October 1946, they occupied Zhangjiakou close to the Great Wall, and cleared much of eastern Inner Mongolia. In northeast China, they fanned out from Shenyang to the Yalu River and extended their positions north and northwestward from Changchun. The well-equipped Kuomintang armies seemed invincible.

In March 1947, Chiang Kai-shek decided to seize Yan'an, the Red capital and the bulwark of Communist power. For this purpose, he mobilized 230,000 troops to attack the city from both sides. The Communist forces in the Northwest then numbered approximately 20,000 men, making a ratio between the two sides of 10 to 1. Under the circumstances, the Communist leaders decided to evacuate the city with all their installations, supplies and equipment. A few days later the Kuomintang troops captured an empty city, gaining banner headlines in newspapers at home and abroad. So elated was Chiang Kai-shek that he saw final victory at hand.

But the Communist forces, now called the People's Liberation Army, carried on with the tried and true strategy of guerrilla and mobile warfare. Rather than defending territory and cities, the PLA disengaged when confronted with an unfavorable balance of forces, harassed the enemy's weak spots, and put out of action as many enemy soldiers as possible. When the PLA destroyed or captured enemy forces, they seized large amounts of modern weaponry as well. Captured Kuomintang troops, many of whom had been forcibly drafted and felt no loyalty to their masters, were recruited whenever possible into the Communist forces. After the evacuation of Yan'an, Mao Zedong and the Central Committee of the Communist Party continued to direct operations against the Kuomintang troops without interruption from a mobile headquarters. The PLA foiled the enemy's strategy of quick and decisive battles on all fronts. In the first year (July 1946 to June 1947) of the war, now called the War of Liberation, the Communist armies deactivated 1,120,000 Kuomintang troops and increased their own numbers to almost 2,000,000 men. The tide of war had turned in favor of the people's forces.

Beginning in July 1947, the People's Liberation Army took the initiative, starting an all-out offensive against the Kuomintang troops. The main force, under Liu Bocheng and Deng Xiaoping, crossed the Huanghe River from north China and drove southward into the heart of Kuomintang-controlled territory. In April 1948 Yan'an was retaken. During the second year of the war, which ended in June 1948, the PLA had liberated 164 cities and wiped out another 1,530,000 Kuomintang troops; its own ranks had grown to number 2,800,000 men. In addition to the increase in numerical strength, they had also gained valuable experience in storming cities and well-defended enemy bastions.

Then came the three major battles that led to the downfall of Chiang Kai-shek's regime. First was the Liaoxi-Shenyang campaign, which liberated the whole of northeast China in 52 days and put 470,000 Kuomintang troops out of action. The PLA by this time had grown to over 3,000,000 men, attaining numerical superiority over the Kuomintang forces for the first time. Second was the Huai-Hai campaign in northern Jiangsu Province, in which another 550,000 Kuomintang troops, including Chiang's best armored units, were defeated. This liberated all of east China north of the Changjiang River. One million PLA men were now poised on the north bank of this major waterway, threatening Nanjing, Shanghai and the heart of Kuomintang rule. Third was the campaign in the Beijing-Tianjin area. When the Kuomintang commanders in Tianjin refused an appeal to lay down their arms, the PLA began a fierce assault which captured the city within 48 hours. Seeing what was in store for them should they further resist, the Kuomintang garrison in Beijing (then called Beiping) surrendered, and the city was liberated peacefully on January 31, 1949. This campaign resulted in another 520,000 Kuomintang troops being either wiped out or reorganized into PLA units. All of north China was now under Communist control.

What was the reason for the disastrous collapse of Chiang Kai-shek's seemingly invincible armies? Contrary to the cries of the "China Lobby" in the United States, it was not due to the lack of American arms and supplies. In the words of General David Barr, head of the U.S. Military Advisory Group to the Nationalist government, "no battle has been lost since my arrival due to lack of ammunition or equipment". Ruefully, he added, "the Kuomintang's military debacles, in my opinion, can be attributed to the world's worst leadership and many other morale-destroying factors that lead to a complete loss of will to fight." Large quantities of American tanks, artillery and other supplies had fallen into the hands of the people's forces. As Mao Zedong had said in 1936, "We rely on the war industries of the imperialist countries and of our enemy. . . . Equipment is delivered to us by the enemy's own transport." In the eyes of the overwhelming majority of the Chinese people, the "mandate of Heaven" had already passed over to the Communist side.

76. THE WAR OF LIBERATION AND THE FOUNDING OF THE PEOPLE'S REPUBLIC

When it was clear that a military victory was out of his grasp, Chiang Kai-shek issued a statement on New Year's Day, 1949, appealing for peace negotiations. The Communists rejected it, knowing that Chiang and his supporters were merely seeking to delay a showdown until more American aid could shore up their loosening military grip on the country.

Some foreign friends, though with good intentions, overestimated Chiang Kai-shek's strength. Fearing U.S. military intervention, they thought the Communists could never win the war. Thus, they advised the Chinese Communist Party not to push the revolution any further, leaving the territory south of the Changjiang River to Chiang Kai-shek's government. Had this advice been followed, China would have become "a house divided", and the people would have continued to suffer internecine strife. The Chinese Communist leaders did not accept this advice, though they knew it was given with good intentions. From the very beginning of the civil war, they had been confident that they would eventually win.

At this juncture, Chiang Kai-shek "retired" from the presidency and Li Zongren (Li Tsung-jen), Chiang's long-time rival from Guangxi Province in southwest China, became acting president with the tacit backing of the United States. Early in April he sent a delegation to Beijing to negotiate with the Communist Party. Even as the negotiations were going on, Chiang was planning to regroup his remaining troops for a counter-offensive against the People's Liberation Army. After 15 days of negotiations, the Kuomintang government rejected the peace agreement that had been reached by the negotiators.

On April 21, 1949, Mao Zedong and Zhu De ordered the PLA to resume the offensive. One million troops camped on the north bank of the Changjiang River immediately sprang into action. Crossing the river, they stormed into Nanjing on April 23 and hoisted the red flag over the "Presidential Palace". Within a few months Communist troops occupied all the major cities, including Shanghai, Wuhan, Xi'an, Changsha and Guangzhou. One province after another was liberated, as the old Kuomintang civilian and military authorities were either defeated, went over to the Communist side, or simply collapsed. The Nationalist central government first moved to Guangzhou, then to Chongqing and Chengdu, and finally to Taiwan under U.S. military protection. By the end of the year, the repressive and corrupt Kuomintang regime, having lost all popular support, had fallen like a house of cards. The Chinese people under the leadership of the Chinese Communist Party had achieved victory.

The People's Republic of China was born on October 1, 1949. At 3:00 p.m., 3,000,000 Beijing citizens gathered in Tian An Men Square to hear Chairman Mao proclaim the founding of the new state. Standing atop Tian An Men, he delivered a soul-stirring speech.

Our nation will from now on become one of the family of peace and freedom-loving nations, working bravely and diligently to create its own civilization and happiness and at the same time promote world peace and freedom. Our nation will never again be insulted, for we have stood up. Our revolution has won the sympathy and rejoicing of the masses of people the world over. We have friends all over the world.

PART III

PEOPLE'S CHINA

77. THE CONSOLIDATION OF POWER

The new People's Republic, established on October 1, 1949, confronted tremendous problems. After a hundred years of foreign aggression and internal disorder, the nation's economy was in a shambles. Steel production, pig iron output and coal production had fallen drastically from the pre-liberation peak year of 1943. Grain output had declined by one quarter and cotton by nearly a half. Years of runaway inflation and Kuomintang indifference to natural disasters had reduced the great majority of the people to abject misery and desperation. Foreign ill-wishers, especially the U.S. government, considered the new government but a fleeting historical apparition and refused even to discuss diplomatic recognition. Chiang Kai-shek, installed on the island of Taiwan, declared that he would strike back within two years.

To consolidate its power, the people's government continued the drive to bring the whole country under its control. The People's Liberation Army moved quickly to liberate Guangzhou and Xiamen in the South; Guilin, Guiyang, Chongqing and Chengdu in the Southwest; and Urumqi in the Northwest. Early in 1950, the PLA recaptured the islands of Hainan and Zhoushan off the southern coast. Following the signing of an agreement for the peaceful liberation of Tibet in May 1951, the PLA entered Lhasa (the capital of Tibet) in October. Within two years, the people's government had achieved the unification of all China, with the exception of Taiwan, Hongkong, Macao and a few small islands still under Kuomintang control.

Political control was, however, only the first task of the people's government. The aim of the revolution was to rid China of feudalism, imperialism and bureaucratic-capitalism — the "three big mountains" oppressing the Chinese people. To eradicate the 2,000-year-old feudal system of land tenure, the new government proclaimed the Land Reform Law in June 1950. Extending policies successfully implemented in areas that had been liberated earlier, land owned by the landlords as well as their farm implements, draft animals, surplus grain and surplus houses were confiscated and redistributed to the tillers of the soil. Landlords who owned industrial and commercial enterprises in the cities and towns were allowed to keep these properties and funds.

By the end of 1952, agrarian reform had been practically completed throughout the country except in some minority nationality regions like Tibet. In the process, while landlord-bullies who had committed heinous crimes such as murder and rape were condemned at mass accusation meetings or punished through court trials, 300 million landless and land-poor peasants received land, tools, animals and seed grain. Freed from exorbitant rent and usurious rates of interest, as well as other forms of exploitation by unscrupulous gentry and warlords, the peasants of China now controlled their own economic and social destinies.

At the same time, the people's government began an assault on the feudal social system which had for so long oppressed women. Feudal custom decreed that women accept as their husbands whomever their parents chose. The Marriage Law of 1950 ushered in a new era for women. It stipulated that marriage be based on free choice of partners and monogamy; the law further prescribed equal rights for both sexes and the protection of the lawful interests of women and children. It prohibited bigamy, concubinage, child betrothal, interference with the remarriage of widows, and the exaction of money or gifts in connection with marriage — all long-standing social evils. A major contribution toward the emancipation of women, the law was heartily welcome by the women of China.

The new government confiscated the holdings of the "big four families", leading bureaucratic-capitalists who had become monopolists through their high positions in the Kuomintang government. These holdings included the formerly Japanese-owned industrial and commercial complexes which they had appropriated after the Japanese defeat. On the eve of liberation, the bureaucratic capitalists controlled two-thirds of China's industrial capital, 90 percent of iron and steel production, 67 percent of electric power, 33 percent of coal production, and all petroleum and nonferrous metal industries. The major banks, railroads, airlines and the dozen largest trading companies were also in their grip. By the end of 1949, the people's government had confiscated over 2,800 such enterprises employing a total of 750,000 workers. Their conversion into state-owned enterprises laid the foundation for the socialist industrialization of China.

Most of the imperialist privileges extorted from China through the unequal treaties had been nominally abolished during the anti-Japanese war, and Japanese property had been taken over after V-J Day. Following liberation the roughly 1,000 non-Japanese foreign businesses in China were encouraged to continue operation under Chinese law. However, because of the abolition of their special privileges and the later (1951) U.S. embargo against China, many closed shop, finding it unprofitable or difficult to continue operation. Some transferred ownership to the people's government by way of payment of taxes and debts. All these establishments were gradually transformed into state-owned enterprises. Because Christian churches, schools, hospitals and charitable institutions came under Chinese ownership and control, many missionaries left for their home countries.

In face of the severe economic and financial situation of the nation, the government stimulated production by restoring state-owned industry and transportation in the cities and undertaking water-control and irrigation works in the rural areas. It established a network of state and cooperative stores for the purchase and distribution of commodities. To stabilize the economy, it rationed food grain and other necessities, fixed prices, allocated supplies and punished speculators. To help privately-owned enterprises producing essential consumer goods, it ensured the supply of raw materials and guaranteed the sale of their products. The government standardized currency and financial controls, adopted a low salary policy for government workers and balanced the budget. These measures quickly brought an end to economic chaos and restored productivity.

By 1952 all sectors of agriculture and industry, with but a few exceptions, had surpassed the highest pre-liberation production levels. The total value of industrial and agricultural output was 77.5 percent higher than that of 1949; industry was up 145 percent and agriculture 48.5 percent. Railroad and highway traffic as well as inland navigation expanded greatly. Workers' wages increased 70 percent and peasants' income rose 30 percent. Both foreign and domestic analysts were amazed by the dramatic successes of the rehabilitation period.

Unlike the Soviet Union, where a dictatorship of the proletariat was established immediately after the October Revolution, the People's Republic of China set up a united-front government of four classes — workers, peasants, petty bourgeoisie such as shopkeepers and professionals, and national bourgeoisie (those with few or no connections with foreign capital). The foundation of this united front was the worker-peasant alliance. While leadership was in the hands of the Communist Party, all democratic parties participated in the deliberations on state affairs. A government based on people's congresses at all levels was set up.

The sudden outbreak of the Korean War in June 1950 also contributed to the strengthening of the new government. When the United States sent troops to the island of Taiwan and the U.S. and U.N. forces marched northward toward the Yalu

First Soviet Congress in Ruijin, Jiangxi Province, November 1931. A provisional government of the Chinese Soviet Republic was set up, with Mao Zedong as chairman.

Members of the Central Bureau of the Soviet Area in 1931. From right: Wang Jiaxiang, Mao Zedong, Xiang Ying, Deng Fa, Zhu De, Ren Bishi and Gu Zuoshen.

A contingent of the Red Army on the Long March.

Chinese civilians buried alive by Japanese troops.

Chinese militia units wreck a Japanese-held railway.

Zhou Enlai (fourth from left) visits the New Fourth Army in central China in 1939. The officers include Chen Yi (first left) and Ye Ting (first right).

United Front: Bishop Logan H. Roots, Anna Louise Strong, Peng Dehuai, Frances Roots and Agnes Smedley at Wuhan in 1938.

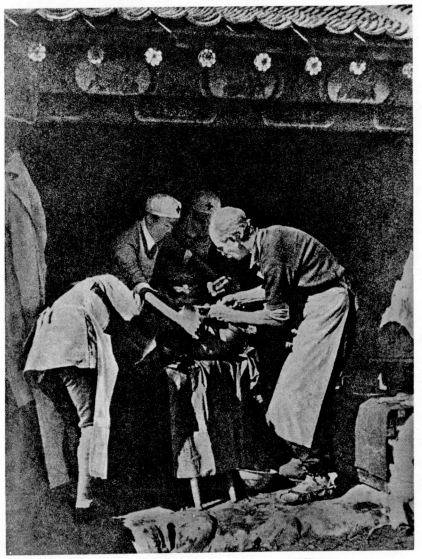

Dr. Norman Bethune operating on a wounded soldier near the battle front.

U.S. Ambassador Patrick J. Hurley with Mao Zedong and Zhou Enlai before their flight to Chongqing, August 1945.

The "Dixie Mission" arrived in Yan'an in July 1944. From right to left: Colonel David Barrett, Mao Zedong, John Service and Zhu De.

The People's Liberation Army captures the Presidential Palace in Nanjing on April 23, 1949.

Chairman Mao Zedong proclaims the birth of the People's Republic of China, October 1, 1949.

River — the border between China and North Korea — all sections of the population rose in patriotic fervor to support the government, which sent volunteer divisions into North Korea to help defend a friendly neighbor as well as its own security. From June 1951 to May 1952, popular contributions amounted to the total price of 3,710 airplanes. Peasants and workers doubled their efforts in production to supply the volunteer fighters on the Korean front. Thus, when China's territory and sovereignty were threatened by foreign aggression, the whole people rallied to the support of the new government.

78. DURING THE KOREAN WAR

In August 1944, with the defeat of the axis powers in sight, the leaders of the Chinese Communist Party began to turn their thoughts toward building a new China in the postwar period. With the devastation suffered by the Soviet Union in the war, its leaders would obviously take the reconstruction of their own country as the first priority. John Stewart Service, then political officer to the U.S. army's observer group in Yan'an, known as the "Dixie Mission", reported his conversation with Mao Zedong in his book *The Amerasia Papers*, Berkeley, 1971. "We do not expect Russian help," Mao Zedong said. "China must industrialize," Mao Zedong continued. "Between the people of China and the people of the United States there are strong ties of sympathy, understanding and mutual interest. Both are essentially democratic and individualistic. Both are by nature peace-loving. . . . America needs an export market for her heavy industry and specialized manufactures. . . . America is not only the most suitable country to assist . . . she is also the only country fully able to participate." Unfortunately, President Roosevelt decided that the United States should continue to support Chiang Kai-shek's Nationalist government, as it had the official backing of the Soviet Union (in the Yalta agreement) and other powers. Should a civil war become unavoidable, Chiang Kai-shek would surely emerge the victor. The subsequent defeat of Chiang Kai-shek's well-equipped armies by the Communist forces was therefore regarded as a quite unexpected calamity by the U.S. government and by Chiang's supporters in the China Lobby.

The U.S. refusal to recognize the new government left the Chinese Communists no alternative but to lean toward the Soviet Union. On June 30, 1949, in commemoration of the 28th anniversary of the Communist Party of China, Mao Zedong wrote:

> Throughout his life, Sun Yat-sen appealed countless times to the capitalist countries for help and got nothing but heartless rebuffs. Only once in his whole life did Sun Yat-sen receive foreign help, and that was Soviet help. . . . Internationally, we belong to the side of the anti-imperialist front headed by the Soviet Union, and so we can turn only to this side for genuine and friendly help, not to the side of the imperialist front.

When the people's government was established on October 1, 1949, the Chinese people were filled with the joy of liberation and hope for a bright future. Internationally, however, China faced hostility from almost all sides except the Soviet Union. Winston Churchill was warning against the "Iron Curtain" and the "menace of the Asiatic hordes". President Truman followed with the doctrine of "the containment of communism". It was in this context that Mao Zedong went to Moscow in December 1949. After several weeks of sojourn in the Soviet Union and negotiations with Stalin and other leaders in the Soviet government, a treaty of friendship, alliance and mutual assistance, as well as several subsidiary agreements, were signed in February 1950 and ratified that autumn.

Materially, China seemed to have gained little from the mutual agreements. The credit of $300 million was less than what Austria had received from the United States after the war.

Politically, however, Mao Zedong's trip was very important. China now had an ally in the powerful Soviet Union and friends in the people's democracies of Eastern Europe. Reversing the tsarist policy of relentless expansion, the Soviet Union thus confirmed its earlier renunciation of attempts to establish a Russian sphere of influence over a wide belt of Chinese territory.

The U.S. entry into the Korean War and President Truman's dispatch of the U.S. Seventh Fleet to the Taiwan Straits in June of 1950 further antagonized the Chinese people and cemented the alliance between China and the Soviet Union. On October 3 Premier Zhou Enlai informed the Indian ambassador that China would not stand by if the U.N. forces crossed the 38th Parallel which divided North and South Korea. The U.S. government and General MacArthur ignored China's warning. A few days later the U.S. First Cavalry Division crossed the 38th Parallel, and the combined forces of 15 other member states of the United Nations drove rapidly northward toward the Yalu River, the border between North Korea and China. At the urgent request of the North Korean government, China responded to this threat to her own borders by sending volunteer divisions to "resist the United States and aid Korea".

After three years of see-saw battles in which millions of people were killed or wounded, an armistice was signed in July 1953, and the opposing forces were left still facing each other roughly along the line of the 38th Parallel. Under U.S. pressure, China was branded an aggressor by the United Nations, while the U.S. Seventh Fleet remained in Chinese waters to protect the Kuomintang government on Taiwan and the off-shore islands. In 1954, the United States signed a treaty of military alliance with Chiang Kai-shek on Taiwan. Thus, Truman's policy of the "containment of communism" had led directly to the U.S. intervention in the Korean conflict, its threat to the borders of China along the Yalu River and military support for the already discredited Kuomintang regime.

In 1951, General Omar Bradley criticized this policy simply and eloquently when he testified, "Red China is not the powerful nation seeking to dominate the world", and called the Korean War "the wrong war, at the wrong place, at the wrong time, and with the wrong enemy". All China's efforts to establish contacts and relations with the United States continued to be rejected by the blind hostility of U.S. policy-makers. The fact that the Taiwan question remains unresolved even today is the direct result of these cold war attitudes of the 1950's.

79. THE FIRST FIVE-YEAR PLAN

With the successful conclusion of China's economic rehabilitation at the end of 1952, the people's government decided to bend its efforts toward laying the preliminary basis for building China into a modern, industrialized, socialist power. The drafting of the First Five-Year Plan (1953-1957) had started as early as 1951, but repeated discussions and revisions delayed its formal adoption until July 1955, at the second session of the First National People's Congress. Outlay for economic and social development was to reach the sum of 76,640 million yuan (equivalent to about U.S. $20,000 million at the time), something unheard of in China's long history.

Taking the economic structure of the Soviet Union as a model, the plan laid special emphasis on the development of heavy industry, for only with heavy industry, the planners then thought, could China hope to modernize its agriculture, transportation and communications, and strengthen its national defense, thus laying the material basis for a constantly developing socialist society. Investment in basic industries such as power plants, coal mines, iron and steel works, machine-building factories and major chemical plants constituted 88.8 percent of the total outlay for industrial capital construction in the five-year period.

Although credits from the Soviet Union were small (only 3 per cent of the total outlay), Soviet aid was invaluable in terms of machinery and equipment, advisers, blueprints and other technical information. Out of the 694 major projects planned, 156 were to be carried out with Soviet equipment and technicians (the number was increased to 211 in 1956).

Through the titanic efforts of the Chinese workers and technicians, a large number of major projects had been completed and put into operation by the end of 1957. Other friendly countries also agreed to help in the building of 27 projects. For the first time, China built airplanes, automobiles, tractors, heavy-duty and precision machine tools, as well as electrical, mining and railroad equipment. The achievements in heavy industry were spectacular indeed.

In the field of agriculture and consumer goods industries, however, the gains were less impressive. On the average, a yearly increase of 19.6 percent in industrial output value and 4.8 percent in agricultural output value between 1953 and 1956 was achieved. Taking into account the population increase of 60-75 million (2 percent per year) during the same period, the living standards of the people improved very little. However, the widespread starvation that had been prevalent in the past was eliminated, a remarkable achievement for a country with such a huge population.

Outstanding progress was also registered in the area of education. Many new schools were established in the interior of the country, and first priority was given to science and engineering in colleges and universities. The teaching of socialist philosophy and morality was introduced into all schools. The number of students in schools at all levels had increased tremendously by 1957. Thus, while the people's government was trying to lay the material basis for a new socialist society, it made great efforts to raise the cultural and educational level of the younger generation.

Impressive though were the achievements of the First Five-Year Plan, certain mistakes were made due to the blind copying of the Soviet model without due regard to China's own conditions. For instance, of the total state investment in capital construction, 58 percent went for industry and only 6.7 percent for agriculture, forestry and water conservation. As a result, the development of agriculture lagged far behind that of industry, creating a serious imbalance in the national economy. This was recognized by Mao Zedong in his talk "On the Ten Major Relationships" in April 1956. He said:

> The emphasis in our country's construction is on heavy industry. The production of the means of production must be given priority, that's settled. But it definitely does not follow that the production of the means of subsistence, especially grain, can be neglected. Without enough food and other daily necessities, it would be impossible to provide for the workers in the first place, and then what sense would it make to talk about developing heavy industry? Therefore, the relationship between heavy industry on the one hand and light industry and agriculture on the other must be properly handled.

In his opinion, a greater emphasis on agriculture would supply more grain to the people and more raw materials for light industry. This would yield more funds in the future to invest in heavy industry and, by ensuring the livelihood of the people, lay a more solid foundation for the development of heavy industry.

There were other shortcomings, too. In their attempt to reach or surpass the high production targets set in the plan, staff members and workers often paid little attention to the quality of their work. The centralized style of leadership from the top left little room for regional or local initiative in the building and running of a factory or mine. In spite of these shortcomings and mistakes, the First Five-Year Plan was carried out with great enthusiasm and tremendous success. The Chinese people began to see that industrialization was not something unattainable. With hard work and eagerness to learn the technical know-how, they believed that they could transform their ancient nation into a modernized socialist country within a relatively short time.

80. THE SOCIALIST TRANSFORMATION

The concept of a society whose members work together for the benefit of all is deeply rooted in Chinese political thought. In the ancient classic *Book of Rites* (*Li Ji*), Confucius eulogized an ideal society which he imagined had existed in remote antiquity. In that period, ". . . a public and common spirit ruled all under the sky. . . . A competent provision was secured for the aged till their death, employment for the able-bodied, and the means of growing up to the young. . . . Robbers, filchers and rebellious traitors did not show themselves, and hence the outer doors remained open, and were not shut. This was the period of what we call the Grand Union." (Translation by James Legge.)

Influenced by such ideals during their childhood, by the Russian Revolution in their youth and especially their study of Marxist theories in connection with their own experience and observation of exploitation by foreign imperialists and native capitalists, the Communist leaders were convinced that only socialism could save China. Immediately after the period of economic rehabilitation, therefore, they adopted in December 1952 the General Line for the Transition to Socialism, which called for the industrialization of the country as well as the gradual transformation to socialist ownership of agriculture, industry, commerce and handicrafts manufacture.

The government had in 1952 prepared the ground for socialist transformation by launching a movement among the national capitalists against bribery, tax evasion, theft of state property, shoddy work on government contracts, and theft of confidential economic information for speculative use. Among government cadres, the armed forces and people's organizations, it had carried out a campaign against corruption, waste and bureaucracy. The government had also initiated a movement to remold the intellectuals' way of thinking so as to encourage them to serve the people and help build China into a socialist country. The Communist Party, having now become a ruling party, warned its members against corruption and urged them to continue to serve the people wholeheartedly. All these measures gave everyone the feeling that a new day was indeed dawning in China.

The core of socialist transformation was to convert the private ownership of land, factories and commercial enterprises to socialist ownership. An outstanding feature of this process in China was that this profound change in the socio-economic structure was accomplished peacefully, step by step. Agricultural and industrial production rose steadily as the transformation progressed, and consequently the people's livelihood improved as well.

In agriculture, the peasants had become owners of their land as a result of the land reform. While this had freed them from paying rent to the landlords, they could hardly make a decent living with their tiny plots, which averaged less than one-seventh of a hectare per person (roughly one-third of an acre). Thus the peasants, with government encouragement and assistance, turned voluntarily to the collective path. Initially they formed mutual-aid teams, in which team members pooled manpower and tools, first during rush seasons and later on a year-round basis. Land, draft animals and farm implements continued to be owned by the individual households, and each retained the harvest from his own land. Regular accounts were kept, and after the harvest those who worked more were paid by those they had helped. This required unified management of land and led to the establishment of elementary or semi-socialist cooperatives.

The publication and mass study of the General Line of the Transitional Period in 1953 accelerated the formation of the semi-socialist agricultural producers' cooperatives in the countryside. Several mutual-aid teams combined together, each member continuing to own his land, draft animals and big farm tools but pooling them for common use. A part of the harvest was divided among the members in proportion to the means of production they had invested. The other part was divided according to the members' work; hence the name, semi-socialist. Soon a contradiction appeared over the division of income between the better-off peasants who had put in more land, tools or animals, and the poorer peasants who had fewer of these but contributed more labor.

Thus the demand rose for the cooperatives to become fully socialist. In this higher form, land became collective property. Draft animals and big farm implements were purchased on long terms from the members by the cooperative. With the establishment of these new agricultural cooperatives, the members were able to plan their farmwork more rationally, undertake the construction of sizeable irrigation works and other projects to improve their land, introduce better seeds and fertilizers and share scientific knowledge. All the income was distributed according to the number of work-days put in by each member. By the end of 1957, as many as 96 percent of the peasant households had joined these fully socialist or higher-type cooperatives.

In industry and commerce, the people's government bought out the national capitalists instead of expropriating their property, as had been done after the October Revolution in Russia. This was possible because members of this class, as patriots, had supported the anti-Japanese war and, unlike the bureaucratic capitalists (officials who had utilized their position to become monopolists), had been sympathetic with or remained neutral in the War of Liberation against the Kuomintang reactionaries. In addition, because of China's economic backwardness, it was wise for the people's government to utilize for a time private enterprises to produce goods needed by the people.

The transition to a socialist form of the capitalist sector of the economy began with the government purchasing the products of private industry. From 1950 on, it began to place orders for processing, while supplying the raw materials, and for the manufacture of goods under government contract. The high tide of socialist transformation in the countryside encouraged the capitalists to go a step further — to convert their private plants into state-private joint enterprises. Up to 1955 the changeover had been made enterprise by enterprise. But in the second half of 1955, it began to proceed by whole trades. In Beijing all formerly private industry became joint-owned in 1956. This was closely followed by Tianjin, Xi'an, Shanghai and other cities.

The same process of socialist transformation also took place in commerce and the handicrafts. Toward the end of 1957, practically all trade was handled by state-private concerns, and 90 percent of handicraftsmen had joined cooperatives.

What happened to the capitalists? Chen Shutong, Chairman of the All-China Federation of Industry and Commerce, said at the time: "The socialist transformation of capitalism does not only change enterprises. It also changes men." Because of their ability and experience, most capitalists became managers, engineers, heads of departments or members of the boards of directors of the state-private joint enterprises. Soon they took a step forward — from profit-sharing to receiving a fixed rate of interest on their investment. The enterprises then became entirely owned by the state, by the whole people.

Thus, while laying the foundation for industrialization with the First Five-Year Plan, the people's government undertook the gigantic task of transforming China's socio-economic structure. Private ownership of the means of production was changed to socialist ownership. In agriculture and handicrafts, this took the form of collective ownership of producers' cooperatives; and in industry and commerce, all enterprises gradually came under state ownership.

81.   THE GREAT LEAP FORWARD

The Great Leap Forward in 1958-1959 was a movement which aimed to transform China from a backward agricultural country into a modern, socialist, industrialized nation within the shortest possible time by mobilizing the energy and initiative of the masses. This policy, initiated by the Communist Party, fired the Chinese people with enthusiasm, but also brought on difficulties which required several years to overcome.

In September 1956, the Eighth National Congress of the Party decided that China's main task was to concentrate all efforts on economic development so as to meet the people's growing material and cultural needs. It adopted the principle of guarding against both conservatism and rash advance, that is, of making steady progress by striking an overall balance. In this spirit, Premier Zhou Enlai curtailed the investment for some capital construction projects which were causing a deficit in the national budget and shortage of materials. However, due to lack of experience in socialist construction and insufficient knowledge of the law of economic growth in China, as well as being smug with their successes and impatient for quick results, Mao Zedong and a number of other Party leaders believed that man's subjective will and efforts could achieve miracles. They thought that since they had defeated the powerful Kuomintang armies by mobilizing the masses, they could build socialism by simply using the same method.

In May 1958, the Party called on the people to "go all out, aim high, and achieve greater, faster, better and more economical results". "Overtake and surpass Britain within 15 years or less in the output of steel and other important products!" became a popular slogan. The 600 million Chinese people were out to reach in a couple of decades levels of production that had taken the advanced Western countries a century or more to attain. In view of China's economic and technological backwardness, this so-called Great Leap Forward was an ambitious endeavor indeed.

In the summer of 1958 several agricultural producers' cooperatives in northern Henan Province pooled their forces to undertake a large irrigation project. On an inspection tour to the province, Mao Zedong praised this new combination, calling it "larger in size and having a higher degree of public ownership" than the cooperatives. This widely-publicized approval led to the rapid spread of the people's communes. At an enlarged Political Bureau meeting of the Communist Party at Beidaihe that August, a resolution was adopted, calling for the formation of people's communes in the rural areas. Within less than two months, 98.2 percent of all farm households had come under this system. About 750,000 cooperatives were merged into 26,000 communes, each with 4,000 to 7,000 households.

With more land, more hands and more funds than the cooperatives had at their command, the communes initiated plans for the all-round development of farming, forestry, animal husbandry, fisheries and sideline production. In addition to boosting grain output, the communes established small industrial plants, schools and cultural centers, nurseries and kindergartens, community mess halls and laundry services. They also took charge of the militia, and became the basic units of government. Under the commune system, it was hoped that the difference between town and country, worker and peasant, and mental and manual labor would vanish fairly rapidly. Although the commune system was not yet the realization of communism, it was mistakenly meant to be a "golden bridge" toward communism.

In industry, very high targets were set in order to get quick results within a short time. Steel output, coal production and electric power were to virtually double between 1957 and 1958. As the demand for steel grew rapidly during this period, the Party issued the call for everybody to make steel. Peasants, students and office workers everywhere rushed to do so. Small blast furnaces and steel works were set up in towns and rural areas. Traveling by train or air at that time, one could see small iron and steel works dotting the landscape; the whole country seemed ablaze with flames of iron- and steel-making.

In this headlong rush, mistakes and shortcomings inevitably occurred. To reach the high targets, workers and peasants often worked to the point of exhaustion. Many local cadres made false reports of their harvests or industrial output, exaggerating achievements in order to win praise. In the people's communes the peasants, believing that communism was near at hand, ate their fill without worrying about tomorrow.

The excessive number of capital construction projects led to a shortage of materials for many factories, and the completion of some essential undertakings had thus to be postponed. Because each unit tried to leap ahead as far as possible without regard to supply, transportation or markets, serious imbalances arose in the national economy. The drive for steel, in particular, proved to be a waste of materials, money and manpower. The steel produced in the "backyard furnaces" by crude methods was of such poor quality that most of it had to be reworked to be of any use. In the end the state had to spend huge funds to make up for the loss.

At the Lushan conference of the Party Central Committee held in July-August 1959, Marshal Peng Dehuai, then Minister of National Defense, pointed out these errors in a letter to Chairman Mao Zedong. He counseled caution and slowing down the pace of socialist construction. When handing the letter out for discussion, Mao Zedong called it a "rightist attack on the Party". He accused Peng of being the "leader of an anti-Party clique", and removed him from his official post. This arbitrary decision did great harm to the democratic life in the Party and brought serious consequences in the future. Peng Dehuai lived in disgrace until his death in 1974 and was only posthumously exonerated in December 1978.

The Great Leap Forward could be considered a romantic period in China's socialist construction. The spirit of "daring to storm the heavens" and "creating a brave new world" permeated the air. Many gigantic projects that under ordinary circumstances would have taken years to finish were completed in a few months' time. Around Beijing, the Ming Tombs Reservoir dam was built with the joint labor of peasants, workers, armymen, students and government cadres in a few months before the advent of the 1958 rainy season. To celebrate the 10th anniversary of the founding of the People's Republic, citizens of Beijing built ten tremendous buildings, including the Great Hall of the People, home of the National People's Congress.

The total disregard of the laws of economics, however, brought on serious imbalances which actually retarded the development of the national economy, and calling any criticism of the errors and shortcomings "an attack from the enemy" inevitably prevented the growth of socialist democracy. One cannot but recall the old saying, "More haste, less speed."

82.   BUILDING SOCIALISM BY SELF-RELIANCE

In 1959-1961, China went through three difficult years brought about by three factors: (1) the worst natural disasters in a century, in which more than half of the cultivated land was hit by drought, floods or hailstorms; (2) economic dislocations caused by excessively high targets and headlong speed in the Great Leap Forward; and (3) the sudden withdrawal of Soviet experts and technical assistance because of ideological and political disagreements between the Chinese and Soviet leaders at the time. Many major projects were left unfinished, without the promised delivery of essential equipment or the blueprints and technical data with which the Chinese engineers and workers could have completed the projects themselves. Some plants had to be shut down because of the shortage of materials and component parts. Agricultural and industrial production sharply declined. The Chinese government had to purchase wheat from abroad for the city dwellers, which used up a third or more of China's total foreign exchange earnings. Even then, allotments of grain rations in the cities were lowered, resulting in widespread malnutrition. But as the leaders chose to share the same hardships and tightened their own belts, the people did not lose their confidence in the leadership of the Party. What a contrast with the Kuomintang officials who in the past amassed huge fortunes while people died of cold and hunger!

To overcome the difficulties, the people's government took steps to correct the "leftist" mistakes in the countryside by reorganizing the communes, abolishing the public canteens and forbidding the transfer of resources from one unit to another without compensation. A three-level system of organization was instituted in the people's communes, consisting of the commune, production brigade and production team at the most basic level — essentially a small village or part of a larger village. Each level had its own resources — draft animals, farm implements or other properties. While land still belonged to the collective, every member was to be paid according to the number of workpoints he or she had earned, with the production team instead of the commune as the basic accounting unit, that is, the level at which the individual's income was determined. To encourage individual initiative, each household was allotted a small private plot of land on which the members could grow their own vegetables and other crops. The members were also allowed to engage in such sidelines as pig- and chicken-raising and basket making, and to sell their products on the free market. Meanwhile, the government raised its purchase prices for grain and other farm produce.

Realizing that food for China's millions came first in importance, the people's government began to take concrete steps to readjust the national economy and implement the policy of "agriculture as the foundation and industry as the leading factor" in the national economy. Millions of people in the urban areas were sent to the countryside, where the labor power grew to over 212 million in 1962, surpassing the total in 1957. All branches of industry were encouraged to support agricultural production. As a result, agriculture gradually recovered, and by 1965 farm output had approached the highest level in history.

The government reduced the number of construction projects in heavy industry, acted to strengthen light industry, and began to promote the development of petroleum production. Outlays for capital construction were slashed between 1960 and 1962, the rate of accumulation for reinvestment was lowered radically, thus increasing the funds available for raising living standards, and steel production targets were lowered. Many heavy industrial plants were shut down, combined with other units or converted to light industrial use.

To increase industrial production, the government initiated a socialist emulation campaign among the workers. The spirit behind this campaign was to "compare with, learn from and catch up with the most advanced and help the less advanced". Technical innovations by individual workers were encouraged, while arrangements for technical exchange were made in the same plants as well as among different plants in cities like Shanghai, Shenyang, Harbin and others. As a result, industrial output increased in quantity and variety and improved in quality.

In 1964 China was able to satisfy more than 85 percent of its machinery needs as compared with 55 per cent in 1957, and 90 percent of its steel requirements. The following table shows briefly China's progress in industrial and agricultural production between 1957 (the end of the First Five-Year Plan) and 1965, the year before the "cultural revolution".

MAIN CATEGORIES OF INDUSTRIAL AND AGRICULTURAL OUTPUT*

(Unit: 1 million)

	1957	1965
Steel (tons)	5.35	12.23
Coal (tons)	131.00	232.00
Electricity (kwh)	19,300.00	67,600.00
Petroleum (tons)	1.46	11.31
Grain (tons)	195.05	194.55
Cotton (tons)	1.64	2.10
Cotton cloth (meters)	5,050.00	6,280.00

Some outstanding achievements during this period merit special mention. First, China became self-sufficient in oil and petroleum products in 1965. China had first discovered oil deposits around Daqing in the Northeast in 1959. Workers from the pre-existing oil fields of Yumen in the Northwest and other parts of China rallied immediately to exploit this new

---

* Figures from *Almanac of China's Economy*, Beijing, 1981.

find. By the end of 1963, China was making several hundred different oil products, including many high-grade ones that formerly had to be imported from abroad. By 1965 China was completely self-sufficient in oil.

Secondly, China exploded its first atom bomb in October 1964, followed by another in May 1965. As the Soviet Union had refused to supply a sample of the atom bomb and the requisite technical know-how, China decided to develop the atom bomb independently so as to break the superpowers' nuclear monopoly. Following the first test explosion, the Chinese government declared: "China will never at any time and under any circumstances be the first to use nuclear weapons."

Thirdly, toward the end of 1964 the Chinese government announced that it had repaid all debts to the Soviet Union — debts contracted largely during the Korean War in the early fifties.

Because of her sad experience first with the Western embargoes and then with the withdrawal of Soviet aid, China emphasizes self-reliance for her modernization although she seeks technology and capital from abroad. She also advocates that the Third World countries should cooperate among themselves but should avoid dependence on outside interests in their efforts to gain economic independence.

83. THE "CULTURAL REVOLUTION"

Many books and articles have been written, pro and con, about China's "great proletarian cultural revolution". Initiated by Mao Zedong to topple "capitalist-roaders" in the Party, the army and the government, and reactionary bourgeois authorities in control of the schools and cultural institutions, it aimed to build China into a genuinely socialist nation without bureaucracy, elitism or inequalities. This high purpose, though far from China's immediate task of strengthening its economic

foundation, gained wide support at the beginning. The mach-
inations of the Lin Biao and Jiang Qing cliques for their
selfish ambitions, however, turned the revolution into a factional power struggle in which countless people were unjustly
accused and mistreated and the building of socialism was often
disrupted. It has been regarded by most people of China,
including the Communist Party leadership, as a national calamity.

The "cultural revolution", which lasted over 10 years from
May 1966 to October 1976, may be divided into three stages:
(1) the launching and development of the revolution under the
direction of Mao Zedong, (2) progress of the revolution and
Lin Biao's plot to assassinate Mao Zedong, and (3) the rise and
fall of the Gang of Four.

1.   The first stage covered roughly three years, starting with
the "May 16 Circular" in 1966 which pointed out the necessity
for the "cultural revolution", and ending with the convening of
the Ninth National Congress of the Party in April 1969 which
named Lin Biao as Mao Zedong's successor.

The "May 16 Circular" maintained that Khrushchev-type re-
visionists had crept into leading positions in the Party and
government, and counter-revolutionary bourgeois intellectuals
were in control of education and culture and that it was right
to rebel and overthrow them all. To do so, the masses had
to be aroused to "expose our dark aspect openly, in an all-
round way and from below", said Mao Zedong. The "four
olds" — old ideas, old culture, old customs and old habits —
had to be destroyed, so that China could avoid back-sliding
into "revisionism", as had happened in the Soviet Union.
Bitter class struggle — the working class against the capitalist
and feudal forces — was to be the order of the day.

A Cultural Revolutionary Group composed of so-called "true
revolutionaries" was set up under the Political Bureau of the
Party. This group replaced the old collective leadership and
eventually became the headquarters that issued orders during
the "cultural revolution".

In their youthful enthusiasm, young rebels in the schools,

organized as Red Guards, plunged into the movement with determination. To smash the "four olds", they broke into the homes of old scholars and professors and raided their collections of books, paintings and valuable antiques. They stormed into ancient temples, smashing Buddhist statues, disfiguring sacred images, and ransacking libraries containing religious texts. The Red Guards sometimes dismantled and destroyed expensive instruments and apparatus, because they regarded scientific laboratories as the strongholds of "reactionary" professors.

Large posters became one of the chief weapons of debate and denunciation. In August 1966, Mao Zedong wrote his own big-character poster, entitled "Bombard the Headquarters". It was an attack against Liu Shaoqi, chairman of the People's Republic. To demonstrate his approval of the young rebels, that fall he reviewed from atop the rostrum of Tian An Men Square in Beijing a total of 13,000,000 Red Guards from all over the country. This started a nationwide movement to drag out the "capitalist-roaders" in the Party, kick aside the Party committees in order to "make revolution", and wipe out the "reactionary line" pursued by Liu Shaoqi and his followers.

In January 1967, the Shanghai rebels headed by Zhang Chunqiao and Wang Hongwen (who later became known as members of the Gang of Four) overturned the old Party leadership in the municipal government and set up a revolutionary committee in its place. Mao Zedong's approval of this action encouraged the rebels everywhere to "seize power" from the old leaders. By September 1968, after 20 months of tumultuous struggles in which the army supported the so-called leftist elements, "revolutionary committees" had been set up in all the provinces (except Taiwan), autonomous regions and major cities like Beijing, Shanghai and Tianjin.

In the scramble for power, disputes developed among the different rebel groups themselves. The Party Central Committee, in its decision on the "cultural revolution" in August 1966, had stipulated that "where there is a debate, it should be conducted by reasoning and not by force". Lin Biao (Defense Minister) and Jiang Qing (Mao Zedong's wife), who had assumed the leadership of the "cultural revolution", however, incited the Red Guards to "create bigger and bigger typhoons" and to resort to weapons if necessary. When a group of experienced veteran revolutionaries protested against the widespread disorder at a February 1967 meeting presided over by Premier Zhou Enlai, both Lin Biao and Jiang Qing branded their complaints as a "countercurrent" against the revolution. Many of the protesters were consequently removed from their positions of power.

To pave the way for their own seizure of power, Lin Biao and Jiang Qing initiated the Mao Zedong personality cult and portrayed themselves as his closest comrades-in-arms. They waved the "Little Red Book" of quotations from his works and proclaimed him to be the greatest genius of the last 2,000 years. Liu Shaoqi, on the other hand, was accused of being "a renegade, traitor and scab" and expelled "forever" from the Party at a Party Central Committee meeting in October 1968.

The Ninth National Congress of the Party was held in April 1969. Lin Biao was named Mao Zedong's successor, and this was even written into a revised Party constitution. At the same congress, Jiang Qing's associates from Shanghai — Zhang Chunqiao, Wang Hongwen and Yao Wenyuan, the three other members of the Gang of Four — were promoted to membership in the Political Bureau of the Central Committee of the Party. Old political leaders were pushed aside but the ultraleftist, self-styled "revolutionaries" gained more power with Mao Zedong's blessing.

2. The second stage — progress of the revolution and Lin Biao's plot to assassinate Mao Zedong and its failure — covered the period from May 1969 to August 1973, the interval between the ninth and tenth congresses of the Party.

To consolidate the "gains" of the "cultural revolution" so that the dictatorship of the proletariat could be strengthened in every factory, village, organization and school, Mao Zedong tried to carry through the policy of "struggle, criticism and transformation" initiated at the beginning of the "cultural revolution". A series of movements were launched, among which were the following:

Party consolidation and rebuilding. Party congresses at all levels were held and new Party committees elected. In this movement, the so-called "renegades, enemy agents and incorrigible capitalist-roaders" were purged while well-known rebel leaders, regarded as "fresh blood", were admitted into the Party. This created serious problems for the Party organization.

Revolutionary criticism. The main target was Liu Shaoqi's book *How to Be a Good Communist* and his "counter-revolutionary revisionist line". Instead of helping the people to gain a more correct understanding of scientific socialism, this movement promoted extreme leftist ideas and created confusion in the minds of many.

Purifying the class ranks. While this movement dealt heavy blows to some undesirable and criminal elements, countless honest supporters of the new government fell victim to false charges and unjust accusations. Great numbers of cadres were mistreated in "cattle pens" (places of confinement set up by rebels to question supposedly "counter-revolutionaries" in their own organization) and thousands were held incommunicado for years for interrogation.

Workers in superstructure positions. Workers' Propaganda Teams entered schools and cultural organizations in July 1968. These teams, totally inexperienced in this kind of work, were to remain in control of these institutions.

Retraining cadres. Cadres were sent to "May 7 Schools" in the countryside to be re-educated by poor peasants through manual labor.

Educational reform. Instead of the old system of entrance examinations, workers, peasants and soldiers sponsored by the local leadership were admitted to the schools, not only to study, but also to control and transform them. The quality of teaching deteriorated greatly.

As these measures reflected the ultra-leftist line, they tended to strengthen the position of Lin Biao, Jiang Qing and other vociferous "revolutionaries".

In March-April 1970 a work session of the Party Central Committee was held to discuss the calling of the Fourth National People's Congress and revision of the Constitution. Dreaming of becoming the president of the republic, on April 11 Lin Biao suddenly proposed that China should have a head of state and Mao Zedong should be elected to that high position. The very next day Mao Zedong rejected his proposal, saying "I will never again do such a thing." Lin Biao, however, would not give up the idea. At a Central Committee meeting of the Party in August that year, Lin Biao repeated his proposal. This time he stated that as Mao Zedong was the genius of our time, he should be made head of state by law. An article on "genius" prepared beforehand by Chen Boda, a leader of the Cutural Revolutionary Group and follower of Lin Biao, was distributed among the members, which created great confusion at the meeting. Seeing through the fraud, Mao Zedong had all discussions of Lin Biao's speech stopped immediately. After the meeting, the Central Committee declared that Chen Boda was under examination. Lin Biao and his followers were dealt a heavy blow.

In despair of ever climbing to top position through peaceful means, Lin Biao, together with his wife and son, decided to resort to military action. Documents discovered later revealed that in October 1970 his son, Lin Liguo, had organized his cohorts into a "Joint Fleet". The following February Lin Liguo was sent to Shanghai to meet with leading members of the "Joint Fleet" and work out a plan for an armed uprising, which they termed "Project 571" (the number 571 has the same pronunciation as "armed uprising" in the Chinese language). Its aim was to seize control of the whole country, or at least to set up a separate government in opposition to the central authority, through an armed uprising, including bombings, assassinations and abductions. Toward the end of March 1971, headquarters personnel was decided upon at a meeting of his chief supporters from Nanjing, Shanghai and Hangzhou (all cities in the lower Changjiang region).

Mao Zedong went on an inspection tour of central and east China in August and September 1971. Wherever he went, he told the local political and military leaders that someone was anxious to be head of state and would not hesitate to split the Party. Receiving this information from his agents, Lin Biao decided to stake all on a single venture — the assassination of Mao Zedong on his journey. The order for this dastardly attempt was given to his cohorts on September 8. Arriving by train at the Shanghai station, Mao Zedong perceived something strange was taking place. Abruptly he ordered the train to pull out and he returned to Beijing on September 12 without advance notice.

Having failed in his plot, Lin Biao commandeered a Trident airplane to Shanhaiguan at the Great Wall near where he was resting. He tried to flee south and set up a separate government in Guangzhou. But Zhou Enlai ordered the airplane to return to Beijing immediately. Under the circumstances, Lin Biao with his wife and son and a few other supporters ran to the plane before daybreak on September 13 and forced the pilot to fly north to seek refuge in the Soviet Union. In the afternoon the plane crashed at Undur Khan in the People's Republic of Mongolia. The sudden death of Lin Biao was a shock to the nation, particularly to those young rebels who had followed his every word in the "cultural revolution".

Mao Zedong then turned to Zhou Enlai to take charge of national affairs. Politically, many veteran revolutionaries accused of being "capitalist-roaders" were rehabilitated, and Deng Xiaoping returned to his position as Vice-Premier. Economically, an overall plan for the nation was worked out by the State Planning Commission, and the principle "to each according to his work", once condemned as "bourgeois right", was re-affirmed. These and other measures helped the recovery and development of agriculture and industry. In the field of education and culture, students were urged to be "Red and expert", and the importance of basic scientific research was emphasized.   In international relations, in October 1971 China regained her legitimate seat in the United Nations by an over-whelming majority in the General Assembly.   The United States decided to withdraw from the long drawn-out war in Viet Nam, a war fought to stop "Chinese expansionism" as openly stated earlier by Secretary of State Dean Rusk.   In February 1972 President Richard Nixon visited China.   The Shanghai Joint Communique that resulted from the visit paved the way to the normalization of relations between the People's Republic of China and the United States.   Chaos seemed to be replaced by orderly progress in China's political and social life.

The Tenth National Congress of the Communist Party was held in Beijing in August 1973.   In his political report, Zhou Enlai condemned the double-faced behavior of the Lin Biao clique.   The congress, however, continued to follow the ultra-leftist political line adopted at the Ninth Congress.   Jiang Qing and her Shanghai associates began to form the Gang of Four in the Political Bureau of the Party.

3.   The third stage lasted from the conclusion of the Tenth Party Congress on August 1973 to the downfall of the Gang of Four in October 1976.   In this period, Jiang Qing and her associates attempted repeatedly to grasp the supreme political power for themselves, but failed.

In 1972 Zhou Enlai proposed the need to criticize the ultra-leftist ideas and anarchism promoted by the Lin Biao clique. Fearing that this might lead to condemnation of their own ideas and actions, Jiang Qing and her gang objected.   Mao Zedong, too, thought the main danger was a swing to the extreme right. In a talk in July 1973, he maintained that Lin Biao, like the Kuomintang reactionaries, was attempting to revive the most conservative tenets of the long outdated worship of Confucius, an ancient Chinese philosopher who had upheld the outworn slave system of his time.   In January 1974, Mao approved the booklet *Lin Biao and the Doctrines of Confucius and Mencius,* compiled under the direction of Jiang Qing.   A movement to criticize Lin Biao and Confucius was thus unfolded throughout the country.

Under Jiang Qing's manipulations, the target of attack was soon shifted from Lin Biao to Premier Zhou Enlai. In letters to government leaders and articles in newspapers, Jiang Qing and company insinuated that Zhou was the "greatest Confucianist" of our time and should be replaced. Meanwhile, by extolling ancient empresses in Chinese history, they attempted to pave the way for Jiang Qing's ascension to the "throne".

In October 1974 Jiang Qing sent Wang Hongwen to see Mao Zedong in an attempt to oust Zhou Enlai from the premiership. Having confidence in Zhou's ability to run the government, Mao rebuked Wang to his face. Later, when Jiang Qing wrote to Mao Zedong on the same subject, Mao Zedong remarked, "It's not for you to form a cabinet," meaning that she should not try to be a big political boss.

The Fourth National People's Congress was held in Beijing in January 1975. Zhou Enlai in his report reiterated the proposition that China should modernize its agriculture, industry, national defense, science and technology by the end of the century so as to move its economy toward the front ranks of the world. Zhou was re-elected Premier despite Jiang Qing's intrigue to oust him. But more of her followers gained leading positions in the government, laying the ground for future troubles.

Zhou Enlai fell ill after the congress and Deng Xiaoping, as Vice-Premier, took over the government functions. Under his direction, many economic, cultural as well as political and military organizations were overhauled and consolidated. Unwilling to take their defeat lying down, the Gang of Four struck back by clamoring against the so-called "bourgeois rights" (referring to such principles as "to each according to his work") and the "danger of empiricism" (referring to experienced veteran leaders). Mao Zedong perceived that Jiang Qing and her gang were incurring widespread resentment. In May 1975 he admonished them to "practice Marxism, unite with others and be open and aboveboard". He also told them not to form a "gang of four".

Jiang Qing and her associates, however, were determined to remove Deng Xiaoping, an obstacle to their seizure of power. They reported to Mao Zedong that Deng Xiaoping was negating the achievements of the "cultural revolution" and was trying to restore the old order. Mao Zedong thereupon started a movement to "beat back the right deviationist attempt to reverse the correct verdicts of the 'cultural revolution'". Deng Xiaoping was denounced by name and confusion was created once again throughout the country.

On January 8, 1976, Premier Zhou Enlai died of cancer. Loved and respected by all the people, his death was mourned by the whole nation. At the beginning of April on the traditional day for sweeping their ancestors' tombs, thousands of Beijing citizens flocked to Tian An Men Square to lay wreaths in memory of the late Premier. Some of the slogans and poems were directed against the evil doings of the Gang of Four. Greatly incensed, the gang branded this mass demonstration a "counter-revolutionary action" and alleged that Deng Xiaoping was its chief instigator and removed him from all his positions.

On July 28 a violent earthquake rocked the Tangshan and Tianjin area in north China, causing heavy damage to life and property. The government rushed men and materials to save the victims. The power-hungry Gang of Four, however, termed this aid a "distraction from the main task of criticizing Deng Xiaoping".

On September 9, 1976, Mao Zedong, the long recognized leader of the Chinese people, passed away, and the whole nation grieved. Regarding the days of national mourning as a golden opportunity, the Gang of Four stepped up their intrigues to seize power for themselves. Usurping the name of "Office of the Central Committee of the Party", they ordered all authorities in the provinces, autonomous regions as well as major municipalities to report to them. They prompted many people to write "letters of loyalty" and "appeals" to Jiang Qing for her to take over the highest power in the land. They secretly distributed large quantities of arms to the Shanghai people's militia units considered to be under their control in preparation for an armed uprising.

At this critical moment, the Political Bureau of the Party took swift action. On the night of October 6, 1976, the Gang of Four were arrested and put in jail, ending an era of turbulence, destruction and persecution. People throughout the country flocked into the streets and sang and danced with jubilation.

Thanks to the enthusiasm of the masses of the people, China's agriculture and industry developed during the "cultural revolution" in spite of leftist disturbances. The peasants went on as usual, earning workpoints in the fields. Grain output increased from 194 million tons in 1965 to 284 million tons in 1975. During the same period, steel production rose from 12.2 to 23.9 million tons, coal from 232 to 482 million tons, electricity from 67,600 to 195,000 million kwh, and crude oil from 11.3 to 77 million tons. (All figures taken from *Almanac of China's Economy*, Beijing, 1981.) Over 4,100 kilometers of rail lines were built across difficult terrain, linking the heartland with frontier regions. The completion of the Changjiang Bridge at Nanjing facilitated transportation between north and south China. At the same time, the successful development of the hydrogen bomb increased China's defense capability, and the launching and recovery of satellites marked China's advance in the field of space research.

Impressive though these achievements were, many people are of the opinion that China would have made much greater progress without the upheavals of the "cultural revolution", which in many ways hampered the development of national economy. In the fields of education, art and literature, had the policy "let a hundred flowers blossom and a hundred schools of thought contend" been adhered to, China would have won many new achievements in these fields as well.

84. LESSONS OF THE "CULTURAL REVOLUTION"

The fall of the Gang of Four was a great victory for the people of China. Hopes ran high that the removal of these conspirators who had masqueraded as "true revolutionaries" would usher in an era of peaceful reconstruction. After many discussions among the leadership as well as among the general masses, there were unanimous views on the reasons for the mistakes in the "cultural revolution" and ways to prevent a recurrence of such a large-scale turmoil. Here are some of the conclusions drawn:

1. Ideologically, the "cultural revolution" was not simply a chance occurrence, but came as a result of leftist misapplication for many years of Marxist ideas of class struggle divorced from the realities of Chinese life. In fact, during the high tide of the socialist transformation of agriculture, private industry and commerce in 1956, the Party had decided to shift the emphasis of its work to the modernization of the Chinese economy. But during the Party rectification campaign in the summer of 1957, a few individuals viciously attacked the Party leadership and socialism. To make a counter-attack was necessary. However, in the "anti-rightist" campaign thus launched the strength and number of enemies were overestimated. Thousands of well-meaning critics of the shortcomings in Party work were also branded as "enemies of the people". The scope of class struggle was steadily broadened until it became the primary task under the socialist system instead of the modernization of Chinese economy. "Class struggle is the key link," Mao Zedong was to insist, "and once you grasp it, you can solve every problem." This separation of theory from reality created constant social tension and disunity and diverted China from the path of peaceful socialist construction.

2. In terms of practical politics, this overemphasis on class struggle under socialism inevitably led to a "leftist" political line. The anti-rightist campaign in 1957 practically killed the

Party's policy of "letting a hundred flowers blossom and a hundred schools of thought contend", a policy aimed to promote the development of arts and sciences in China. At the Lushan conference of the Party Central Committee in 1959, Mao Zedong mistook Marshal Peng Dehuai's correct criticism of the shortcomings of the Great Leap Forward for an act of bitter class struggle. In the course of the Socialist Education Movement in the early 1960s, Mao Zedong began to suspect many honest and hard-working cadres to be "capitalist-roaders" within the Party. He began to view Liu Shaoqi as the leader of a "bourgeois headquarters" seeking the restoration of capitalism in China. Many intellectuals were accused of being "reactionaries" controlling the schools and cultural life of the people. The "cultural revolution" was then launched in the name of combating "revisionism", a term which few truly understood. This gave the Lin Biao and Jiang Qing cliques the opportunity to stir up turmoil in the land, through which they hoped to realize their ambitions to grasp political power.

3. Organizationally, the creation of the "Cultural Revolutionary Group" eventually destroyed the collective leadership of the Party. It enabled careerists, conspirators and opportunists of all sorts to climb into high and even key positions. Pretending to be "true revolutionaries", the Lin Biao and Jiang Qing cliques raised the slogan "Kick aside the Party committee to make revolution". Inexperienced revolutionary youths in many cities were misled by these fiery words. They began to storm Party headquarters and set up "revolutionary committees" of their own. In this scramble for power, factional strifes inevitably developed, and chaos spread throughout the country. The principle of democratic centralism — democracy under the guidance of a time-tested central leadership — was completely forgotten.

4. The "ultra-leftist" political line also helped usher in the wrong methods used in the "cultural revolution". The socialist system is quite new in China. Owing to China's centuries-old feudal history, the remnants of old ideas and habits remain

strong in many places even today. Some veteran revolutionaries, now officials in the government, have become bureaucratic in style or even corrupt. Enemies of socialism and foreign agents do exist, and they try by every means to undermine the new order. However, these weaknesses of the new society must be overcome by strengthening Party discipline and developing socialist democracy and legality. Party members must be taught to hold on to the Yan'an tradition — wholehearted service to the people instead of seeking personal interests and privileges. Everybody should be equal before the law. A person, no matter how high he is in the government or Party, must obey the Constitution and laws of the land. During the "cultural revolution", however, the overthrow of all old-time leaders, good or bad, was advocated by the Lin Biao and Jiang Qing cliques. They also called for a "complete dictatorship" over all intellectuals and put forth the fallacy that "the more learning one possesses, the more reactionary one becomes". They incited their factions to fight with every weapon at their disposal, resulting in many injuries and deaths and destruction of property. This lawlessness weakened socialism instead of strengthening and consolidating it.

After the fall of the Gang of Four, the Party's leaders came to see that they had to heal the wounds of the "cultural revolution" before the confidence and support of the people could be regained. All cases were reexamined; those persons previously persecuted were exonerated or rehabilitated, and compensation was made for their financial losses. Tens of thousands of people who had been humiliated for being "counter-revolutionaries" or "foreign agents" began to be regarded again as honest and loyal citizens. Intellectuals were now recognized as part of the working class. On the other hand, the ringleaders of the Lin Biao and Jiang Qing cliques and the Gang of Four themselves were publicly tried and duly punished for their criminal acts, to the relief and joy of millions.

The leaders also agreed that although Mao Zedong had personally launched the "cultural revolution", they could not lay all the blame for its aberrations on him alone. Since socialism was entirely new to China, many veteran revolutionaries lacked the knowledge or experience necessary to manage this new system. In spite of Mao Zedong's misjudgments and errors in his later years, his contributions to the victory of the Chinese revolution far outweighed his shortcomings. Mao Zedong Thought was not a merely personal product but rather the collective wisdom of countless revolutionaries and their leaders, among whom he was the most outstanding. As the integration of Marxist theories with concrete Chinese conditions, it remains to this day the guide to China's future development.

The havoc wrought by the "cultural revolution" brought home to the leaders that the correct road for China's advance had been pointed out over 20 years before — the modernization of agriculture, industry, national defense, science and technology. Today the leadership agrees that these "four modernizations" should once again become the main task of the people, a new Long March that will take decades to reach its goal.

85. POST-1978 ECONOMIC CHANGES

"At present, the four modernizations constitute the pivot of our political life," declared Ye Jianying, Chairman of the Standing Committee of the National People's Congress, at the celebration of the 30th anniversary of the People's Republic on October 1, 1979. Since the national economy suffered great imbalance during the "cultural revolution", the first battle was to plan and begin implementing a series of economic readjustments and reforms. Meanwhile, to raise the living standards of the people, it was necessary to improve family planning so as to reduce the natural rate of population growth. The Third Plenary Session of the 11th Central Committee held in December 1978 was a new turning point in the history of the Chinese Communist Party. The basic policies worked out at the meeting heralded a number of important changes in national construction.

A. Agriculture

To provide food for China's huge population with the limited available arable land is a gigantic task. Although agriculture had been recognized as the foundation of the Chinese economy as early as 1957, this idea was never fully carried out, as the emphasis continued to be the development of heavy industry. Therefore, the government decided that its first task was to accelerate the development of agriculture by mobilizing the peasants' initiative. While land ownership remains collective, the socialist principle "to each according to his work" is being implemented by the introduction of a responsibility system under which individual households contract to produce certain quotas on assigned sections of land, with the right to keep everything over the quota. This system is also being bettered and instituted in forestry, animal husbandry, fish raising and sideline production. Payment is always linked to output. Since 1978, the small private plots have been restored, on which each family can grow its own vegetables and other crops, and the free markets reopened. The prices of farm machines, chemical fertilizers and insecticides have been lowered, while the state's purchasing prices of grain and other farm products have been raised. These measures have increased the peasants' income and heightened their interest in better farming techniques.

In the past, because of the overemphasis on grain production, forests and pasture lands were sometimes destroyed in an attempt to convert them into grain fields. Now this practice is being replaced by a well-rounded development of farming, forestry, animal husbandry, fisheries and sideline occupations compatible with local conditions. This diversification is helping to convert the traditional subsistence economy of China's rural areas into a more modern and specialized one which can serve both local and national needs.

Climatic and soil conditions are now being taken into consideration. In the Inner Mongolia Autonomous Region, for instance, the acreage for grain crops has been reduced, while that for sugar beets and oil-bearing crops has been increased. Fields totally unsuited for grain crops are being reconverted into forests and pastures, with good results.   On Hainan Island in the far south, the planting of rubber trees and coffee shrubs in place of grain crops has brought prosperity to the inhabitants in recent years.

The people's communes are being changed to purely economic units, rather than also serving as the local units of government.   This separation of political from economic functions enables the commune leaders to devote all their time and energies to promoting production.   Various forms of cooperation between scientists and peasants are also being encouraged to increase agricultural output.

The above measures have already achieved remarkable results.   The annual growth rate of agricultural output averaged 5.6 percent between 1979 and 1981, up from only 2.9 percent in the 20 years between 1958 and 1978. It is hoped that as the peasants become more prosperous, they will be able to buy farm machines on a cooperative basis and thus advance along the socialist road of agricultural mechanization on a sounder basis than before.

B. Industry

In the past, China went after rapid development of production and large-scale capital construction in a blind fashion, particularly in heavy industry.   Between 1958 and 1978, the annual growth rate of industrial output averaged over 10 percent, and capital construction funds accounted for 30 percent or more of national income.   As a result of this one-sided emphasis on growth, raising the people's living standards was not always given proper attention.   Starting in 1978, the government began to slow down the growth rate of heavy industry from 13.5 percent in 1978 to 8 percent in 1979, and then again to 6 percent in 1980.   During the same period, expenditures for capital construction were likewise reduced.   More emphasis was placed on the development of agriculture and light industry.

Meanwhile, the income of workers and cadres was raised through wage increases and bonuses of various kinds. Higher purchasing prices were set for farm products. These, combined with other factors, resulted in a deficit in the national budget, which the government is now trying to correct.

After a series of readjustments and reforms, the ratio of output values among agriculture, light industry and heavy industry in 1983 improved greatly as compared with previous years. This is shown in the following table:

OUTPUT VALUES AS PROPORTION OF NATIONAL PRODUCTION*

	Agriculture	Light Industry	Heavy Industry
1960	21.8	26.1	52.1
1965	37.3	32.3	30.4
1978	27.8	31.1	41.1
1980	30.0	32.9	37.1
1983	34.0	32.1	33.9

The situation in 1960 was extremely lopsided, with heavy industry predominant in the national economy. After a few years of readjustment, the situation had improved greatly by 1965. This more balanced development was disrupted by the ten years of the "cultural revolution", and the situation in 1978 had again become lopsided in favor of heavy industry. The adjustments made after 1978 improved the picture considerably. By 1983, a much better balance had been brought about among the three sectors.

C. Foreign Ties

During the "cultural revolution", the Lin Biao and Jiang Qing cliques deprecated foreign culture, science and technology; China entered a period of "splendid isolation". The present leadership saw the errors in this nearsighted mentality. They realized that China has much to gain by opening its doors to scientific knowledge, technological equipment and capital

---

* Figures from *Almanac of China's Economy*, Beijing, 1982.

investment from abroad. Since 1979 the government has passed laws and regulations concerning joint enterprises between Chinese and foreign capital, has established special economic zones where foreign investors enjoy certain advantages, and has begun joint prospecting and exploitation of offshore oil resources. These measures have attracted capital investment from overseas Chinese and foreign businessmen, thus increasing cooperation between China and foreign countries. This open policy toward the outside world, together with the basic principle of self-reliance, has helped China complete some major industrial projects, balance international receipts and payments, facilitate technical and managerial reforms in a number of industries and accelerate economic development.

Looking at the economic picture as a whole, it is clear that the Chinese economy is stronger and more vital than ever before. Although standards of living are still low, the general feeling among the people is that, after so many years of trial and error, they are now headed in the right direction and can look forward to a more abundant and decent life in the future.

D. The Year 2000

The goal of modernization by the end of the century, as outlined by General Secretary Hu Yaobang at the 12th Congress of the Communist Party in September 1982, is to "quadruple the gross annual value of industrial and agricultural products in the year 2000". Real personal income will rise proportionally. To reach this target, the plans envisage two major stages: (1) the laying of a solid foundation during the 1980s, and (2) a period of vigorous economic expansion in which the growth rate should reach 8 percent or more per year during the 1990s. The tasks in the first stage are to strengthen agriculture, energy resources, transport and communications, to reorganize industries and increase labor efficiency, and to raise the levels of science, technology and education. Only on this solid foundation can China hope to reach the rapid rate of growth expected in the second stage. An important component of these plans is reduction of the population growth rate to keep China's population within 1,200 million by the end of the century.

86.   FOREIGN FRIENDS OF THE CHINESE REVOLUTION

"We have friends all over the world." This assertion of Mao Zedong on the eve of the founding of the People's Republic was true then and remains true today.

As early as 1850 Karl Marx predicted that "when our European reactionaries in their flight to Asia . . . come at length to the Great Wall of China, to the gates which lead to the stronghold of arch-conservatism, who knows if they will not find there the inscription: 'République Chinoise, Liberté, Egalité, Fraternité' ". Lenin had great respect for Dr. Sun Yat-sen and sent representatives offering advice and aid in his revolutionary activities.   Thanks to Stalin and the Communist International, the first Kuomintang-Communist united front was formed, which led to the revolutionary upsurge of 1925-1927.

During the anti-Japanese war, aside from Russian flyers and military advisers who helped defend Chinese territory, Communist leaders from Japan, Korea and Viet Nam went to Yan'an and helped the Eighth Route Army in the war against Japan.   They linked the victory of the Chinese people's resistance to Japanese aggression and the defeat of the axis powers in World War II with the fate of their own country and of mankind.   So numerous were the friends who contributed generously of their time, money, energies and even lives to the cause of the Chinese revolution that it is impossible to mention them all.

However, some are particularly well-known among the Chinese people.

Foremost is **Dr. Norman Bethune** (1890-1939), a skilled Canadian surgeon who organized frontline medical services for the Eighth Route Army and who died at his post in a mountain village in north China.   After serving in Spain, providing medical aid to the Spanish Republicans fighting the German- and Italian-backed fascists, Bethune arrived in China at the beginning of 1938. He went to the Communist headquarters at Yan'an and devoted himself to organizing medical field units and training young medical workers, besides treating patients day and night.

In October 1939, he cut his finger while performing an emergency operation under enemy fire. Because of Chiang Kai-shek's blockade of the Border Region, sulfa-drugs were unavailable. Before his death of blood poisoning, he said to his Chinese comrades, "The last two years have been the most significant, the most meaningful years of my life."

He died on November 12, 1939. Filled with grief, Mao Ze-dong in an article in memory of Bethune called on the Chinese people to learn from his absolute selflessness and international-ist spirit. His tomb and the International Peace Hospital he founded have been moved to Shijiazhuang, capital of Hebei Province in north China. His name has become a household word in China.

Dr. Dwarkanath Kotnis (1910-1942) came to China in September 1938 as one of five members of an Indian Medical Mission sent by the Indian National Congress. (The other members were Drs. M. Atal, Cholkar, Basu and Mukherjee.) Knowing from childhood the sufferings of the Indian people under British colonial rule, Kotnis was extremely sympathetic to the Chinese people's resistance to Japanese imperialist aggression. He was inspired by the idea that the people of the two great countries of China and India should work like brothers in their struggle for national independence.

In his four years in China he worked ceaselessly under extremely difficult conditions in the north China guerrilla areas. Dr. Kotnis worked hard to train Chinese students and became the first director of the Bethune International Peace Hospital. Aside from heavy administrative duties, he performed hundreds of operations in a year. In 1942 the Japanese invaders extended their "mopping up" operations to the mountain areas of western Hebei Province, where the hospital and the medical school were situated. Dr. Kotnis led his colleagues and students in playing "hide and seek" with the enemy, moving the hospital with the patients at night. He gave lectures in the open air to his students during respites in the enemy bombing attacks. There was an acute shortage of salt, cooking oil and grain — the bare necessities of life — due to the enemy's "scorched earth" policy. Undernourished and overworked, Dr. Kotnis was advised to leave the front to rest. But like Dr. Bethune before him, he refused to leave his post. Finally, on December 9, 1942, he died of malnutrition and exhaustion, leaving his young Chinese wife and an infant son who symbolized the bond of friendship between the peoples of China and India.

Agnes Smedley (1892-1950) came to Shanghai in 1929 as the correspondent of the *Frankfurter Zeitung* of Germany. Born into a poor family in the state of Missouri in the United States, she had suffered privations and hardships from childhood and had to struggle to get an education. She had been arrested and imprisoned in New York for her close involvement with the Indian nationalist movement. While in Berlin in the 1920s, she had met Nehru, the future Prime Minister of India, and also became close to many members of the German left-wing movement.

As soon as she landed in Shanghai, then the largest treaty port in China, she was struck by the incredible sufferings of the Chinese workers. She wrote a series of powerful reports which were later collected in her book, *Chinese Destinies*. She became a friend of the great Chinese writer Lu Xun and worked with Soong Ching Ling in the League for Civil Rights. She took part in many revolutionary activities in the face of the Kuomintang White terror.

When the anti-Japanese war began in 1937, Smedley went to the Communist-controlled Border Region in the Northwest. There she had long interviews with Zhu De, Commander-in-Chief of the Eighth Route Army. These talks are recorded in her last book, *The Great Road*, a biography of Zhu De published in 1956 after her death.

Because of ill health, she left the New Fourth Army and returned to the United States. There she completed her books on wartime China. In February 1949, she was suddenly called a Soviet spy by General Douglas MacArthur's headquarters. She went to Britain with the intention of returning to the new China. She died after surgery for stomach ulcers in London on May 6, 1950. According to the wishes expressed in her will, she is buried in the Revolutionary Cemetery outside Beijing.

Edgar Snow (1906-1972) is best known for his 1938 book *Red Star over China* — a masterpiece of truthful reporting on the Communist Border Region blockaded by the Kuomintang. It opened the eyes of millions of readers in China and abroad who had previously regarded the Communists as "Red bandits", as they were called by the Kuomintang.

When Snow arrived in Shanghai in 1928 as an adventurous young man, he intended to stay only six weeks in China. Instead he stayed 13 years. While teaching at Yanjing University, established by American missionaries, he studied the Chinese language, befriended the Chinese students and joined in their patriotic demonstrations. He translated Lu Xun's biting short stories into English. When the Communists had completed the Long March and set up their new base in northern Shaanxi, he had the courage to go there and find out the truth about the revolution. Through long interviews with Mao Zedong and contacts with other Communist leaders and ordinary people, he learned much about China's past, present and future. After the Japanese imperialists launched their all-out invasion of China in 1937, he became a co-sponsor with Rewi Alley, from New Zealand, of the Chinese Industrial Cooperatives (Indusco, or "Gung Ho", the "Work-Together Movement") which set up many small workshops to enable the Chinese people to carry on the war against Japan economically. He also helped Soong Ching Ling start the China Defense League in Hongkong, which told the world about the Chinese people's struggles and collected medical aid for the Eighth Route Army and guerrilla fighters behind Japanese lines. He regarded as his life work the promotion of the understanding and friendship between the Chinese and American peoples.

After the founding of the People's Republic, Snow returned to China on three visits, in 1960, 1964 and 1970. In his book, *The Other Side of the River* (New York, 1961), he faithfully recorded the great changes brought about by the Chinese people in all the areas he had visited so long ago. Before he died in Switzerland, he had written: "I love China. I should like part of me to stay there after death as it always did during life." Today part of his ashes are buried on a beautiful hillside of the Peking University campus.

Anna Louise Strong (1885-1970) first came to China in 1925 when a revolutionary upsurge was sweeping south China under the leadership of the first Kuomintang-Communist united front. She sympathetically reported on the great Hongkong strike against British imperialism. When she went to the rural areas of Hunan Province in 1927, she predicted: "It will be such peasants and workers who will have the courage to carry their country out of the feudal ages into the modern world." She became an enthusiastic supporter of the Chinese revolution to the end of her life.

During the Chinese people's war of resistance against Japanese aggression from 1937 to 1945, she paid two visits to China. She reported the battles waged against the Japanese invaders by the people's forces under the leadership of the Communist Party and exposed the crimes of the Kuomintang in opposing the Communists and sabotaging the anti-Japanese war. In 1946 she flew to China for the fifth time and visited Yan'an and other liberated areas. It was during this visit that Mao Zedong, in an interview, made his famous statement, "All reactionaries are paper tigers."

In 1958, after overcoming many obstacles, she came to China for the sixth time at the age of 72 and made Beijing her home. In her regular reports, *Letter from China*, she told her readers throughout the world about China's achievements in socialist revolution and construction. Enthusiastically she reported on the people's communes and acclaimed the emancipation of the Tibetan serfs.

She died in 1970 at the age of 84, and like Agnes Smedley, she is buried in the Revolutionary Cemetery outside Beijing.

Rewi Alley (born in 1897) is a New Zealander who fought in World War I in France. In April 1927, he arrived in Shanghai right after Chiang Kai-shek had betrayed the Chinese revolution. As chief factory inspector in the International Settlement, he saw the miserable conditions of the Chinese workers. With his strong sense of justice, he became sympathetic to the Chinese people and increasingly indignant at the Kuomintang reactionaries.

In 1929, he traveled to Inner Mongolia as chief technical adviser on famine relief. The refugees, including women and children, were dying by the thousands on the roadside. He wrote: "One can see horrors enough in one day in this place to last a lifetime." In 1931-1932, he was director of dike repair work at Hankou after a disastrous flood of the Changjiang River. While the streets were full of refugees, the Kuomintang officials feasted each other with champagne dinners out of public relief funds. But he had faith in the common people. He believed they were capable of solving their problems through common struggles.

Following the outbreak of the anti-Japanese war in 1937, Rewi Alley devoted his efforts to establishing industrial cooperatives. Known as "Indusco", the movement grew so rapidly that by October 1940 more than 2,300 small factories — including machine shops, textile and flour mills, sugar and oil refineries, as well as shops making medicines, uniforms and hand grenades — were spread across sixteen provinces. A quarter of a million people depended on Indusco for a livelihood. In addition, 40,000 affiliated home-industry spinners and weavers were engaged in filling Indusco orders to make blankets for the Chinese army. The Bailie School for technical training of young Chinese boys was set up at Shuangshipu, later moved to Shandan, Gansu Province, in the Northwest.

After the founding of the People's Republic of China, Rewi

Alley became a peace activist, a traveler, a poet and writer. He translated many ancient and modern Chinese poems into English, and his numerous books and articles recorded the achievements of the Chinese people in building a modern socialist nation. He is still continuing his activities today.

Dr. Ma Haide (George Hatem) came to China in 1933 after graduation from the medical school of the University of Geneva, Switzerland. Born in 1910 in Buffalo, N.Y. of Lebanese descent, he had been a brilliant student. He set up an office in Shanghai specializing in treating VD patients, and the business flourished. He got acquainted with Soong Ching Ling, Agnes Smedley, Rewi Alley and other progressives, and soon became dissatisfied with his success. To Edgar Snow whom he met in Xi'an on their way to Yan'an he said, "The medical profession is a failure if we can't give all children of even the humblest parentage an equal start in life — the same food and proper care that only the wealthy can afford now. If that's what these people up there are aiming at, I'm with them. Anyway, I want to see for myself." He has been with the Chinese Communists ever since.

At first, Dr. Ma was one of the only two doctors with Western medical training in the Border Region, the other being a Chinese doctor trained in a missionary hospital. He helped greatly the work of Dr. Bethune, the Indian Medical Team, and later the Chinese Industrial Cooperatives in the Border Region. Tireless in treating the sick and wounded, he handled over 40,000 cases between 1944 and 1947 alone.

After liberation, he became adviser to the Ministry of Public Health of the people's government, and chief of staff of the Institute of Dermatology and Venereal Diseases of the Chinese Academy of Medical Sciences. In the 1950s, he helped wipe out VD in the frontier regions like Inner Mongolia and Xinjiang, a remarkable achievement which greatly benefited the local population. Since then he has been trying to eliminate leprosy along the coastal provinces of China. Now a citizen of new China, he has become a member of the Standing Committee of the national Chinese People's Political Consultative

Conference, an advisory body of prominent leaders from all walks of life to China's supreme organ of power, the National People's Congress. He has also been active in promoting the mutual understanding and friendship between the Chinese and American peoples.

In the course of China's protracted revolution, countless people of different countries, at one time or another, gave their moral or material support to the just aspirations of the Chinese people. Some devoted their time and talent to solicit aid for the Chinese cause, while others stood firmly on the side of the Chinese people at a time when their own governments were adopting a hostile policy toward the revolution. A few brave persons came and joined the arduous struggles alongside the Chinese fighters, and laid down their lives for a cause which they considered just. The total number of these friends was so great that, to the author's regret, space does not allow him to list even the prominent ones. The Chinese people will forever cherish their friendship.

AFTERWORD

The people of China today face three gigantic tasks: (1) stepping up modernization of agriculture, industry, national defense, science and technology so as to make China a strong socialist nation; (2) striving for reunification of the country, particularly the return of Taiwan to the motherland, and (3) opposing hegemonism and helping safeguard world peace together with the other Third World countries and peace-loving people everywhere. None of these tasks can be accomplished without strenuous and sustained efforts.

Now China is in a period of peaceful reconstruction. Contemporary Chinese history is like a mighty river and there may be twists and turns and even turbulent waves ahead. Some onlookers may regard pieces of deadwood or other flotsam on the surface as signs of decay or objects for derision. But the general direction of the mainstream is unmistakable. Over one billion people, nearly a quarter of the human race, are united in an endeavor to transform a society, only recently semi-feudal and semi-colonial, into a modern socialist state so as to lead a richer material and cultural life and contribute their share to world civilization as they did in the past. Whatever successes or failures they may register by the end of the century, these can only serve as the basis for further efforts and progress. Their experience will be useful not only to themselves but possibly also to all those who, in this present world of so much chaos and brutality, are trying to build a better world for all people.

APPENDIX I

CHRONOLOGY OF IMPORTANT EVENTS
(1839-1983)

1839   Commissioner Lin Zexu arrives in Guangzhou; opium burned; British cabinet declares war on China

1840   First Opium War begins

1841   Britain occupies Hongkong

1842   Treaty of Nanjing — the first of China's unequal treaties with foreign countries — signed

1844   Sino-U.S. Treaty of Wangxia signed; Sino-French Treaty of Huangpu signed

1851   Taiping peasant revolution led by Hong Xiuquan breaks out in Guangxi in southwest China

1853   Taiping Heavenly Kingdom set up at Nanjing; Little Sword Society rises in revolt in Shanghai; Taiping forces approach Tianjin in north China

1854   Zeng Guofan organizes Hunan army to fight the Taipings

1856   Second Opium War begins

1860   Frederick T. Ward organizes "Volunteers" in Shanghai to fight the Taipings; tsarist Russia occupies Vladivostok and all territory east of the Wusuli River; the Yuan Ming Yuan outside Beijing looted and burned by British and French troops; Treaty of Beijing signed, ending Second Opium War

1861   Zongli Yamen set up to handle China's foreign relations; China's Maritime Customs Service set up;
Emperor Xian Feng dies; Empress Dowager Ci Xi
becomes power behind the throne

1862-77 Yakub-beg revolt in Xinjiang supported by Britain
and the Ottoman Empire

1865   Jiangnan Arsenal established in Shanghai

1866   Fuzhou Navy Yard set up

1871   Ili in Xinjiang occupied by Russian troops

1879   Ryukyu Islands annexed by Japan

1881   Treaty of Ili signed, China loses more territory in
northwest to tsarist Russia

1883-85 Sino-French War; China renounces all rights in Viet
Nam

1890   Hanyang Steel Works set up

1893   Yadong in Tibet opened to foreign trade under British pressure

1894   Sino-Japanese War; Sun Yat-sen organizes *Xing
Zhong Hui* in Hawaii

1895   Treaty of Shimonoseki signed, Sino-Japanese War
ends; Japan occupies Taiwan; Kang Youwei petitions Emperor Guang Xu to institute reforms

1898   China forced to lease: (1) Qingdao in Shandong
Province to Germany, (2) Lüda (Lüshun and Dalian)
to tsarist Russia, (3) Guangzhouwan in Guangdong
Province to France, and (4) Kowloon near Hongkong
to Britain; Britain obtains Weihaiwei in Shandong
Province as naval base to counter Russian influence
in northeast China; "Hundred Days' Reform" crushed
by Empress Dowager Ci Xi

1899   "Open Door Doctrine" proposed by U.S. Secretary of
State John Hay; Boxer Movement spreads from
Shandong Province to Beijing

1900   Allied troops of eight nations enter Beijing

1901   Boxer Protocol signed; Zongli Yamen changed to
Waiwubu (Ministry for Foreign Affairs)

1903   Tibet invaded by British troops

1904-05   Russo-Japanese War fought in northeast China; Sun
           Yat-sen organizes *Tong Meng Hui* in Tokyo

1907   Revolutionary attempt led by Xu Xilin and Qiu Jin
           fails, both executed

1908   Death of Emperor Guang Xu and Empress Dowager
           Ci Xi; Puyi enthroned as child-emperor

1911   October 10: revolution breaks out in Wuchang,
           signaling end of monarchy and beginning of the Re-
           public; Sun Yat-sen elected provisional president

1912   Yuan Shikai becomes President of the Republic of
           China; Kuomintang formed

1914   World War I begins; Japan declares war against
           Germany and occupies Qingdao in Shandong Prov-
           ince

1915   Twenty-one Demands presented by Japan; Yuan Shi-
           kai attempts to restore the monarchy by assuming
           the throne himself

1916   Death of Yuan Shikai; in-fighting begins among war-
           lords

1917   China joins the Allies against Germany; October So-
           cialist Revolution in Russia

1919   May Fourth Movement; Chinese delegation refuses
           to sign Versailles Treaty

1921   Foundation of Chinese Communist Party

1922   Washington Conference and Nine-Power Treaty;
           Hongkong seamen's strike

1923   Railway workers' strike suppressed by warlord Wu
           Peifu

1924   First Kuomintang-Communist united front; Chiang
           Kai-shek becomes head of Huangpu Military Academy

1925   March 12: Sun Yat-sen dies; May 30th Movement
           sweeps China

1926   "March 18 massacre" in Beijing; Northern Expedi-
           tion commences from Guangzhou; revolutionary
           government set up at Wuhan

1927   April 12: Chiang Kai-shek turns against revolution and begins to slaughter Communists, workers and peasants; Wuhan government also betrays revolution in July

August 1:   Communists stage Nanchang Uprising, now called Army Day

September: Mao Zedong decides to lead Red forces on strategic retreat into the Jinggang Mountains

December: Guangzhou Commune

1928   Chiang Kai-shek in control of most of China; disastrous famine in north China

1930   Left-wing Writers League formed in Shanghai; Chiang Kai-shek defeated in first encirclement campaign against Red base areas

1931   September 18: "Shenyang Incident", Japanese army takes over northeast China; Soviet government set up at Ruijin in Jiangxi Province

1932   Japanese troops attack Shanghai, heroically defended by the 19th Route Army; Japan creates puppet state of "Manchukuo", Chiang Kai-shek leads fourth encirclement campaign against Red base areas

1933   "Christian General" Feng Yuxiang forms Anti-Japanese Allied Army at Zhangjiakou; Chiang Kai-shek begins fifth encirclement campaign against Red base areas

1934   Kuomintang launches New Life Movement; Red Army starts the Long March

1935   Zunyi meeting, Mao Zedong elected leader of CCP

1936   Lu Xun, famous writer, dies in Shanghai;
December: Xi'an Incident, Chiang Kai-shek abducted and then released by two of his generals

1937   Second Kuomintang-Communist united front; July 7, Lugouqiao Incident, Japan begins large-scale invasion of China

1938   Japan occupies major cities of China; Chiang Kai-shek retreats to Chongqing in Sichuan Province

1940   Japanese puppet government set up under Wang Jingwei at Nanjing

1941   January: Southern Anhui Incident, Communist-led New Fourth Army attacked by Kuomintang troops

June: Nazi Germany invades the USSR

December: Pearl Harbor bombed by Japanese planes

1945   May: Unconditional surrender by Germany

August: The Soviet Union declares war against Japan; United States drops atom bombs on Hiroshima and Nagasaki; Japan surrenders

October: Chongqing Agreement between Kuomintang and Communists

December: General George Marshall arrives in China

1946   Chiang Kai-shek starts civil war against Communists; Marshall mission thwarted

1947   March: Kuomintang troops occupy Yan'an; Communists issue call to "Overthrow Chiang Kai-shek and liberate all China"; Red Army re-named People's Liberation Army

1948   April: Yan'an recovered by People's Liberation Army

November: All northeast China liberated from the Kuomintang

1949   January: Beijing liberated peacefully; Huaihai campaign concluded

April: Nanjing, capital of "Nationalist China", liberated by People's Liberation Army

October 1: Founding of People's Republic of China; Chiang Kai-shek and Kuomintang government retreat to island of Taiwan

1950   Sino-Soviet Alliance signed in Moscow; Chinese Volunteers sent to North Korea to help resist U.S. and U.N. troops

1951   Tibet liberated peacefully; Three-Anti, Five-Anti, and Thought Reform campaigns

1952   Sino-Japanese trade agreement signed in Beijing

1953   Death of Stalin; cease-fire agreement in Korean War; First Five-Year Plan begins

1954   Agricultural cooperatives set up, beginning of collectivization; China and India agree on Five Principles of Peaceful Co-existence; First National People's Congress adopts Constitution; Chinese Volunteers return to China from Korea

1955   April: Zhou Enlai attends Bandung Conference of Asian-African Countries
November: CCP passes resolution on socialist transformation of capitalist industry and commerce

1956   The "Hundred Flowers" policy in art and literature;
November: Zhou Enlai visits seven Asian countries

1957   CCP unfolds rectification campaign; anti-rightist campaign

1958   The Great Leap Forward; people's communes organized in rural areas

1959   Tibetan reactionary leaders stage abortive rebellion; border clashes between China and India

1960   July: USSR recalls all technicians from China

1961   China and North Korea sign Friendship, Cooperation and Mutual Assistance Treaty

1962   October-November: border war between China and India

1963   August: Zhou Enlai proposes total destruction of nuclear weapons to all governments; China self-sufficient in oil and petroleum products

1964   October: China explodes first atom bomb

1965   Tibet Autonomous Region established

1966   May: The "great proletarian cultural revolution" begins

1967   June: China explodes first hydrogen bomb

1968   Liu Shaoqi expelled "forever" from CCP; bridge

across the Changjiang River at Nanjing completed

1969 March: Chinese and Soviet troops clash at Zhenbao Island in Heilongjiang Province

1970 April: China launches first earth satellite

1971 July: Henry Kissinger's first trip to China; President Nixon invited to China

September 13: Lin Biao killed

October 25: People's Republic of China seated in United Nations; Kuomintang government on Taiwan expelled

1972 February: President Richard Nixon Visits China; Shanghai Communique signed

September: Premier Tanaka visits China; Sino-Japanese diplomatic relations normalized

1974 Criticize Lin Biao and Confucius campaign

1975 January: Fourth National People's Congress convenes; Premier Zhou Enlai proposes policy of "four modernizations"

April 5: Chiang Kai-shek dies on Taiwan

May: China establishes relations with EEC

1976 January 8: Premier Zhou Enlai dies in Beijing

April: Tian An Men Square Incident; Deng Xiaoping ousted; Hua Guofeng becomes Premier

July 6: Zhu De, Commander-in-Chief of the People's Liberation Army, dies

July 28: Tangshan earthquake

September 9: Mao Zedong dies at 82

October 6: Gang of Four arrested

1977 Deng Xiaoping rehabilitated; President Tito visits China

1978 February-March: Fifth National People's Congress; new Constitution adopted

August: Sino-Japanese Peace and Cooperation Treaty signed in Beijing

December: Third Plenum of 11th Central Committee of CCP, deciding socialist modernization to be central task

1979   January 1: Full diplomatic relations established between China and the United States; U.S.-Taiwan relations changed to "unofficial" channels

February-March: Chinese troops launch punitive counter-offensive against Viet Nam and then withdraw

1980   February: Hu Yaobang becomes General Secretary of CCP; Liu Shaoqi posthumously rehabilitated

September: Zhao Ziyang becomes Premier

1981   January: Gang of Four sentenced by Special Tribunal

May 29: Soong Ching Ling dies

September 20: China launches three satellites propelled by a single rocket

October 9: 70th anniversary of 1911 Revolution; Hu Yaobang designates the three main tasks: (1) socialist modernization; (2) reunification of the whole country, including Taiwan; (3) safeguarding world peace

1982   August 17: China-U.S. Joint Communique on gradually reducing and finally resolving the issue of U.S. arms sales to Taiwan issued

September: British Prime Minister Thatcher visits China

October: China launches a submarine-based carrier rocket; China's national census shows its population tops 1,000 million

December: China adopts Sixth Five-Year Plan (1981-1985); Premier Zhao Ziyang embarks on visits to eleven African countries

1983   Li Xiannian elected President of the People's Republic; Premier Zhao Ziyang visits New Zealand and Australia; French President Mitterrand visits China; China launches a scientific experimental satellite

APPENDIX II

GUIDE TO SOME GEOGRAPHICAL NAMES

New Spelling or Name	Chinese	Old Spelling or Name
Aihui	爱 珲	Aigun
Beijing	北 京	Peking, Peiping
Changjiang River	长 江	Yangtze River
Chengde	承 德	Jehol
Chengdu	成 都	Chengtu
Chongqing	重 庆	Chungking
Dalian	大 连	Dairen, Dalny
Duolun	多 伦	Dolonor
Fuzhou	福 州	Foochow
Guangzhou	广 州	Canton
Guilin	桂 林	Kweilin
Guiyang	贵 阳	Kweiyang
Vladivostok	海 参 崴	Haishenwei
Hangzhou	杭 州	Hangchow
Heilong River	黑 龙 江	Amur River

Huanghe River	黄 河	Yellow River
Huangpu	黄 埔	Whampoa
Huangpu River	黄 浦 江	Whangpoo River
Huhhot	呼和浩特	Huhehot
Jinan	济 南	Tsinan
Jinggang Mountains	井 岗 山	Chingkang Mountains
Jiulong	九 龙	Kowloon
Lanzhou	兰 州	Lanchow
Lugouqiao (Bridge)	芦 沟 桥	Lukouchiao, Marco Polo Bridge
Luoyang	洛 阳	Loyang
Lüshun	旅 顺	Lushun, Port Anthur
Nanjing	南 京	Nanking
Penghu Islands	澎湖群岛	Pescadores
Pingxingguan	平 型 关	Pinghsingkuan Pass
Qingdao	青 岛	Tsingtao
Ruijin	瑞 金	Juichin
Shanhaiguan	山 海 关	Shanhaikuan
Shenyang	沈 阳	Mukden
Shenzhen	深 圳	Shumchun
Suzhou	苏 州	Soochow
Tianjin	天 津	Tientsin
Urumqi	乌鲁木齐	Urumchi
Wangxia	望 厦	Wanghsia
Wusuli River	乌苏里江	Ussuri River
Wuxi	无 锡	Wusih

Xi'an	西 安	Sian
Xiamen	厦 门	Amoy
Yan'an	延 安	Yenan
Yantai	烟 台	Chefoo
Zhangjiakou	张 家 口	Changkiakou, Kalgan
Zhenjiang	镇 江	Chenkiang
Zhoushan Islands	舟山群岛	Choushan Archipelago
Zhujiang	珠 江	Pearl River
Zunyi	遵 义	Tsunyi

Provinces and Autonomous Regions:

Anhui	安 徽	Anhwei
Fujian	福 建	Fukien
Gansu	甘 肃	Kansu
Guangdong	广 东	Kwangtung
Guangxi	广 西	Kwangsi
Guizhou	贵 州	Kweichow
Hebei	河 北	Hopei, Chili
Heilongjiang	黑 龙 江	Heilungkiang
Henan	河 南	Honan
Hubei	湖 北	Hupeh
Hunan	湖 南	Hunan
Inner Mongolia	内 蒙 古	Inner Mongolia
Jiangsu	江 苏	Kiangsu
Jiangxi	江 西	Kiangsi
Jilin	吉 林	Kirin
Liaoning	辽 宁	Liaoning, Fengtien

Ningxia	宁	夏	Ninghsia
Qinghai	青	海	Chinghai
Shaanxi	陕	西	Shensi
Shandong	山	东	Shantung
Shanxi	山	西	Shansi
Sichuan	四	川	Szechuan
Taiwan	台	湾	Taiwan
Xinjiang	新	疆	Sinkiang
Yunnan	云	南	Yunnan
Zhejiang	浙	江	Chekiang

INDEX

中国近代史话

苏开明 著

*

新世界出版社出版
外文印刷厂印刷
中国国际图书贸易总公司发行
（中国国际书店）
北京399信箱
1985年第一版
1986年第二次印刷
编号：（英）17223—151
00700（精）
00500（平）
11—E—1955